EXPLORING WINDOWS® 95

AND ESSENTIAL COMPUTING CONCEPTS

EXPLORING WINDOWS® 95

AND ESSENTIAL COMPUTING CONCEPTS

Robert T. Grauer / Maryann Barber

University of Miami

Prentice Hall, Englewood Cliffs, New Jersey 07632

Library of Congress Cataloging-in-Publication Data

Grauer, Robert T., [date]
   Exploring Windows 95 and essential computing concepts / Robert T.
Grauer, Maryann Barber.
     p. cm.
  Includes index.
  ISBN 0-13-504077-9
  1. Operating systems (Computers)   2. Microsoft Windows 95.
  I. Barber, Maryann M.   II. Title.
  QA76.76.063G727 1995
  005.4′469—dc20

                                    95-30343
                                           CIP

Acquisitions editor: Carolyn Henderson
Editorial/production supervisor: Greg Hubit Bookworks
Interior and cover design: Suzanne Behnke
Manufacturing buyer: Paul Smolenski
Managing editor: Katherine Evancie
Editorial assistant: Audrey Regan
Production coordinator: Renée Pelletier

© 1996 by Prentice-Hall, Inc.
Simon & Schuster / A Viacom Company
Upper Saddle River, New Jersey 07458

Printed in the United States of America
10 9 8 7 6 5 4

ISBN 0-13-504077-9

Prentice Hall International (UK) Limited, *London*
Prentice Hall of Australia Pty. Limited, *Sydney*
Prentice Hall of Canada Inc., *Toronto*
Prentice Hall Hispanoamericano, S.A., *Mexico*
Prentice Hall of India Private Limited, *New Delhi*
Prentice Hall of Japan, Inc., *Tokyo*
Simon & Schuster Asia Pte. Ltd., *Singapore*
Editora Prentice Hall do Brasil, Ltda., *Rio de Janeiro*

CONTENTS

PREFACE   ix

1

Introduction: Welcome to Windows 95   1

CHAPTER OBJECTIVES   1
OVERVIEW   1
The Nature of Software   2
The Desktop   2
The Mouse   3
Online Help   5
Learning by Doing   7
HANDS-ON EXERCISE 1: WELCOME TO WINDOWS 95   7
Working in Windows   12
    Anatomy of a Window   12   Moving and Sizing a Window   13
    Pull-down Menus   14   Dialog Boxes   15   The Mouse versus the
    Keyboard, and Other Shortcuts   15
Formatting a Disk   17
HANDS-ON EXERCISE 2: WORKING IN WINDOWS   17
Customizing Windows   23
    The Control Panel   23
The Tile and Cascade Commands   24
HANDS-ON EXERCISE 3: CUSTOMIZING WINDOWS   26
Summary   33
Key Words and Concepts   33
Multiple Choice   34
Exploring Windows 95   36
Practice with Windows 95   39
Case Studies   43

2

The Common User Interface: The WordPad and Paint Accessories 45

CHAPTER OBJECTIVES 45
OVERVIEW 45
The Common User Interface 46
The WordPad Accessory 48
    The File Menu 48   The Edit Menu 50   The Format Menu 50
    Toolbars 51
HANDS-ON EXERCISE 1: THE WORDPAD ACCESSORY 53
The Paint Accessory 61
HANDS-ON EXERCISE 2: THE PAINT ACCESSORY 63
Multitasking 70
HANDS-ON EXERCISE 3: MULTITASKING 72
Summary 77
Key Words and Concepts 78
Multiple Choice 78
Exploring Windows 95 81
Practice with Windows 95 83
Case Studies 86

3

Managing Files and Folders: My Computer and the Explorer 89

CHAPTER OBJECTIVES 89
OVERVIEW 89
My Computer 90
Files and Folders 92
    File Type 92   Browsing My Computer 93
Learning by Doing 94
HANDS-ON EXERCISE 1: MY COMPUTER 95
File Operations 103
    Moving and Copying a File 103   Backup 104   Deleting Files 104
HANDS-ON EXERCISE 2: FILE OPERATIONS 105
Windows Explorer 113
Learning by Doing 115
HANDS-ON EXERCISE 3: WINDOWS EXPLORER 116
Tips and Tricks 123
    The Find Command 123   Shortcuts 125
HANDS-ON EXERCISE 4: TIPS AND TRICKS 127

Summary   133
Key Words and Concepts   134
Multiple Choice   134
Exploring Windows 95   136
Practice with Windows 95   140
Case Studies   144

4

Beyond the PC: Local Area Networks, E-mail, Information Services   145

CHAPTER OBJECTIVES   145
OVERVIEW   145
Local Area Networks   146
    Security   147   Network Neighborhood   148
HANDS-ON EXERCISE 1: LOCAL AREA NETWORKS   150
Communicating with the Outside World   156
    Modems   156   The Hyper Terminal Accessory   157
    The Phone Dialer Accessory   158   Microsoft Fax   160
Information Services   163
Learning by Doing   164
HANDS-ON EXERCISE 2: USING A MODEM   164
E-mail   173
    The Microsoft Exchange   174   The Internet   176
HANDS-ON EXERCISE 3: E-MAIL   177
Summary   182
Key Words and Concepts   183
Multiple Choice   183
Exploring Windows 95   185
Practice with Windows 95   187
Case Studies   190

APPENDIX A: MIGRATING FROM WINDOWS 3.1   191

APPENDIX B: A PC BUYING GUIDE   207

APPENDIX C: INTRODUCTION TO MULTIMEDIA   221

APPENDIX D: THE INTERNET AND WORLD WIDE WEB   237

INDEX   257

PREFACE

Exploring Windows 95 and Essential Computing Concepts is the first book in the *Exploring Windows* series to focus on the new operating system. It also includes several additional topics that are not part of Windows 95 per se, but which are very often presented in the introductory applications course. Students want to know how to buy a PC. They want to use e-mail, the Internet, and the World Wide Web. They are intrigued by multimedia. And they need to learn about local area networks so that they will understand the environment in which they will be working. Inclusion of these topics, plus hands-on coverage of how to use Windows 95, make *Exploring Windows 95 and Essential Computing Concepts* a truly unique textbook and the ideal way to master key computing concepts as well as the powerful new operating system.

Each book in the *Exploring Windows* series is suitable on a stand-alone basis for any course that teaches a specific application; alternatively, several modules can be packaged together for a single course that teaches multiple applications. Other series titles include *Microsoft Word Version 7.0, Microsoft Excel Version 7.0, Microsoft PowerPoint Version 7.0, Microsoft Access Version 7.0, Microsoft Office 7.0* (a combination of chapters from the individual books), *Exploring Lotus 95, Exploring WordPerfect 95,* and *Exploring the Internet.* All of the books possess a common design, pedagogy, and writing style that is appropriate for microcomputer application courses in both two- and four-year schools.

The *Exploring Windows* series will appeal to students in a variety of disciplines including business, liberal arts, and the sciences. Each book has a consistent presentation that stresses the benefits of the Windows environment, especially the common user interface, multitasking, and the extensive on-line help facility. Students are taught concepts, not just keystrokes or mouse clicks, with hands-on exercises in every chapter providing the necessary practice to master the material.

The *Exploring Windows* series is different from other books, both in its scope as well as in the way in which material is presented. Students learn by doing. Concepts are stressed and memorization is minimized. Shortcuts and other important information are consistently highlighted in the many tips that appear throughout the series. Every chapter contains an average of three directed exercises at the computer. Equally important are the less structured end-of-chapter problems that not only review the information, but extend it as well. The end-of-chapter material is a distinguishing feature of the entire series, an integral part of the learning process, and a powerful motivational tool for students to learn and explore.

Exploring Windows 95 and Essential Computing Concepts is accompanied by a comprehensive Instructor's Resource Manual with tests, transparency masters, and student/instructor resource disks. Instructors can also use the Prentice Hall Computerized Online Testing System to prepare customized tests and may obtain Interactive Multimedia courseware as a further supplement. *Exploring Windows 95 and Essential Computer Concepts* is part of the Prentice Hall custom binding program.

FEATURES AND BENEFITS

Exploring Windows 95 and Essential Computing Concepts is written for the computer novice and assumes no previous knowledge of Windows 3.1. Appendix A is included for the knowledgeable Windows user to aid his or her migration to the new interface.

A unique buying guide presents a thorough introduction to PC hardware from the viewpoint of purchasing a computer. Students learn the subtleties in selecting a configuration, how to extend the warranty of a new computer, and the advantages of a mail-order purchase.

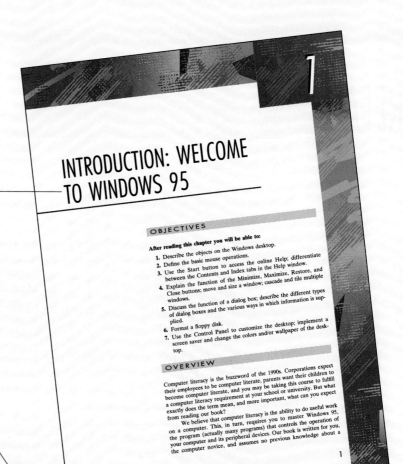

INTRODUCTION: WELCOME TO WINDOWS 95

OBJECTIVES

After reading this chapter you will be able to:

1. Describe the objects on the Windows desktop.
2. Define the basic mouse operations.
3. Use the Start button to access the online Help; differentiate between the Contents and Index tabs in the Help window.
4. Explain the function of the Minimize, Maximize, Restore, and Close buttons; move and size a window; cascade and tile multiple windows.
5. Discuss the function of a dialog box; describe the different types of dialog boxes and the various ways in which information is supplied.
6. Format a floppy disk.
7. Use the Control Panel to customize the desktop; implement a screen saver and change the colors and/or wallpaper of the desktop.

OVERVIEW

Computer literacy is the buzzword of the 1990s. Corporations expect their employees to be computer literate, parents want their children to become computer literate, and you may be taking this course to fulfill a computer literacy requirement at your school or university. But what exactly does the term mean, and most important, what can you expect from reading our book?

We believe that computer literacy is the ability to do useful work on a computer. This, in turn, requires you to master Windows 95, the program (actually many programs) that controls the operation of your computer and its peripheral devices. Our book is written for you, the computer novice, and assumes no previous knowledge about a

1

THE PERSONAL COMPUTER

The personal computer is a marvel of miniaturization and technology. We take it for granted, but the IBM PC, which jump-started the industry, is just a teenager. IBM announced the PC in 1981 (three years after the Apple II) and broke a long-standing corporate tradition by going to external sources for supporting hardware and software. The *microprocessor* inside the PC was produced by *Intel Corporation.* The operating system was developed by *Microsoft Corporation.*

In terms of today's capabilities, IBM's initial offering was hardly spectacular. A fully loaded system with two floppy disk drives (a hard disk was not available), monochrome monitor, and 80 cps (character per second) dot matrix printer sold for $4425. Software was practically nonexistent. Lotus 1-2-3 had not yet been released, and WordPerfect was a little-known program not yet modified to run on the PC. Yet the PC, with little software and limited hardware, was an instant success for two reasons. The IBM name, and its reputation for quality and service, meant that corporate America could order the machine and be assured that it would perform as promised.

Of equal, or even greater, significance, was the PC's open design, which meant that independent vendors could offer supporting products to enhance performance. This was accomplished through *expansion slots* that held additional circuit boards that added functionality to the basic PC. IBM made public the technical information to create *expansion cards* (also knows as adapters) so that other companies could build peripherals for the PC, thus enhancing its capabilities. Today you can purchase expansion cards that add sound, increase the number of colors, resolution, and speed of the monitor, or add peripheral devices such as CD-ROMs and tape-backup units that did not exist when the PC was introduced.

PC-compatibles, computers based on the same microprocessor and able to run the same software, began to appear as early as 1982 and offered superior performance for less money. Companies and individuals who were once willing to pay a premium for the IBM name began ordering the "same" machine from other vendors. PC has become a generic term for any computer based on Intel-compatible microprocessors and capable of running Microsoft Windows.

Figure B.1 illustrates a typical Windows workstation. We view the system from the front (Figure B.1a), the rear (Figure B.1b), and from inside the system unit (Figure B.1c). Your system will be different from ours, but you should be able to recognize the various components as they are discussed in this appendix. Whether you choose a desktop or tower for your system unit, or whether you purchase a laptop or notebook computer, you will have to decide on each component of your system.

LET YOUR FINGERS DO THE WALKING

A single issue of a computer magazine contains advertisements from many vendors, making it possible to comparison shop from multiple mail-order vendors from the convenience of home. Computer magazines are also the source of the latest technical information, and thus a subscription to a magazine is a must for the serious user. Our three favorites (*PC Computing, PC Magazine,* and *Windows Magazine*) are found on most newsstands.

THE MICROPROCESSOR

The capability of a PC depends in large part on the microprocessor on which it is based. Intel microprocessors are currently in their fifth generation, with each

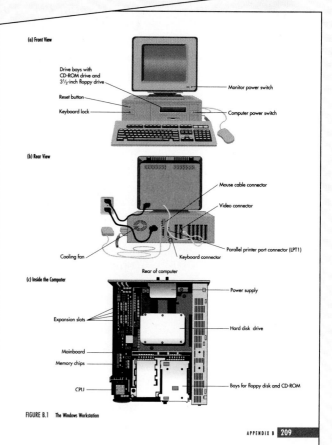

(a) Front View

Drive bays with CD-ROM drive and 3½-inch floppy drive

Reset button

Keyboard lock

Monitor power switch

Computer power switch

(b) Rear View

Mouse cable connector

Video connector

Parallel printer port connector (LPT1)

Cooling fan

Keyboard connector

Rear of computer

(c) Inside the Computer

Power supply

Expansion slots

Hard disk drive

Mainboard

Memory chips

Bays for floppy disk and CD-ROM

CPU

FIGURE B.1   The Windows Workstation

If you are lucky enough to have a PC at home, then you have (or should have) a modem, which is the interface between the PC and the telephone system. We show you how to use the Hyper Terminal accessory to access a remote computer through your modem. We describe the use of the Microsoft Fax accessory to send and receive faxes through your computer. We also explore the use of information services such as the Microsoft Network, CompuServe, America Online, and Prodigy. The chapter describes the capabilities of these services in general terms and suggests ways in which they can enhance your use of the PC.

The last part of the chapter is devoted to e-mail and discusses the basic commands that are present in any e-mail system. It includes an introduction to the Internet (a vast global network of computers) and shows you how to send e-mail to anyone with an Internet address. (Appendix D presents additional information on the Internet and shows you how to browse the World Wide Web.) All told, this is a comprehensive and ambitious chapter, but it is also a chapter that you will enjoy tremendously.

LOCAL AREA NETWORKS

A network is a combination of hardware and software that enables computers to communicate with one another. It may be large enough to encompass computers around the world or it may be limited to the computers on your floor or in your building. The latter is known as a *local area network* or LAN.

The computer that you use at school or work is probably connected to a local area network. The idea behind a LAN is very simple—to enable the connected computers to share resources such as application software, hardware, and data. One printer, for example, can support multiple PCs because not everyone needs to print at the same time.

Networks are common today, but that was not always true. Without a network, you often created a file on one computer, then carried the disk to another machine in order to use the laser printer. Or you might have borrowed a disk containing a specific file to load it on your computer. Or you might have left a message for a friend or colleague in his or her in-box, only to have it get lost under a pile of paper.

All of these situations are examples of network applications, implemented informally in a *sneaker net*, whereby you transferred a file to a floppy disk, put on your sneakers, and ran down the hall to deliver the disk to someone else. A local area network automates the process, and while sneaker net may not sound very impressive, it does illustrate the concept rather effectively.

Figure 4.1 represents a conceptual view of a LAN consisting of multiple workstations, two laser printers, two CD-ROM drives, and two network drives, all connected to a server. A *workstation* (also known as a client or a node) is any PC on which an individual works. There can be different types of workstations (different computers) connected to the network as seen in the figure.

A *server* is a more powerful PC that controls the way the individual workstations share resources. The hard disk(s) attached to the server stores the software and data shared by the individual workstations. The network software handles all requests for network services. Larger networks may have multiple servers, each dedicated to a specific task. A *file server* provides a common place to store data and provides rapid access to that data. A *printer server* manages all printing for the network.

Application programs are stored on a server rather than on individual machines. To use an application, you click the icon to load the program, which issues a request to the network software. The software checks that you are permitted access to the program, then it loads the application into your PC's memory, and the application appears on your screen.

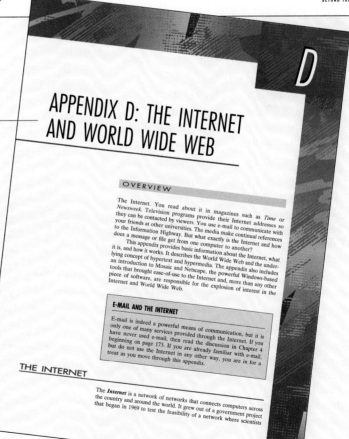

FIGURE 4.1   A Local Area Network

The document used with the application may be stored on either a local or a network drive. If the document is stored locally, the network does not come into play. If, however, the document is kept on the network, the server will check that the document is not already in use, then it will open the document for you. It will also prevent other users from gaining access to that document as long as it is open on your machine.

While you're working, other people on the network may load the word processor, but no one else can access your particular document. Anyone attempting to do so gets a message saying the file is in use, because the network locks out everyone else from that file. You finish editing and save the file. Then you execute the print command, and the network prints the document on a network printer(s).

BEYOND THE LAN

A user of a local area network can gain access to other networks and even to mainframe computers through *bridges* or *gateways* installed on the network. The operation of these devices is transparent to the user, but they make it possible for a computer on one network to address a computer on another network as though both machines were on the same network.

Chapter 4 on local area networks explains the basics of networking and e-mail. Students learn the Domain Name System and how to send e-mail across the Internet. A separate appendix explains how the Internet works in terms that are understandable to the beginner and also introduces the reader to the World Wide Web.

APPENDIX D: THE INTERNET AND WORLD WIDE WEB

OVERVIEW

The Internet. You read about it in magazines such as *Time* or *Newsweek*. Television programs provide their Internet addresses so they can be contacted by viewers. You use e-mail to communicate with your friends at other universities. The media make continual references to the Information Highway. But what exactly is the Internet and how does a message or file get from one computer to another?

This appendix provides basic information about the Internet, what it is, and how it works. It describes the World Wide Web and the underlying concept of hypertext and hypermedia. The appendix also includes an introduction to Mosaic and Netscape, the powerful Windows-based tools that brought ease-of-use to the Internet and, more than any other piece of software, are responsible for the explosion of interest in the Internet and World Wide Web.

E-MAIL AND THE INTERNET

E-mail is indeed a powerful means of communication, but it is only one of many services provided through the Internet. If you have never used e-mail, then read the discussion in Chapter 4 beginning on page 173. If you are already familiar with e-mail, but do not use the Internet in any other way, you are in for a treat as you move through this appendix.

THE INTERNET

The *Internet* is a network of networks that connects computers across the country and around the world. It grew out of a government project that began in 1969 to test the feasibility of a network where scientists

237

A different title bar is highlighted in each figure, corresponding to the active window. The *active window* contains the application on which you are presently working; it is the Recycle Bin in Figure 1.9a and the Control Panel in Figure 1.9b. To change the active window, just click in a different window or click the corresponding button on the Taskbar.

Each window in Figure 1.9 (whether tiled or cascaded) contains the elements essential to every Windows application. Each window has a control menu box as well as a title bar with a Minimize, Maximize, and Close button. A horizontal scroll bar is present in the Recycle Bin window of Figure 1.9a because not all of the detail information for a specific file is visible. A vertical scroll bar is also present in this window because the Recycle Bin contains more files than can be seen at one time. The toolbar and status bar are not displayed for the Recycle Bin but are present in the other windows. The menu bar is found in all three windows.

HANDS-ON EXERCISE 3

Customizing Windows

Objective: Tile and cascade open windows; create a shortcut on the desktop to open the Control Panel; customize the desktop and Taskbar. Use Figure 1.10 as a guide in the exercise.

STEP 1: Open the Control Panel

➤ Load Windows. Double click the **My Computer icon.** Double click the **Control Panel icon** within My Computer to open the Control Panel. Do not be concerned about the contents of the windows or their size or position on the desktop.

➤ Point to an empty space on the **Taskbar** (you can't point to a button). Click the **right mouse button** to display a menu as shown in Figure 1.10a. Click the **Cascade command** to cascade the windows.

ONE WINDOW OR MANY

If opening the Control Panel causes the My Computer window to disappear (and its button to vanish from the Taskbar), you need to set an option to open each folder in a separate window. Pull down the View menu, click Options, click the Folder tab, then click the option button to use a separate window for each folder. Click the OK command button to accept this setting and return to the desktop

---

STEP 2: The Active Window

➤ Click and drag the **title bar** of the top window (the Control Panel in Figure 1.10b) so that the size and position of the windows on your desktop match Figure 1.10b. The view in your windows may be different from ours.

➤ Click anywhere in the My Computer window to make it the active window. The title bar for My Computer is highlighted and all subsequent commands affect just this window:

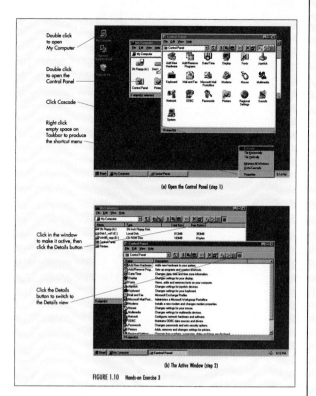

Double click to open My Computer

Double click to open the Control Panel

Click Cascade

Right click empty space on Taskbar to produce the shortcut menu

(a) Open the Control Panel (step 1)

Click in the window to make it active, then click the Details button

Click the Details button to switch to the Details view

(b) The Active Window (step 2)

FIGURE 1.10 Hands-on Exercise 3

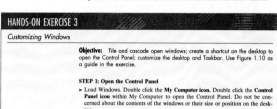

A total of 15 in-depth hands-on exercises guide the reader at the computer. Each of these tutorials is illustrated with large, full-color screen captures that are clear and easy to read. Each tutorial is accompanied by numerous tips that present different ways to accomplish a given task, but in a logical and relaxed fashion. The authors are constantly anticipating mistakes that students will make and tell the reader how to recover from problems that may occur.

Appendix C on multimedia explains the basics of this rapidly emerging technology and describes how multimedia is implemented in Windows 95. Students learn the basics of sound and video files and are introduced to the subtleties of file compression.

THE BASICS OF MULTIMEDIA

Everyone has their favorite multimedia application. But did you ever stop to think of how the application was created? Or of the large number of individual files that are needed for the sound and visual effects that are at the heart of the application? We said at the beginning of this appendix that multimedia combines the text and graphics capability of the PC with high-quality sound and video. In this section we look at the individual components, the sound and video files, that comprise a multimedia application.

Sound

The sound you hear from your PC is the result of a sound file (stored on disk or a CD-ROM) being played through the sound card in your system. There are, however, two very different types of sound files, a WAV file, and a MIDI file. Each is discussed in turn.

A *WAV file* is a digitized recording of an actual sound (a voice, music, or special effects). It is created by a chip in the sound card, which converts a recorded sound (e.g., your voice by way of a microphone) into a file on disk. The sound card divides the sound wave into tiny segments (known as samples) and stores each sample as a binary number. The quality of the sound is determined by two factors—the sampling rate and the resolution of each sample. The higher each of these values, the better the quality, and the larger the corresponding file.

The *sampling rate* (or frequency) is the number of samples per second and is expressed in KHz (thousands of samples per second). The higher the sampling rate, the more accurately the sound will be represented in the wave file. Common sampling rates are 11KHz, 22KHz, and 44KHz.

The *resolution* is the number of bits (binary digits) used to store each sample. The more bits, the better. The first sound cards provided for only eight bits. Sixteen bits are standard in today's environment.

WAV files, even those that last only a few seconds, grow large very quickly. Eight-bit sound, for example, at a sampling rate of 11KHz (11,000 samples a second) requires approximately 11KB of disk space per second. Thirty seconds of sound at this sampling rate will take some 330KB. If you improve the quality by using a 16-bit sound card, and by doubling the sampling rate to 22KHz, the same 30 seconds of sound will consume 1.3MB or almost an entire high-density floppy disk!

A *MIDI file* (Musical Instrument Digital Interface) is very different from a WAV file and is used only to create music. It does not store an actual sound, but rather the instructions to create that sound. Thus, a MIDI file is the electronic equivalent of sheet music. The advantage of a MIDI file is that it is much more compact than a WAV file because it stores instructions to create the sound rather than the actual sound. A WAV file, however, can represent any type of sound (a voice, music, or special effects) because it is a recorded sound. A MIDI file can store only music.

Video

An *AVI* (Audi-Video Interleaved) *file* is the Microsoft standard for a digital video (i.e., a multimedia) file. It takes approximately 4.5MB to store one second of uncompressed color video in the AVI format. That may sound unbelievable, but you can verify the number with a little arithmetic.

A single VGA screen contains approximately 300,000 (640 × 480) pixels, each of which requires at least one byte of storage. Allocating one byte (or 8 bits)

APPENDIX L 223

Concepts are emphasized in addition to covering keystrokes and mouse clicks, so that the reader appreciates the theory behind the applications. Students are not just taught what to do, but are provided with the rationale for why they are doing it, enabling them to extend the information to additional learning on their own. Problem solving and troubleshooting are stressed throughout.

Abundant and thought-provoking exercises, found at the end of every chapter, review and extend the material in different ways. There are objective multiple-choice questions, conceptual problems that do not require interaction with the computer ("Exploring Windows 95"), directed computer exercises ("Practice with Windows 95"), and less structured case studies that encourage the reader to pursue further exploration and independent study.

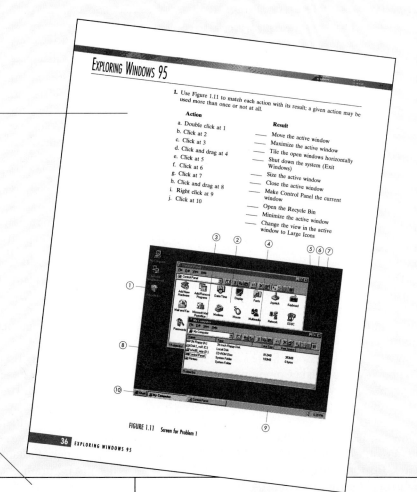

EXPLORING WINDOWS 95

1. Use Figure 1.11 to match each action with its result; a given action may be used more than once or not at all.

Action
a. Double click at 1
b. Click at 2
c. Click at 3
d. Click and drag at 4
e. Click at 5
f. Click at 6
g. Click at 7
h. Click and drag at 8
i. Right click at 9
j. Click at 10

Result
___ Move the active window
___ Maximize the active window
___ Tile the open windows horizontally
___ Shut down the system (Exit Windows)
___ Size the active window
___ Close the active window
___ Make Control Panel the current window
___ Open the Recycle Bin
___ Minimize the active window
___ Change the view in the active window to Large Icons

FIGURE 1.11 Screen for Problem 1

e. What is the effect of dragging the icon for the Elvis After document to the icon for drive A? To the icon for the Data folder?
f. How do you copy the Excel Criteria file to the Asg.120 folder? How do you move the file to that folder?
g. How do you find the file called Term Paper, which you know is somewhere on your system?
h. How do you create a shortcut icon for the printer? What would happen if you drag a file icon to the shortcut icon for the printer?
i. What happens if you double click the icon for Jessica on the desktop? If you double click the icon for the Shortcut to Jessica?
j. What would happen if you delete the icon for Jessica? If you delete the icon for Shortcut to Jessica?

PRACTICE WITH WINDOWS 95

1. **Screen capture:** Prove to your instructor that you have done the hands-on exercises in the chapter by capturing a screen from each exercise and then printing the captured screen in a document to which you add your name. Figure 3.15, for example, occurs in step 6 of exercise 4 (and corresponds to Figure 3.10f) and proves that Jessica Grauer did her homework.

   The instructions below show you how to create a document similar to the one in Figure 3.15 using the Paint accessory:

   a. Do the hands-on exercise until you come to the screen you want to capture. Press the Print Screen key to copy the screen to the clipboard (an area of memory that is available to every Windows application).
   b. Click the Start button, click Programs, click Accessories, then click Paint to open the Paint accessory. If necessary, click the Maximize button so that the Paint window takes the entire desktop.
   c. Pull down the Edit menu. Click Paste to copy the screen from the clipboard to the drawing.
   d. Click the text tool (the capital A), then click and drag in the drawing area to create a dotted rectangle that will contain the message to your instructor. Type the text indicating that you did your homework. Click outside the rectangle to deselect it.
   e. Pull down the File menu and click the Page Setup command to display the Page Setup dialog box. Click the Landscape option button. Change the margins to one inch all around.
   f. Pull down the File menu a second time. Click Print. Click OK.
   g. Click the Close button to exit Paint.

2. **Organize your work:** A folder may contain documents, programs, or other folders. The My Classes folder in Figure 3.16, for example, contains five folders, one folder for each class you are taking this semester, and in similar fashion, the Correspondence folder contains two additional folders according to the type of correspondence. We use folders in this fashion to organize our work, and we suggest you do likewise.

   The best way to practice with folders is on a floppy disk as was done in Figure 3.16. Accordingly:

   a. Format a floppy disk, or alternatively, use the floppy disk you have been using throughout the chapter.

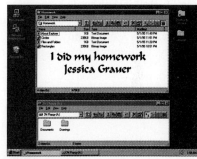

FIGURE 3.15 Practice Exercise 1

FIGURE 3.16 Practice Exercise 2

Acknowledgments

We want to thank the many individuals who helped bring this project to fruition. We are especially grateful to our editors at Prentice Hall, Carolyn Henderson and P. J. Boardman, without whom the series would not have been possible. Cecil Yarbrough did an outstanding job in checking the manuscript for technical accuracy. Gretchen Marx of Saint Joseph College created the test bank. Carlotta Eaton of Radford University produced an outstanding set of Instructor Manuals. Greg Hubit was in charge of production. Suzanne Behnke created the functional and appealing design. Nancy Evans and Deborah Emry, our marketing managers at Prentice Hall, developed the innovative campaigns that helped make the series a success.

We also want to acknowledge our reviewers, who, through their comments and constructive criticism, made this a far better series.

Lynne Band, Middlesex Community College
Stuart P. Brian, Holy Family College
Carl M. Briggs, Indiana University School of Business
Larry S. Corman, Fort Lewis College
Kimberly Chambers, Scottsdale Community College
Alok Charturvedi, Purdue University
Jerry Chin, Southwest Missouri State University
Dean Combellick, Scottsdale Community College
Cody Copeland, Johnson County Community College
Paul E. Daurelle, Western Piedmont Community College
David Douglas, University of Arkansas
Raymond Frost, Central Connecticut State University
James Gips, Boston College
Vernon Griffin, Austin Community College
Wanda D. Heller, Seminole Community College
Bonnie Homan, San Francisco State University
Ernie Ivey, Polk Community College
Mike Kelly, Community College of Rhode Island

Jane King, Everett Community College
John Lesson, University of Central Florida
Mary McKenry Percival, University of Miami
David B. Meinert, Southwest Missouri State
Alan Moltz, Naugatuck Valley Technical Community College
Delores Pusins, Hillsborough Community College
Gale E. Rand, College Misericordia
Judith Rice, Santa Fe Community College
David Rinehard, Lansing Community College
Marilyn Salas, Scottsdale Community College
John Shepherd, Duquesne University
Mike Thomas, Indiana University School of Business
Sally Visci, Lorain County Community College
David Weiner, University of San Francisco
Connie Wells, Georgia State University
Wallace John Whistance-Smith, Ryerson Polytechnic University
Jack Zeller, Kirkwood Community College

A final word of thanks to the unnamed students at the University of Miami who make it all worthwhile. And most of all, thanks to you, our readers, for choosing this book. Please feel free to contact us with any comments and suggestions. We can be reached most easily on the Internet.

Robert T. Grauer
RGRAUER@UMIAMI.MIAMI.EDU
http://www.bus.miami.edu/~rgrauer

Maryann Barber
MBARBER@UMIAMI.MIAMI.EDU
http://www.bus.miami.edu/~mbarber

INTRODUCTION: WELCOME TO WINDOWS 95

OBJECTIVES

After reading this chapter you will be able to:

1. Describe the objects on the Windows desktop.
2. Define the basic mouse operations.
3. Use the Start button to access the online Help; differentiate between the Contents and Index tabs in the Help window.
4. Explain the function of the Minimize, Maximize, Restore, and Close buttons; move and size a window; cascade and tile multiple windows.
5. Discuss the function of a dialog box; describe the different types of dialog boxes and the various ways in which information is supplied.
6. Format a floppy disk.
7. Use the Control Panel to customize the desktop; implement a screen saver and change the colors and/or wallpaper of the desktop.

OVERVIEW

Computer literacy is the buzzword of the 1990s. Corporations expect their employees to be computer literate, parents want their children to become computer literate, and you may be taking this course to fulfill a computer literacy requirement at your school or university. But what exactly does the term mean, and more important, what can you expect from reading our book?

We believe that computer literacy is the ability to do useful work on a computer. This, in turn, requires you to master Windows 95, the program (actually many programs) that controls the operation of your computer and its peripheral devices. Our book is written for you, the computer novice, and assumes no previous knowledge about a computer or about Windows. Our goal is to get you "up and running" as quickly as possible so that you can do the work you want to do.

We begin with an introduction to the Windows desktop, the graphical user interface that lets you work in intuitive fashion by pointing at icons and clicking the mouse. We show you how to use the online help facility to look up information when you need it. We identify the basic components of a window and describe how to execute commands and supply information through various types of dialog boxes. We also show you how to customize Windows so that it is better suited to your personal needs and work habits.

You will find our book to be a combination of concepts and hands-on exercises. The concepts explain the theory behind what you are doing and the exercises enable you to you sit down at the computer and apply what you learn. You are about to embark on a wonderful journey with an unlimited number of potential applications. Be patient, be inquisitive, and enjoy!

THE NATURE OF SOFTWARE

Sit down in front of a computer and you see *hardware,* that is, physical equipment such as a monitor, system unit, or mouse. The hardware is useless, however, without *software* (computer programs consisting of instructions to the hardware), and it is the availability of software that justifies the purchase of hardware. The software drives the hardware and dictates the uses to which the computer will be put. It is the software that determines how successful a computer system will be in satisfying your needs.

Software is divided broadly into two classes: *system software* (referred to as the operating system) and *application software.* You may already be familiar with different kinds of application software such as word processors, spreadsheets, or games. The wonderful thing about application software is that changing from one application to another completely changes the personality of the computer. The same computer that is used for word processing can also be used to communicate with online databases in cities thousands of miles away, prepare long-range financial forecasts, or perform hundreds of other tasks merely by changing the application program.

The operating system serves a much different function and acts as "middle man" between the application software and the hardware. An application program requests the services of the operating system whenever it needs to interact with the hardware. In other words, the application program does not communicate directly with the hardware, but does so through the operating system, which in turn locates the data on a disk, accepts information from a keyboard, directs output to the printer, and so on.

Microsoft Windows® Version 3.1 (which runs under MS-DOS) is today's most widely used operating system for the PC with an estimated 120 million copies sold to date. Windows applications have effectively replaced their text-based counterparts that dominated the first decade of the personal computer. *Windows 95* is the long-awaited successor to Windows 3.1. (Appendix A summarizes the changes and improvements in Windows 95 over its predecessor.)

THE DESKTOP

Windows 95 creates a working environment for your computer that parallels the working environment at home or in an office. You work at a desk. Windows operations take place on the *desktop.*

There are physical objects on a desk such as folders, a dictionary, a calculator, or a phone. The computer equivalents of those objects appear as *icons* (pictorial symbols) on the desktop. Each object on a real desk has attributes (properties) such as size, weight, and color. In similar fashion, Windows assigns properties to every object on its desktop. And just as you can move the objects on a real desk, you can rearrange the objects on the Windows desktop.

Figure 1.1a displays the desktop when Windows is first installed on a new computer. This desktop has only a few objects and is similar to the desk in a new office, just after you move in. Figure 1.1b displays a different desktop, one with three open windows, and is similar to a desk during the middle of a working day. Do not be concerned if your Windows desktop is different from ours. Your real desk is arranged differently from those of your friends and so your Windows desktop will also be different.

The simplicity of the desktop in Figure 1.1a helps you to focus on what's important. The ***Start button,*** as its name suggests, is where you begin. Click the Start button (mouse operations are explained in the next section) and you see a menu that provides access to any program (e.g., Microsoft Word or Microsoft Excel) on your computer. The Start button also gives you access to an online Help facility that provides information about every aspect of Windows.

In addition to the Start button, the desktop in Figure 1.1a contains three objects, each of which has a special purpose. ***My Computer*** enables you to browse the disk drives (and optional CD-ROM drive) that are attached to your computer. My Computer is discussed briefly in this chapter and again in Chapter 3. ***Network Neighborhood*** extends your view of the computer to include the accessible drives on the network to which your machine is attached, if indeed it is part of a network. (You will not see this icon if you are not connected to a network.) Network Neighborhood is discussed in Chapter 4. The ***Recycle Bin*** lets you recover a file that was previously deleted and is covered in Chapter 3.

Each object in Figure 1.1a contains additional objects that are displayed when you open (double click) the object. Double click My Computer in Figure 1.1a, for example, and you see the objects contained in the My Computer window of Figure 1.1b. Double click Network Neighborhood and you will see all of the drives available on your network.

Two additional windows are open on the desktop in Figure 1.1b and correspond to programs that are currently in use. Each window has a title bar that displays the name of the program and the associated document. (The Start button was used to open each program, Microsoft Word and Microsoft Excel in Figure 1.1b.) You can work in any window as long as you want, then switch to a different window. ***Multitasking,*** the ability to run several programs at the same time, is one of the major benefits of the Windows environment. It lets you run a word processor in one window, a spreadsheet in a second window, communicate online in a third window, run a game in a fourth window, and so on.

The ***Taskbar*** at the bottom of the desktop shows all of the programs that are currently running (open in memory). It contains a button for each open program and lets you switch back and forth between those programs, by clicking the appropriate button. The Taskbar in Figure 1.1a does not contain any buttons (other than the Start button) since there are no open applications. The Taskbar in Figure 1.1b, however, contains three additional buttons, one for each open window.

THE MOUSE

The mouse is indispensable to Windows and is referenced continually in the hands-on exercises throughout the text. There are four basic operations with which you must become familiar:

Double click to browse disk drives

Double click to access network drives

Double click to recover deleted files

Click here to begin

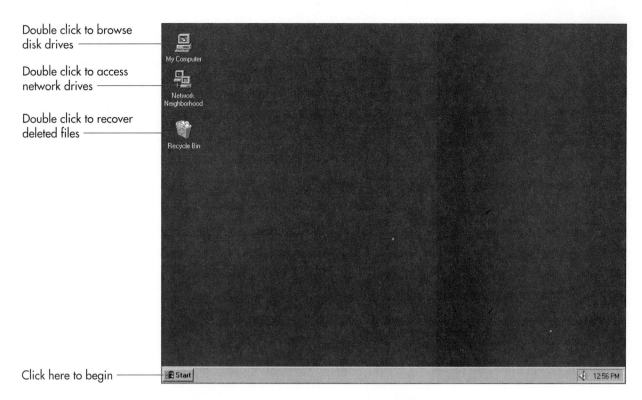

(a) New Desktop

Microsoft Word is in memory

Microsoft Excel is in memory

My Computer shows disk drives and folders

Menu produced by clicking the Start button

Taskbar shows all programs currently running

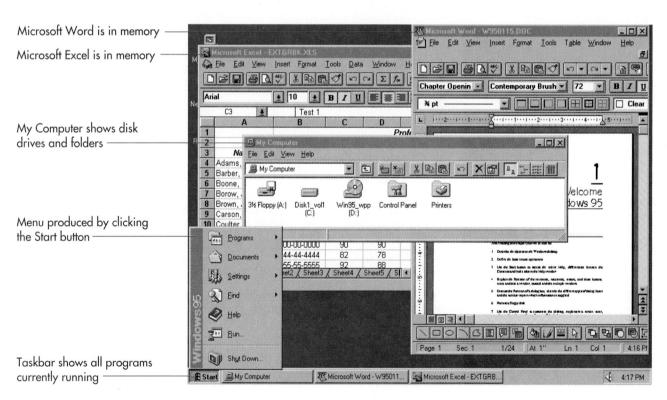

(b) A Working Desktop

FIGURE 1.1   The Windows Desktop

- To *point* to an object, move the mouse pointer onto the object.
- To *click* an object, point to it, then press and release the left mouse button; to *right click* an object, point to the object, then press and release the right mouse button.
- To *double click* an object, point to it, then quickly click the left button twice in succession.
- To *drag* an object, move the pointer to the object, then press and hold the left button while you move the mouse to a new position.

The mouse is a pointing device—move the mouse on your desk and the *mouse pointer,* typically a small arrowhead, moves on the monitor. The mouse pointer assumes different shapes according to the location of the pointer or the nature of the current action—for example, a double arrow when you change the size of a window, an I-beam to insert text, a hand to jump from one Help topic to the next, or a circle with a line through it to indicate that an attempted action is invalid.

The mouse pointer will also change to an hourglass to indicate Windows is processing your last command, and that no further commands may be issued until the action is completed. The more powerful your computer, the less frequently the hourglass will appear; and conversely, the less powerful your system, the more you see the hourglass.

ONLINE HELP

Windows 95 has an extensive *online Help* facility that contains information about virtually every topic in Windows. We believe that the best time to learn about Help is as you begin your study of Windows. Help is available at any time, and is accessed most easily by clicking the *Help command* in the Start menu, which produces the Help window in Figure 1.2.

The *Contents tab* in Figure 1.2a is similar to the table of contents in an ordinary book. The major topics are represented by books, each of which can be opened to display additional topics. Each open book will eventually display one or more specific topics, which may be viewed and/or printed to provide the indicated information.

The *Index tab* in Figure 1.2b is analogous to the index of an ordinary book. Type the first several letters of the topic to look up, click the topic when it appears in the window, then click the Display button to view the descriptive information as shown in Figure 1.2c. The Help information is task-specific and describes how to accomplish the desired task.

You can print the contents of the Help windows in Figures 1.2a and 1.2b by clicking the Print command button at the bottom of a window. You can also print the contents of the display window in Figure 1.2c by right clicking in the window, then clicking the Print topic command from the shortcut menu.

READ THE MANUAL

The answer to almost anything you need to know about Windows is available through online Help if only you take the trouble to look. The Help facility is intuitive and easy to use. The Help displays are task-specific and fit in a single screen to keep you from having to scroll through large amounts of information.

Contents tab is selected ——

Books represent major topics ——

Open book displays
more specific topics ——

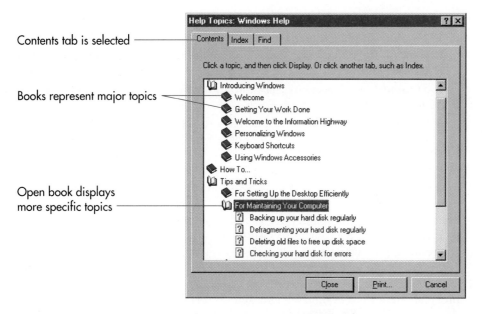

(a) Contents Tab

Index tab is selected ——

Type first letters of topic ——

Click desired topic ——

Click Display button ——

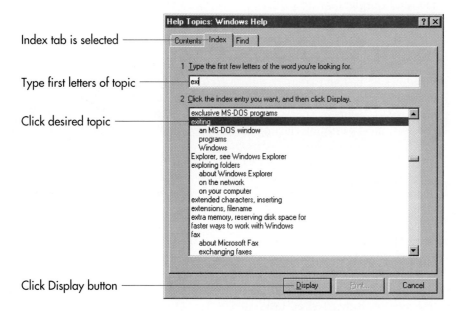

(b) Index Tab

Descriptive information describes
how to accomplish the task ——

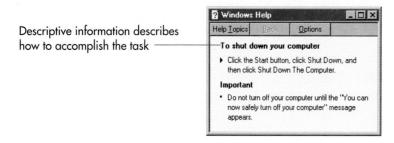

(c) Help Display

FIGURE 1.2   Online Help

Learning is best accomplished by doing, and so we come to the first of the many hands-on exercises that appear throughout the book. The exercises enable you to apply the concepts you have learned, then extend those concepts to further exploration on your own.

Our first exercise welcomes you to Windows 95, shows you how to take the guided tour provided by Microsoft, and demonstrates the use of online Help to implement a screen saver. A *screen saver* is a special program that protects your monitor by producing a constantly changing pattern after a designated period of inactivity. It is a delightful way to personalize your computer and an excellent illustration of how online Help can aid you in accomplishing a specific task.

THERE'S ALWAYS A REASON

We would love to tell you that everything will go perfectly, that you will never be frustrated, and that the computer will always perform exactly as you expect. Unfortunately, that is not going to happen, because a computer does what you tell it to do, which is not necessarily what you want it to do. There can be a tremendous difference! There is, however, a logical reason for everything the computer does or does not do; sooner or later you will discover that reason, at which point everything will fall into place.

HANDS-ON EXERCISE 1

Welcome to Windows 95

Objective: Turn the computer (and its peripherals) on; start Windows 95; use the online Help facility to implement a screen saver. Use Figure 1.3 as a guide in the exercise.

STEP 1: Turn the Computer On

➤ The floppy drive should be empty prior to starting your machine. This ensures that the system starts by reading files from the hard disk (which contains the Windows files), as opposed to a floppy disk (which does not).

➤ The number and location of the on/off switches depend on the nature and manufacturer of the devices connected to the computer. In any event:

- Turn on the monitor if it has a separate switch.
- Turn on the printer.
- Turn on the power switch of the system unit.

➤ Your system will take a minute or so to get started, after which you should see the desktop in Figure 1.3a (the Start menu is *not* yet visible). Do not be concerned if the appearance of your desktop is different from ours.

➤ You may (or may not) see the Welcome message in Figure 1.3a. All of the command buttons merit further exploration, which we will do at a later time. But for now, we ask that you click the **Close button** if you see the Welcome message.

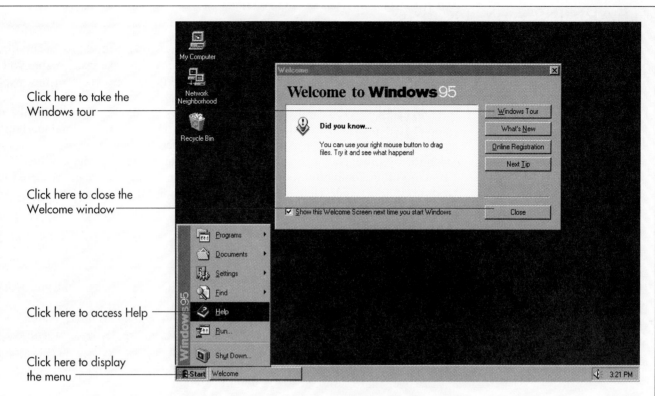

Click here to take the Windows tour

Click here to close the Welcome window

Click here to access Help

Click here to display the menu

(a) Welcome to Windows 95 (step 1)

FIGURE 1.3 Hands-on Exercise 1

➤ Click the **Start button** to display the Start menu. Again, do not be concerned if your Start menu is different from ours, or if your icons are smaller (or larger) than ours.

➤ Click the **Help command** as shown in Figure 1.3a.

MASTER THE MOUSE

Moving the mouse pointer is easy, but it takes practice to move it to an exact position on the screen. If you're having trouble, be sure the mouse is perpendicular to the system unit. Move the mouse to the left or right and the mouse pointer moves left or right on the screen. Move the mouse forward or back, and the pointer moves up or down.

STEP 2: Ten Minutes to Windows

➤ If necessary, click the **Contents tab** in the Help Topics dialog box as shown in Figure 1.3b. All of the books on your screen will be closed.

➤ Click the topic **Ten Minutes to Using Windows,** then click the **Display button** to begin the Windows tour. (You can double click the topic to avoid having to click the Display button.)

➤ You should see the menu in Figure 1.3c. Click the **Book icon** next to Using Help to learn about the Help facility.

Click the Contents tab

Double click here to
begin the Windows tour

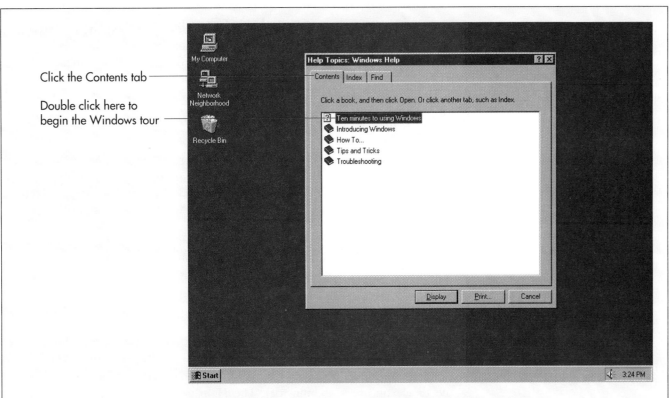

(b) Help Contents (step 2)

Click here to exit the tour

Click here to learn about
the Help facility

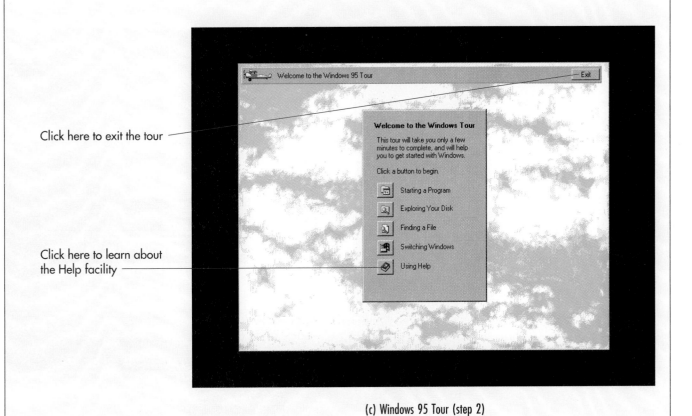

(c) Windows 95 Tour (step 2)

FIGURE 1.3   Hands-on Exercise 1 (continued)

➤ Follow the instructions provided by Windows until you complete the session on Help. Click the **Exit button** at the upper right of the screen, then click the **Exit Tour button** to return to the Desktop and continue with the exercise.

WHAT'S NEW IN WINDOWS 95

Our book is written for the novice and assumes no knowledge of Windows 3.1. If you have used Windows before, you are no doubt curious as to the changes and improvements in Windows 95. Click the Start button, click Help, then click the Index tab. Type "new" (the first few letters in the word(s) you are looking for), double click "new features" when it appears as an index entry, then select the listed topic(s) and display the information. You can also turn to Appendix A on page 191 for more detailed information.

STEP 3: Help Index

➤ Let's apply what you've learned in the Windows tour to implement a screen saver. Click the **Start button** on the Taskbar, then click the **Help command.**

➤ Click the **Index tab** as shown in Figure 1.3d. Type **sc** (the first letters in "screen," the topic you are searching for). The Help system automatically displays the topics beginning with the letters you enter.

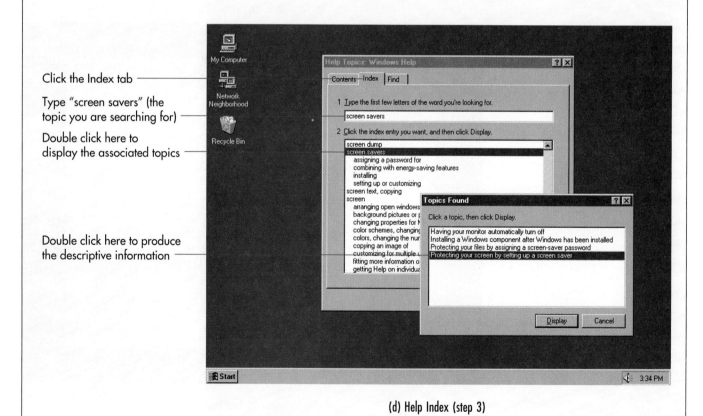

(d) Help Index (step 3)

FIGURE 1.3   Hands-on Exercise 1 (continued)

➤ Click **screen savers** from the list of displayed topics, then click the **Display command button** (or double click the topic to avoid having to click the command button).

➤ You will see a second dialog box listing the available topics under Screen Savers. Double click the topic that begins **Protecting your screen** as shown in Figure 1.3d.

DOUBLE CLICKING FOR BEGINNERS

If you are having trouble double clicking, it is because you are not clicking quickly enough, or more likely, because you are moving the mouse (however slightly) between clicks. Relax, hold the mouse firmly on your desk, and try again.

STEP 4: Implement a Screen Saver

➤ You should see the Help screen in Figure 1.3e. Click the **Shortcut Jump button** to display the **Display Properties dialog box** shown in Figure 1.3e.

➤ Click the **down arrow** in the Screen Saver list box to display the available screen savers. Click one or more of the available screen savers until you come to one you like.

➤ Click the **OK command button** to accept the screen saver and exit the dialog box. Click the **Close button** to close the Windows Help window.

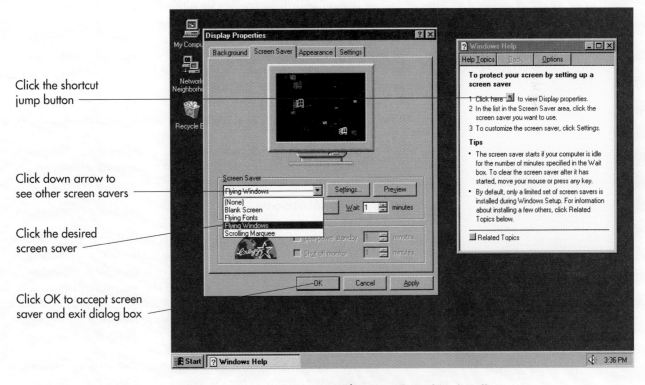

Click the shortcut jump button

Click down arrow to see other screen savers

Click the desired screen saver

Click OK to accept screen saver and exit dialog box

(e) Implementing a Screen Saver (step 4)

FIGURE 1.3   Hands-on Exercise 1 (continued)

STEP 5: Exit Windows

➤ Click the **Start button,** then click the **Shut Down command.** You will see a dialog box asking whether you're sure that you want to shut down the computer. (The option button to shut down the computer is already selected.)

➤ Click the **Yes command button,** then wait as Windows gets ready to shut down your system. Wait until you see another screen indicating that it is OK to turn off the computer.

➤ Turn off the power to your system if you do not want to continue with the next exercise at this time, or press **Ctrl, Alt,** and **Del** to restart the system. (Press and hold the **Ctrl** and **Alt keys** with your left hand as you click the **Del key** with your right.)

WORKING IN WINDOWS

One of the most significant benefits of the Windows environment is the common user interface and consistent command structure that are imposed on every Windows application. This provides a sense of familiarity from one application to the next in that all applications follow the same conventions and work basically the same way. Once you learn the basic concepts and techniques, you can apply that knowledge to every Windows application.

To use Windows effectively, you need to know the different parts of a window. You need to be able to select items from a dialog box and to execute commands from a pull-down menu. You also need to be able to move and size objects on the desktop. Each of these topics is discussed in the next several pages, after which you will have an opportunity to practice in a hands-on exercise.

Anatomy of a Window

Figure 1.4 displays a typical window and labels its essential elements. Every window has the same components as every other window, which include a control menu box, a title bar, a Minimize button, a Maximize or Restore button, and a Close button. Other elements, that may or may not be present, include a horizontal and/or vertical scroll bar, a menu bar, a status bar, and a toolbar. Every window also contains additional objects (icons) that pertain specifically to the program or data associated with that window.

The *title bar* appears at the top of the window and displays the name of the window—for example, My Computer in Figure 1.4. The *control menu box* (an icon at the extreme left of the title bar) provides access to a pull-down menu that lets you select operations relevant to the window. The *Minimize button* shrinks

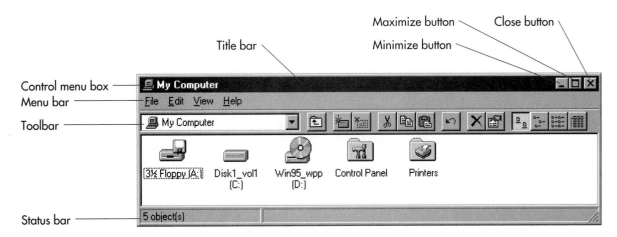

FIGURE 1.4   Anatomy of a Window

the window to a button on the Taskbar, but the program remains in memory. The *Maximize button* enlarges the window so that it takes up the entire desktop. The *Restore button* (not shown in Figure 1.4) appears instead of the maximize button after a window has been maximized, and restores the window to its previous size. The *Close button* closes the window and removes it from the desktop.

The *menu bar* appears immediately below the title bar and provides access to pull-down menus as discussed in the next section. A *toolbar* appears below the menu bar and lets you execute a command by clicking an icon, as opposed to pulling down a menu. The *status bar* is found at the bottom of the window and displays information about the window as a whole or about a selected object within a window.

A *vertical (horizontal) scroll bar* appears at the right (bottom) border of a window when its contents are not completely visible and provides access to the unseen areas. Scroll bars do not appear in Figure 1.4 since all five objects in the window are visible. (Scrolling is illustrated in step 4 of the next hands-on exercise, which begins on page 17.)

MY COMPUTER

My Computer lets you browse the disk drives (and CD-ROM) on your system. It is present on every desktop, but the contents depend on the specific configuration. Our system, for example, has one floppy drive, one hard disk, and a CD-ROM, each of which is represented by an icon within the My Computer window. To open My Computer, double click its icon on the desktop. To see the files on a specific device, double click the device icon; for example, double click the icon for drive A to see the contents of the floppy disk in drive A. My Computer is discussed in detail in Chapter 3.

Moving and Sizing a Window

Any window can be sized or moved on the desktop through appropriate actions with the mouse. To *size a window,* point to any border (the mouse pointer changes to a double arrow), then drag the border in the direction you want to go—inward to shrink the window or outward to enlarge it. You can also drag a corner (instead of a border) to change both dimensions at the same time. To ***move a window,*** while retaining its current size, click and drag the title bar to a new position on the desktop.

Pull-down Menus

The menu bar provides access to pull-down menus that enable you to execute commands within an application (a program). A pull-down menu is accessed by clicking the menu name or by pressing the Alt key plus the underlined letter in the menu name; for example, press Alt+V to pull down the View menu. Three pull-down menus associated with My Computer are shown in Figure 1.5.

The commands within a menu are executed by clicking the command once the menu has been pulled down, or by typing the underlined letter (for example, C to execute the Close command in the File menu). Alternatively, you can bypass the menu entirely if you know the equivalent keystrokes shown to the right of the command in the menu (e.g., Ctrl+X, Ctrl+C, or Ctrl+V to cut, copy, or paste as shown within the Edit menu.) A ***dimmed command*** (e.g., the Paste command in the Edit menu) means the command is not currently executable; some additional action has to be taken for the command to become available.

An ***ellipsis*** (...) following a command indicates that additional information is required to execute the command; for example, selection of the Format command in the File menu requires the user to specify additional information about the formatting process. This information is entered into a dialog box (discussed in the next section), which appears immediately after the command has been selected.

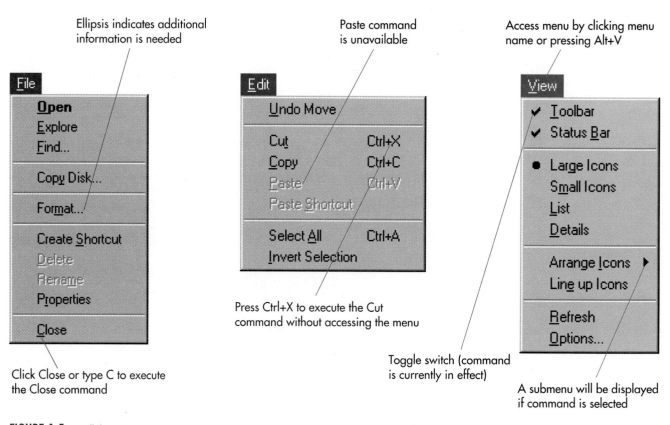

FIGURE 1.5   Pull-down Menus

A check next to a command indicates a toggle switch, whereby the command is either on or off. There is a check next to the Toolbar command in the View menu of Figure 1.5, which means the command is in effect (and thus the toolbar will be displayed). Click the Toolbar command and the check disappears, which suppresses the display of the toolbar. Pull down the menu again, click the command a second time, and the check reappears, as does the toolbar in the associated window.

An arrowhead after a command (e.g., the Arrange Icons command in the View menu) indicates a **submenu** will follow with additional menu options.

Dialog Boxes

A *dialog box* appears when additional information is needed to execute a command. The Format command, for example, requires information about which drive to format and the type of formatting desired.

Option (radio) buttons indicate mutually exclusive choices, one of which must be chosen—for example, one of three Format Type options in Figure 1.6a. Click a button to select an option, which automatically deselects the previously selected option.

Check boxes are used instead of option buttons if the choices are not mutually exclusive or if an option is not required. Multiple boxes can be checked as in Figure1.6a, or no boxes may be checked as in Figure 1.6b. Individual options are selected (cleared) by clicking on the appropriate check box.

A *text box* is used to enter descriptive information such as Bob's Disk in Figure 1.6a. A flashing vertical bar (an I-beam) appears within the text box (when the text box is active) to mark the insertion point for the text you will enter.

A *list box* displays some or all of the available choices, any one of which is selected by clicking the desired item. A *drop-down list box,* such as the Capacity list box in Figure 1.6a, conserves space by showing only the current selection. Click the arrow of a drop-down list box to produce a list of available options. An *open list box,* such as those in Figure 1.6b, displays the choices without having to click the down arrow. (A scroll bar appears within an open list box if all of the choices are not visible at one time and provides access to the hidden choices.)

A *tabbed dialog box* provides multiple sets of options. The dialog box in Figure 1.6c, for example, has two tabs, each with its own set of options. Click either tab (the General tab is currently selected) to display the associated options.

All dialog boxes have a title bar that contains a What's This button (in the form of a question mark) and a Close button. The *What's This button* provides help for any item in the dialog box; click the button, then click the item in the dialog box for which you want additional information. The Close button at the right of the title bar closes the dialog box.

All dialog boxes also contain one or more *command buttons,* the function of which is generally apparent from the button's name. The Start button, in Figure 1.6a, for example, initiates the formatting process. The OK command button in Figure 1.6b accepts the settings, then closes the dialog box. The Cancel button does just the opposite, and ignores (cancels) the settings and closes the dialog box with no further action.

The Mouse versus the Keyboard, and Other Shortcuts

Almost every command in Windows can be executed in many different ways, using either the mouse or the keyboard. Most people start with the mouse but add keyboard shortcuts as they become more proficient. There is no right or wrong technique, just different techniques, and the one you choose depends entirely on personal preference in a specific situation. If, for example, your hands are already on

Drop-down list box shows
current selection only

Option buttons indicate
mutually exclusive choices

Text box is used to enter
descriptive information

Check boxes indicate choices
that are not mutually exclusive

Click here to see
other options

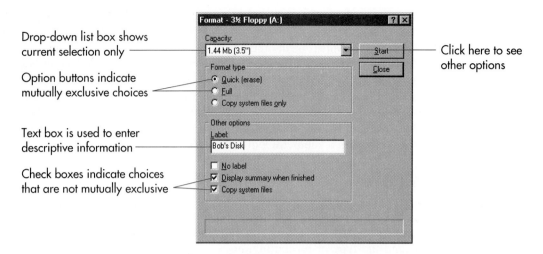

(a) Option Buttons and Check Boxes

Command buttons

Open list box displays
multiple options

Scroll bar indicates that
not all options are visible

No boxes are checked

Title bar

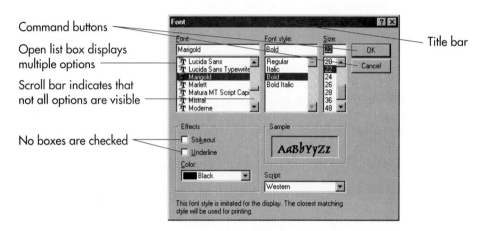

(b) List Boxes

Tab

Command buttons

Close button

What's This button

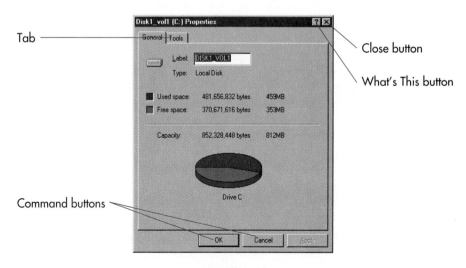

(c) Tabbed Dialog Box

FIGURE 1.6   Dialog Boxes

the keyboard, it is faster to use the keyboard equivalent. Other times, your hand will be on the mouse and that will be the fastest way. Toolbars provide still other ways to execute common commands.

In the beginning you may wonder why there are so many different ways to do the same thing, but you will eventually recognize the many options as part of Windows' charm. It is not necessary to memorize anything, nor should you even try; just be flexible and willing to experiment. The more you practice, the faster all of this will become second nature to you.

FORMATTING A DISK

All disks have to be formatted before they can hold data. The formatting process divides a disk into concentric circles called tracks, then further divides each track into sectors. You don't have to worry about formatting a hard disk, as that is done at the factory prior to the machine being sold. You do, however, have to format a floppy disk in order for Windows to read from and write to the disk. The procedure to format a floppy disk is described in step 5 of the following exercise.

FORMAT AT THE PROPER CAPACITY

You must format a floppy disk at its rated capacity or else you may be unable to read the disk. There are two types of 3½-inch disks, double density (720KB) and high density (1.44MB). The easiest way to determine the type of disk you have is to look at the disk itself for the labels DD or HD, for double and high density, respectively. You can also check the number of square holes in the disk; a double-density disk has one, whereas a high-density disk has two.

HANDS-ON EXERCISE 2

Working in Windows

Objective: Open My Computer, then use the View menu to change the appearance of the icons in the resulting window. Move and size a window on the desktop. Format a floppy disk. Use Figure 1.7 as a guide in the exercise.

STEP 1: Open My Computer

➤ Turn on the computer and load Windows as you did in the previous exercise. Click the **Close command button** if you see the Welcome to Windows 95 window.

➤ Point to the **My Computer icon,** click the **right mouse button,** then click the **Open command** from the shortcut menu. (Alternatively, you can double click the icon to open it directly.)

➤ My Computer will open into a window as shown in Figure 1.7a. Do not be concerned if the contents of your window or its size and position on the desktop are different from ours.

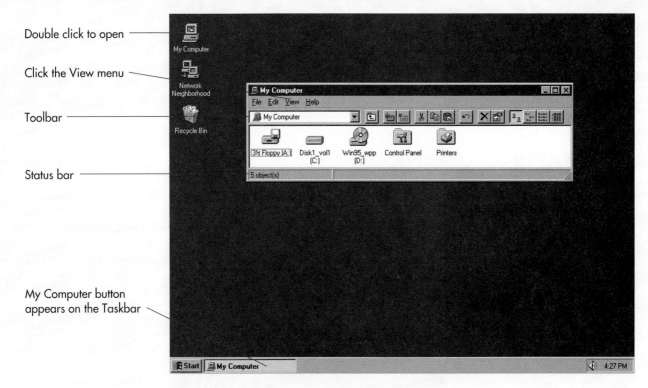

Double click to open

Click the View menu

Toolbar

Status bar

My Computer button
appears on the Taskbar

(a) Open My Computer (step 1)

FIGURE 1.7 Hands-on Exercise 2

STEP 2: The View Menu

➤ Pull down the **View menu** (point to the menu and click) or press Alt+V as shown in Figure 1.7b.

➤ Make or verify the following selections. (You have to pull down the menu each time you choose a different command.)

- The **Toolbar command** should be checked. The Toolbar command functions as a toggle switch. Click the command and the toolbar is displayed. Pull down the menu again, click the command a second time and the toolbar disappears.

- The **Status Bar command** should be checked. The Status Bar command also functions as a toggle switch.

- **Large icons** should be selected.

➤ Pull down the **View menu** a final time. Click the **Arrange icons command** and (if necessary) click the **AutoArrange command** so that a check appears. Click outside the menu (or press the **Esc key**) if the command is already checked.

TOOLTIPS

Point to any button on the toolbar and Windows displays the name of the button, which is indicative of its function. Point to the clock at the extreme right of the Taskbar and you will see a ToolTip with today's date. Point to the Start Button and you will see a ToolTip telling you to click here to begin.

Drag the title bar to move the window (when menu is closed)

Click and drag a border to size the window (when menu is closed)

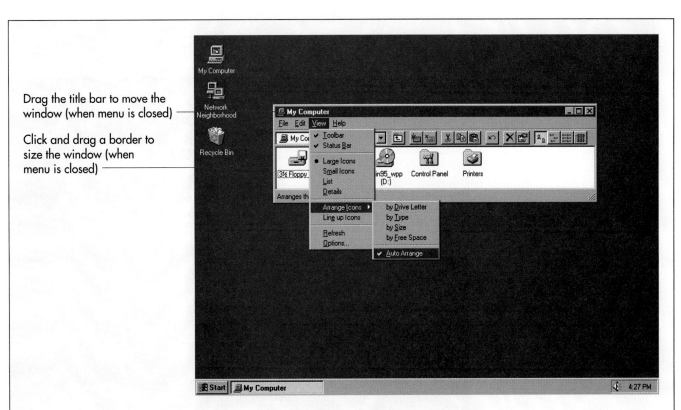

(b) The View Menu (step 2)

FIGURE 1.7   Hands-on Exercise 2 (continued)

STEP 3: Move and Size the Window

➤ Move and size the My Computer window on your desk to match the display in Figure 1.7b.

- Click the **Restore button** (which appears only if the window has been maximized) or else you will not be able to move and size the window.

- To change the width or height of the window, click and drag a border (the mouse pointer changes to a double arrow) in the direction you want to go. Drag the border inward to shrink the window or outward to enlarge it.

- To change the width and height at the same time, click and drag a corner rather than a border.

- To change the position of the window, click and drag the title bar.

- Click the **maximize button** so that the window expands to fill the entire screen. Click the **restore button** (which replaces the maximize button and is not shown in Figure 1.7a) to return the window to its previous size.

- Click the **minimize button** to shrink the My Computer window to a button on the Taskbar. My Computer is still open and remains active in memory.

- Click the **My Computer button** on the Taskbar to reopen the window.

STEP 4: Scrolling

➤ Pull down the **View menu** and click **Details** (or click the **Details button** on the toolbar). You are now in the Details view as shown in Figure 1.7c.

➤ Click and drag the bottom border of the window inward so that you see the vertical scroll bar in Figure 1.7c. The scroll bar indicates that the contents of the window are not completely visible.

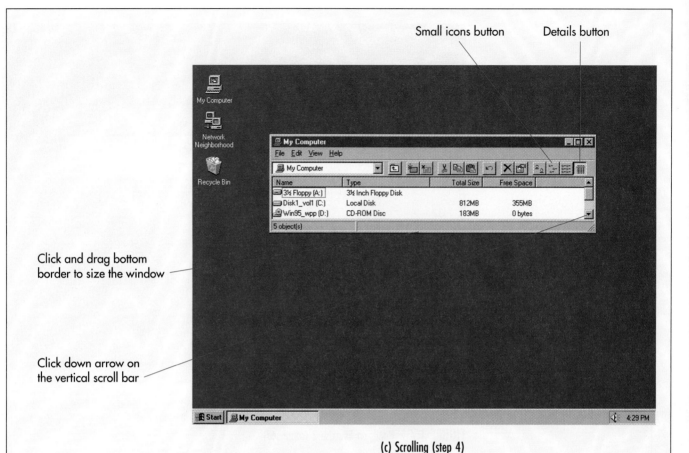

Small icons button   Details button

(c) Scrolling (step 4)

FIGURE 1.7   Hands-on Exercise 2 (continued)

Click and drag bottom border to size the window

Click down arrow on the vertical scroll bar

- Click the **down arrow** on the scroll bar. The top line (for drive A) disappears from view and a new line containing the Control Panel comes into view.
- Click the **down arrow** a second time, which brings the Printers folder into view at the bottom of the window as the icon for drive C scrolls off the screen.
➤ Click the **Small icons button** on the toolbar. Size the window so that the scroll bar disappears when the contents of the window become completely visible.
➤ Click the **Details button** on the toolbar. The scroll bar returns because you can no longer see the complete contents. Move and/or size the window to your personal preference.

THE DETAILS VIEW

The Details view provides information about each object in a folder—for example, the capacity (total size) and amount of free space on a disk. To switch to the Details view, pull down the View menu and click Details. You can also click the Details button on the toolbar provided the toolbar is displayed.

STEP 5: Format a Floppy Disk

➤ Place a floppy disk in drive A, then click the icon for **drive A.** Pull down the **File menu** and click **Format.**

➤ You will see the dialog box in Figure 1.7d. Move the dialog box by clicking and dragging its **title bar** so that your screen matches ours.

➤ Click the **What's This button** (the mouse pointer changes to a question mark). Click the **Full option button** (under Format type) for an explanation. Click anywhere in the dialog box to close the pop-up window.

➤ Set the formatting parameters as shown in Figure 1.7d:

• Set the **Capacity** to match the floppy disk you purchased (see boxed tip on page 17).

• Click the **Full option button** to choose a full format. This option is well worth the extra time as it ensures the integrity of your disk. (The quick option can be used only if a disk was previously formatted.)

• Click the **Label text box** if it's empty or click and drag over the existing label if there is an entry. Enter a new label such as **Bob's Disk** as shown in Figure 1.7d.

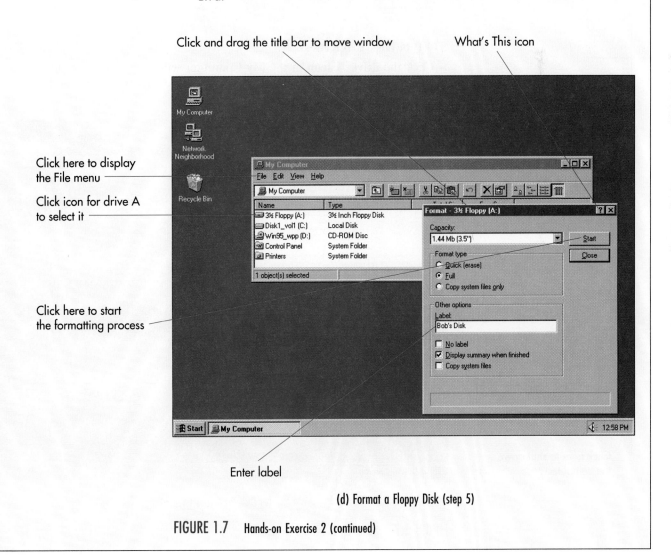

(d) Format a Floppy Disk (step 5)

FIGURE 1.7   Hands-on Exercise 2 (continued)

➤ Click the **Start command button** to begin the formatting operation. This will take about a minute and you can see the progress of the formatting process at the bottom of the dialog box.

➤ After the formatting process is complete, you will see an informational dialog box with the results of the formatting operation. Read the information, then click the **Close command button** to close the informational dialog box.

➤ Click the **Close button** to close the Format dialog box.

WHAT'S THIS?

The What's This button (a question mark) appears in the title bar in every dialog box. Click the question mark, then click the item you want information about, and the information appears in a pop-up window. To print the contents of the pop-up window, click the right mouse button inside the window, and click Print Topic. Click outside the pop-up window to close the window and continue working.

STEP 6: Disk Properties

➤ Click the **drive A icon** in the My Computer window, click the **right mouse button** to display a shortcut menu, then click the **Properties command.**

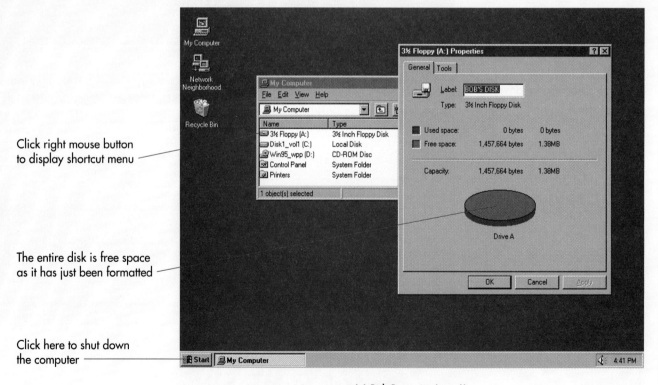

Click right mouse button to display shortcut menu

The entire disk is free space as it has just been formatted

Click here to shut down the computer

(e) Disk Properties (step 6)

FIGURE 1.7   Hands-on Exercise 2 (continued)

➤ You should see the Properties dialog box in Figure 1.7e although you may have to move and size the window to match our figure. The pie chart displays the percentage of free and unused space.

➤ Click **OK** to close the Properties dialog box. Click the **Close button** to close My Computer.

PROPERTIES EVERYWHERE

Windows assigns properties to every object on the desktop and stores those properties with the object itself. Point to any object on the desktop, including the desktop itself, click the right mouse button to display a shortcut menu, then click Properties to display the property sheet for that object.

STEP 7: Exit Windows

➤ Click the **Start button,** then click the **Shut Down command.** You will see a dialog box asking whether you're sure that you want to shut down the computer. (The option button to shut down the computer is already selected.)

➤ Click the **Yes command button,** then wait as Windows gets ready to shut down your system. Wait until you see another screen indicating that it is OK to turn off the computer.

CUSTOMIZING WINDOWS

You can customize every aspect of the Windows environment. You can add icons to the desktop, move icons from one place to another, or remove the icons altogether. You can change the colors of the desktop, reverse the action of the left and right mouse buttons, or change the resolution of your monitor. Many of these changes are accomplished through the Control Panel, which is accessed through the My Computer icon.

The Control Panel

The *Control Panel* contains the utility programs (tools) used to change the hardware or software settings on your system. The tools in the Control Panel are displayed in Figure 1.8 (you may have a different number of icons, depending on the hardware devices in your configuration).

The Control Panel window has the same components as every other window. The title bar displays the name of the window and contains the Control menu box, and the Minimize, Maximize (or Restore), and Close buttons. The menu bar provides access to the pull-down menus. The toolbar provides an alternate way to execute common commands. The status bar displays information about the selected icon.

Each icon in the Control Panel provides access to a property sheet or program, which changes (configures) a different aspect of the Windows environment. To access a specific icon, click the icon, then pull down the File menu and click the Open command (or simply double click the icon). The name of the icon is indicative of its function. Additional information can be obtained through the Help facility. The changes available through the Display icon will be illustrated in the next hands-on exercise when we modify the colors of the desktop.

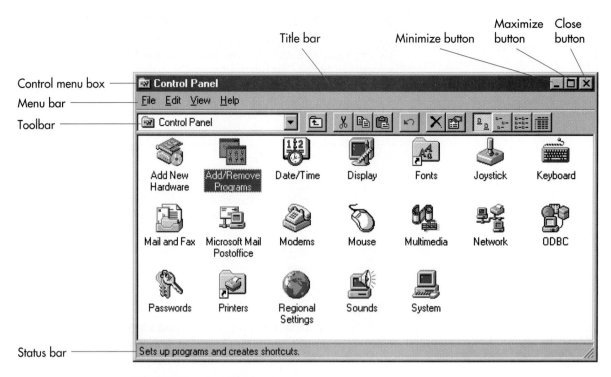

FIGURE 1.8   The Control Panel

SHORTCUTS

One of the best ways to customize Windows is to create a shortcut in the form of an additional icon on the desktop that lets you go directly to a frequently used program. The Control Panel, for example, is accessed through My Computer; that is, you have to open My Computer in order to get to the Control Panel. You can, however, bypass My Computer by creating a shortcut icon on the desktop that takes you directly to the Control Panel. See steps 4 and 5 on pages 29 and 30.

THE TILE AND CASCADE COMMANDS

One of the advantages of Windows is the ability to work on several programs at the same time, each of which is open in its own window. Each window can be moved or sized individually, but it is often faster to change the appearance of multiple windows at the same time. This is accomplished through the Tile and Cascade commands, which are accessed by right clicking the Taskbar. (See step 3 in the next hands-on exercise.)

The Tile and Cascade commands are illustrated in Figure 1.9. The *Tile command* in Figure 1.9a resizes each open window, then arranges the windows vertically (or horizontally) on the desktop. The *Cascade command* in Figure 1.9b layers the open windows one on top of another, bringing one window to the front while keeping the title bar of the remaining windows visible. Tiling is preferable when you are working with two or more applications simultaneously and want to see the contents of all windows. Cascading is better when you are working primarily with one application and need to see as much of that window as possible, while still seeing part of the other window.

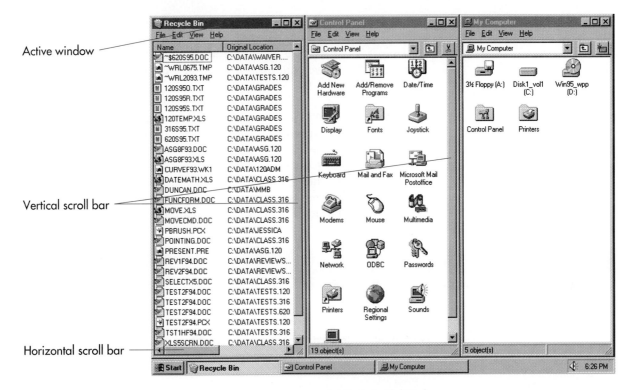

Active window

Vertical scroll bar

Horizontal scroll bar

(a) Vertically Tiled Windows

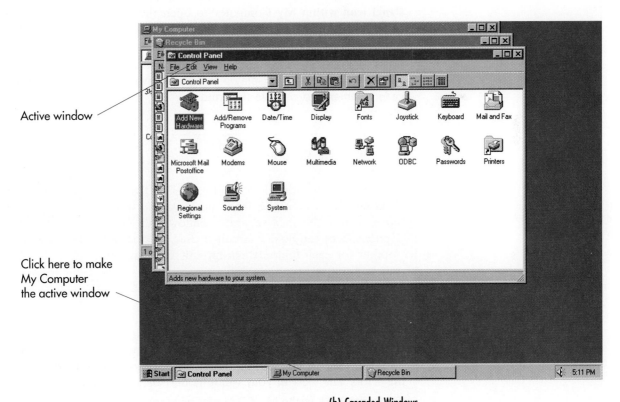

Active window

Click here to make
My Computer
the active window

(b) Cascaded Windows

FIGURE 1.9   Arranging the Desktop

A different title bar is highlighted in each figure, corresponding to the active window. The *active window* contains the application on which you are presently working; it is the Recycle Bin in Figure 1.9a and the Control Panel in Figure 1.9b. To change the active window, just click in a different window or click the corresponding button on the Taskbar.

Each window in Figure 1.9 (whether tiled or cascaded) contains the elements essential to every Windows application. Each window has a control menu box as well as a title bar with a Minimize, Maximize, and Close button. A horizontal scroll bar is present in the Recycle Bin window of Figure 1.9a because not all of the detail information for a specific file is visible. A vertical scroll bar is also present in this window because the Recycle Bin contains more files than can be seen at one time. The toolbar and status bar are not displayed for the Recycle Bin but are present in the other windows. The menu bar is found in all three windows.

HANDS-ON EXERCISE 3

Customizing Windows

Objective: Tile and cascade open windows; create a shortcut on the desktop to open the Control Panel; customize the desktop and Taskbar. Use Figure 1.10 as a guide in the exercise.

STEP 1: Open the Control Panel

➤ Load Windows. Double click the **My Computer icon.** Double click the **Control Panel icon** within My Computer to open the Control Panel. Do not be concerned about the contents of the windows or their size or position on the desktop.

➤ Point to an empty space on the **Taskbar** (you can't point to a button). Click the **right mouse button** to display a menu as shown in Figure 1.10a. Click the **Cascade command** to cascade the windows.

ONE WINDOW OR MANY

If opening the Control Panel causes the My Computer window to disappear (and its button to vanish from the Taskbar), you need to set an option to open each folder in a separate window. Pull down the View menu, click Options, click the Folder tab, then click the option button to use a separate window for each folder. Click the OK command button to accept this setting and return to the desktop

STEP 2: The Active Window

➤ Click and drag the **title bar** of the top window (the Control Panel in Figure 1.10b) so that the size and position of the windows on your desktop match Figure 1.10b. The view in your windows may be different from ours.

➤ Click anywhere in the My Computer window to make it the active window. The title bar for My Computer is highlighted and all subsequent commands affect just this window:

Double click
to open
My Computer

Double click
to open the
Control Panel

Click Cascade

Right click
empty space on
Taskbar to produce
the shortcut menu

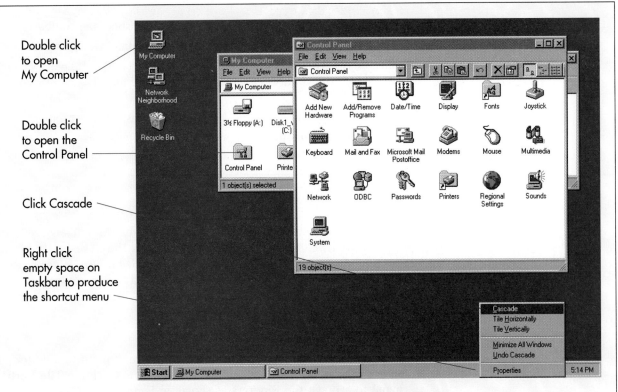

(a) Open the Control Panel (step 1)

Click in the window
to make it active, then
click the Details button

Click the Details
button to switch to
the Details view

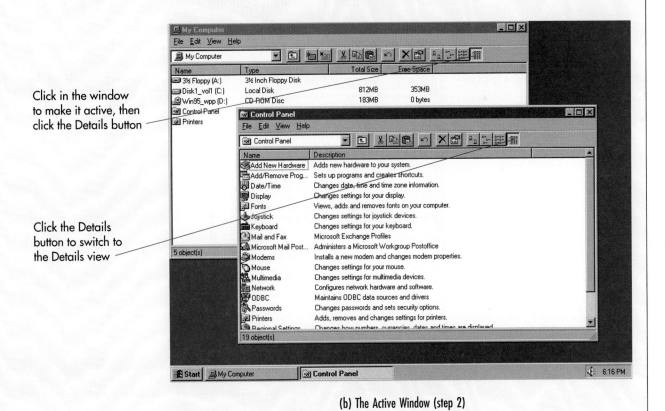

(b) The Active Window (step 2)

FIGURE 1.10   Hands-on Exercise 3

- If necessary, pull down the **View menu** to display the toolbar.
- Click the **Details button** to switch to the Details view.

➤ Click anywhere in the Control Panel window to make it the active window. The title bar for the Control Panel is highlighted and all subsequent commands affect just this window:

- If necessary, pull down the **View menu** to display the toolbar.
- Click the **Details button** to switch to the Details view.

CUSTOMIZE THE MOUSE

Customize the mouse to reverse the actions of the left and right buttons and/or implement other changes. Double click the Mouse icon in the Control Panel, click the Buttons tab in the Mouse Properties sheet, then click the appropriate (Left-handed or Right-handed) option button.

STEP 3: Tile the Windows

➤ Point to an empty space on the **Taskbar** (you can't point to a button). Click the **right mouse button** to display the shortcut menu. Click the **Tile Vertically command** to arrange the windows as shown in Figure 1.10c.

➤ **Right click the Taskbar.** Click the **Tile Horizontally command** to tile the windows horizontally rather than vertically.

Click here to close the Control Panel window

Pull down the View menu and click Large Icons

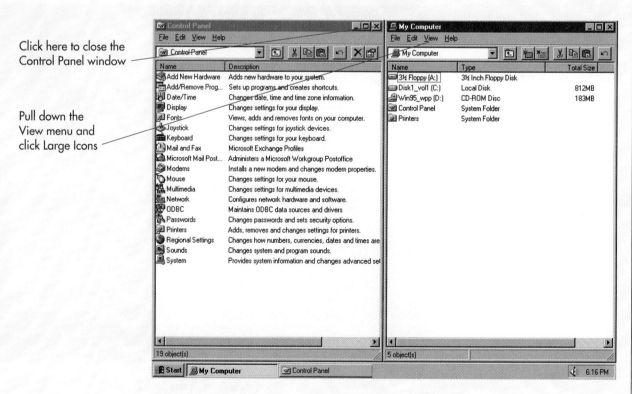

(c) Tile the Windows (step 3)

FIGURE 1.10   Hands-on Exercise 3 (continued)

➤ **Right click the Taskbar** a third (and final) time. Click the **Undo Tile command** to reverse the horizontal tiling and again match Figure 1.10c.

➤ Click in the **My Computer window** (or click the **My Computer button** on the Taskbar) to make it the active window. Pull down the **View menu** and click **Large icons** to change the view in this window.

➤ Click in the **Control Panel window** (or click the **Control Panel button** on the Taskbar) to make the Control Panel the active window. Click the **Close button** to close the window.

THE UNDO COMMAND

The Undo command is available in every Windows application to reverse (undo) the most recent command. The command is also available from the Taskbar to reverse the Tile and/or Cascade commands. Point to the Taskbar, click the right mouse button, then click the Undo command to restore the arrangement on your desktop.

STEP 4: Create a Shortcut to the Control Panel

➤ Point to the **Control Panel icon** in the My Computer window, click the **right mouse button,** and drag the icon from the window to the desktop as shown in Figure 1.10d. Release the mouse.

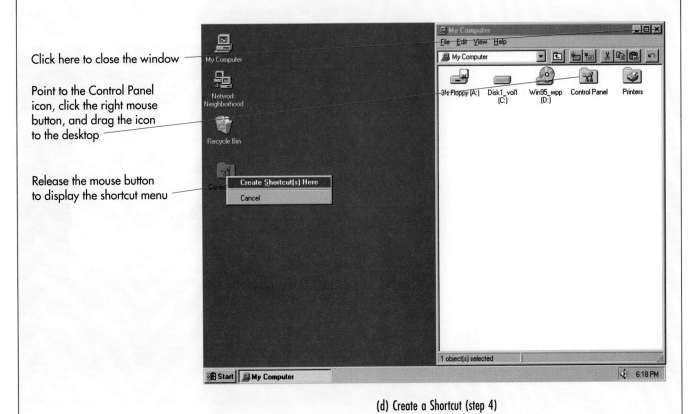

Click here to close the window

Point to the Control Panel icon, click the right mouse button, and drag the icon to the desktop

Release the mouse button to display the shortcut menu

(d) Create a Shortcut (step 4)

FIGURE 1.10   Hands-on Exercise 3 (continued)

➤ Click **Create Shortcut Here** to close the menu and create the shortcut. Note the following:

- The icon for the shortcut resembles the Control Panel icon in My Computer except that it contains a curved arrow indicating a shortcut.
- To move the Shortcut, click and drag the icon to a new location on the desktop.

➤ Click the **Close button** in the My Computer window.

STEP 5: Try the Shortcut

➤ Double click the **Shortcut to the Control Panel icon** to reopen the Control Panel in its previous position.

➤ Windows remembers the size and position of an open window and uses those settings whenever it reopens the window. Move and size the Control Panel window to match the display in Figure 1.10e.

- To change the height *or* width of the window, click and drag a border.
- To change the height *and* width simultaneously, click and drag a corner.
- To change the position of the window, click and drag the title bar.
- Click the **Large icons button** to change to this view.

➤ Double click the **Display icon** to open the Properties sheet for the desktop. Click the **Minimize button** in the Control Panel window to shrink the window to a button on the Taskbar.

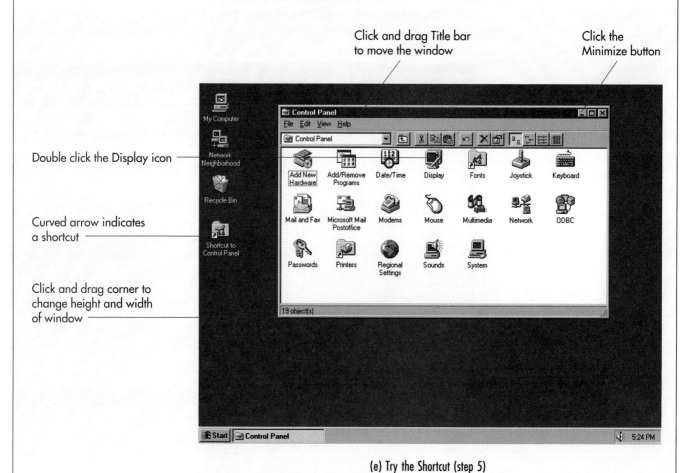

(e) Try the Shortcut (step 5)

FIGURE 1.10   Hands-on Exercise 3 (continued)

STEP 6: Customize the Desktop

➤ Click the **Appearance tab** in the Display Properties dialog box as shown in Figure 1.10f.

➤ Click the **down arrow** in the **Scheme list box** to select a different color scheme. Click the **Apply command button** to apply the new color scheme and continue working. Experiment with one or two additional color schemes until you are satisfied.

➤ Click the **Background tab** to select a pattern and/or a wallpaper for the desktop. Click the **Apply command button** to apply the pattern or wallpaper.

➤ Click the **OK command button** to exit the Properties sheet.

SET A TIME LIMIT

You can spend (waste) untold hours in pursuing the ideal color scheme or wallpaper selection for your desktop. Set a time limit before you start (10 or 15 minutes), then quit when you have spent the allotted time. Tomorrow is another day.

STEP 7: Customize the Taskbar

➤ Point to an empty area on the **Taskbar,** click the **right mouse button** to display a shortcut menu, then click **Properties** to display a dialog box for the Taskbar as shown in Figure 1.10g.

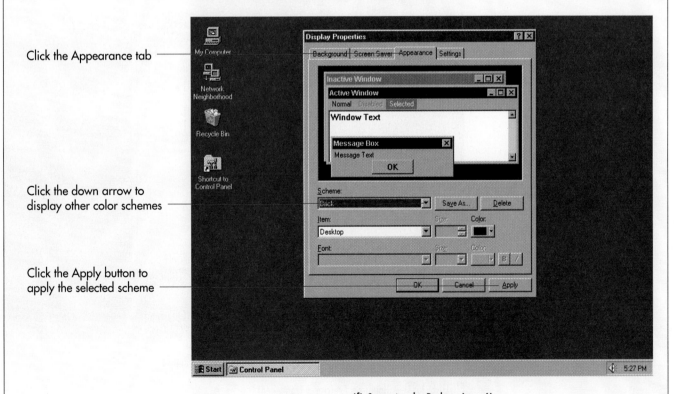

Click the Appearance tab

Click the down arrow to
display other color schemes

Click the Apply button to
apply the selected scheme

(f) Customize the Desktop (step 6)

FIGURE 1.10   Hands-on Exercise 3 (continued)

➤ Click the **Show small icons** check box on and off to see its effect. Choose the option you prefer (small or large icons). Click the **OK command button** to accept the option and exit the Properties sheet.

THE RIGHT MOUSE BUTTON

The right mouse button is the fastest way to change the properties of any object on the desktop or even the desktop itself. Point to a blank area on the desktop, click the right mouse button, then click Properties in the shortcut menu to display the dialog box (Properties sheet) for the desktop. In similar fashion, you can right click the Taskbar to change its properties. You can also right click any icon on the desktop or any icon in a window.

STEP 8: Exit Windows

➤ Click the **Start button** to display the Start menu, which displays the icons in the size you selected, then exit from Windows as you have done in the previous exercises.

➤ Click the **Shut Down** command, click the **Yes command button,** and then wait until you see the screen indicating it is OK to turn off the computer.

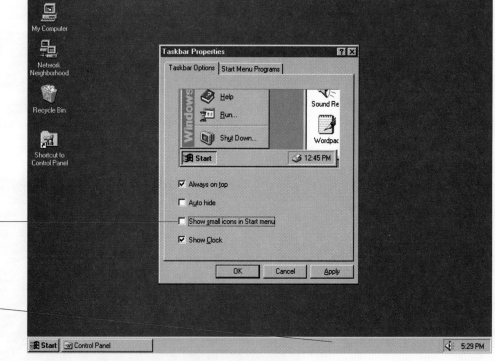

Click to select/deselect this choice

Right click empty space on Taskbar to produce the shortcut menu

(g) Customize the Taskbar (step 7)

FIGURE 1.10   Hands-on Exercise 3 (continued)

Windows 95 is a computer program (actually many programs) that controls the operation of your computer and its peripherals. It is the successor to Windows 3.1, which is the most common operating system for desktop and portable PCs.

All Windows operations take place on the desktop. The Start button, as its name suggests, is where you begin. Online Help is accessed by clicking the Help command from the Start menu.

The mouse is essential to Windows and has four basic actions: pointing, clicking (with the left or right button), double clicking, and dragging. The mouse pointer assumes different shapes according to the nature of the current action.

Every window on the desktop contains the same basic elements, which include a title bar, a control menu box, a Minimize button, a Maximize or Restore button, and a Close button. Other elements that may be present include a menu bar, vertical and/or horizontal scroll bars, a status bar, and a toolbar. All windows may be moved, sized, tiled, or cascaded.

A dialog box supplies information needed to execute a command. Option buttons indicate mutually exclusive choices, one of which must be chosen. Check boxes are used if the choices are not mutually exclusive or if an option is not required. A text box supplies descriptive information. A (drop-down or open) list box displays multiple choices, any of which may be selected. A tabbed dialog box provides access to multiple sets of options.

My Computer enables you to browse the disk drives attached to your system. My Computer is present on every desktop, but its contents depend on your specific configuration. Every aspect of Windows can be customized through the Control Panel, which is accessed through My Computer.

KEY WORDS AND CONCEPTS

Active window
Application software
Cascade command
Check box
Click
Close button
Command buttons
Contents tab
Control Panel
Desktop
Dialog box
Dimmed command
Double click
Drag
Drop-down list box
Ellipsis
Hardware
Help command

Help Index
Horizontal scroll bar
Index tab
List box
Maximize button
Menu bar
Minimize button
Mouse pointer
Move a window
Multitasking
My Computer
Network Neighborhood
Online Help
Open list box
Option buttons
Point
Recycle Bin
Restore button

Right click
Screen saver
Size a window
Software
Start button
Status bar
Submenu
System software
Tabbed dialog box
Taskbar
Text box
Tile command
Toolbar
Vertical scroll bar
What's This button
Windows 95

MULTIPLE CHOICE

1. Which of the following is true?
   (a) Double clicking the icon of an open Help book will close the book
   (b) Double clicking the icon of a closed Help book will open the book
   (c) Both (a) and (b)
   (d) Neither (a) nor (b)

2. Which of the following is true regarding a dialog box?
   (a) Option buttons indicate mutually exclusive choices
   (b) Check boxes imply that multiple options may be selected
   (c) Both (a) and (b)
   (d) Neither (a) nor (b)

3. Which of the following is the first step in sizing a window?
   (a) Point to the title bar
   (b) Pull down the View menu to display the toolbar
   (c) Point to any corner or border
   (d) Pull down the View menu and change to large icons

4. Which of the following is the first step in moving a window?
   (a) Point to the title bar
   (b) Pull down the View menu to display the toolbar
   (c) Point to any corner or border
   (d) Pull down the View menu and change to large icons

5. A right-handed person will normally:
   (a) Click the left mouse button to select an item
   (b) Click the right mouse button to display a shortcut menu
   (c) Both (a) and (b)
   (d) Neither (a) nor (b)

6. How do you exit Windows?
   (a) Click the Start button, then click the Shut Down command
   (b) Right click the Start button, then click the Shut Down command
   (c) Click the End button, then click the Shut Down command
   (d) Right click the End button, then click the Shut Down command

7. How do you access Help?
   (a) Click the Start button, then click the Help command
   (b) Click the Help button, then click the Start command
   (c) Right click the Start button, then click the Help command
   (d) Right click the Help button, then click the Start command

8. How do you open My Computer?
   (a) Double click the My Computer icon on the desktop
   (b) Right click the My Computer icon on the desktop, then click the Open command
   (c) Both (a) and (b)
   (d) Neither (a) nor (b)

9. How do you open the Control Panel?
    (a) Double click the Control Panel icon within My Computer
    (b) Double click a shortcut icon on the desktop
    (c) Both (a) and (b)
    (d) Neither (a) nor (b)

10. Which of the following is considered an application program?
    (a) Windows 95
    (b) Microsoft Word
    (c) Both (a) and (b)
    (d) Neither (a) nor (b)

11. Which button appears immediately after a window has been maximized?
    (a) The Close button
    (b) The Restore button
    (c) Both (a) and (b)
    (d) Neither (a) nor (b)

12. What happens to a window that has been minimized?
    (a) The window is still visible but it no longer has a minimize button
    (b) The window shrinks to a button on the Taskbar
    (c) The window is closed and the application is removed from memory
    (d) The window is still open but the application has been removed from memory

13. Which of the following commands will display equal-sized windows on the desktop, with one window partially on top of the next?
    (a) Minimize all windows
    (b) Tile Horizontally
    (c) Tile Vertically
    (d) Cascade

14. What is the significance of three dots next to a command in a pull-down menu?
    (a) The command is not currently accessible
    (b) A dialog box will appear if the command is selected
    (c) A help window will appear if the command is selected
    (d) There are no equivalent keystrokes for the particular command

15. What is the significance of a faded (dimmed) command in a pull-down menu?
    (a) The command is not currently accessible
    (b) A dialog box will appear if the command is selected
    (c) A help window will appear if the command is selected
    (d) There are no equivalent keystrokes for the particular command

ANSWERS

1. c	**6.** a	**11.** b
2. c	**7.** a	**12.** b
3. c	**8.** c	**13.** d
4. a	**9.** c	**14.** b
5. c	**10.** b	**15.** a

1. Use Figure 1.11 to match each action with its result; a given action may be used more than once or not at all.

Action

a. Double click at 1
b. Click at 2
c. Click at 3
d. Click and drag at 4
e. Click at 5
f. Click at 6
g. Click at 7
h. Click and drag at 8
i. Right click at 9
j. Click at 10

Result

_____ Move the active window

_____ Maximize the active window

_____ Tile the open windows horizontally

_____ Shut down the system (Exit Windows)

_____ Size the active window

_____ Close the active window

_____ Make Control Panel the current window

_____ Open the Recycle Bin

_____ Minimize the active window

_____ Change the view in the active window to Large Icons

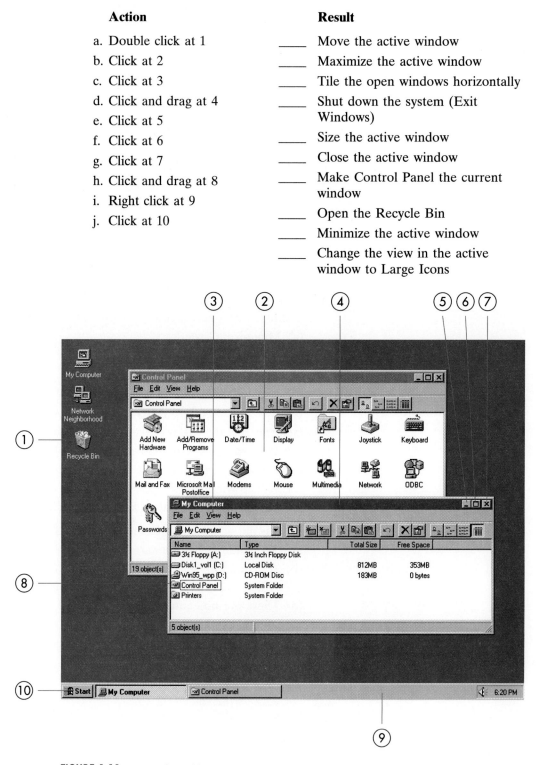

FIGURE 1.11   Screen for Problem 1

2. Each of the messages in Figure 1.12 occurred (or could have occurred) during the various hands-on exercises in the chapter. Indicate the probable cause of each error and the necessary corrective action.

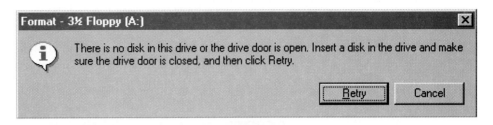

(a) Message 1

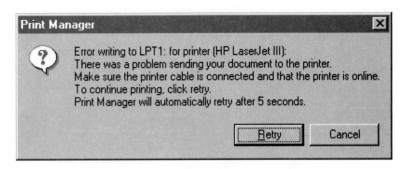

(b) Message 2

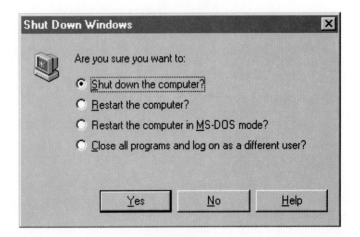

(c) Message 3

(d) Message 4

FIGURE 1.12   Informational Messages for Problem 2

3. Troubleshooting: The best time to learn about troubleshooting is when everything is going smoothly. Answer the following with respect to the screen in Figure 1.13:

   a. How do you display the screen in Figure 1.13?
   b. Which books are open? Which books are closed?
   c. How do you open a closed book? How do you close an open book?
   d. Are the contents of the window completely visible? What happens if you click the up (down) arrow in the vertical scroll bar?
   e. How do you print a Help topic?

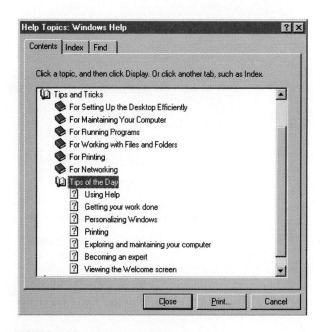

FIGURE 1.13   Screen for Problem 3

4. Answer the following with respect to the My Computer configuration in Figure 1.14:

   a. In which view is My Computer displayed? How do you change the view?
   b. Why are the horizontal and vertical scroll bars missing from the figure?
   c. How many floppy drives are on the system? Which letter is associated with each drive?

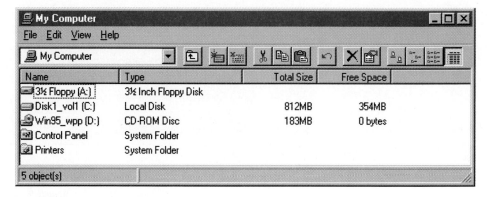

FIGURE 1.14   Screen for Problem 4

d. How many hard drives are on the system? Which letter is associated with each drive?

e. What is the total storage capacity of the system's hard disk(s)? How much space is still available?

f. Is a CD-ROM present?

g. What happens if you double click the icon for drive A? For drive C?

h. What happens if you right click the icon for drive A? For drive C?

5. Answer the following with respect to the desktop in Figure 1.15:

a. Are the windows tiled or cascaded? How do you change the arrangement?

b. Which windows contain a scroll bar? A menu bar? A toolbar?

c. Which windows contain a Minimize button? A Maximize button? A Close button? A Restore button?

d. Which window is the active window? What view is used in that window? Would changing the view in this window affect the view in any other window?

e. How would you maximize the window containing the Control Panel? How would you minimize the window?

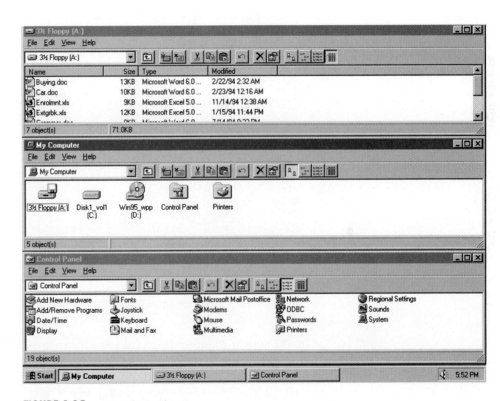

FIGURE 1.15   Screen for Problem 5

PRACTICE WITH WINDOWS 95

1. Register Now: Do this exercise only if you are working on your own computer. It is good practice always to register every program you purchase, so that the vendor can notify you of new releases and/or other pertinent infor-

mation. Windows 95 provides an online capability whereby you can register via modem. To register your copy of Windows 95:

   a. Click the Online Registration command button in the Welcome to Windows screen that appears when Windows is loaded, *or*

   b. Click the Start button, click the Find command, click Files and Folders, then enter Welcome in the Named text box. Click the Find Now command button, then double click the icon next to the Welcome program when it appears in the dialog box.

Either way you should see the Online Registration window in Figure 1.16. Click the Next command button and follow directions.

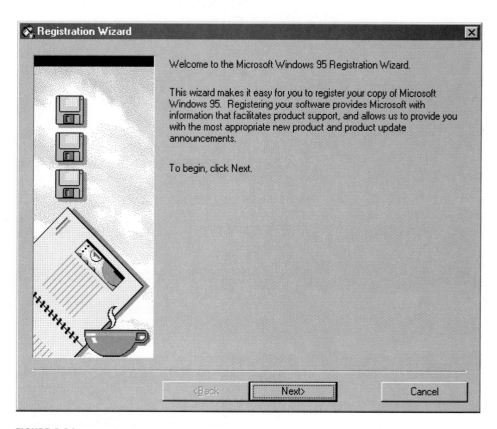

FIGURE 1.16   Registration Screen (Practice Exercise 1)

2. Screen Capture: Prove to your instructor that you have done the hands-on exercises in the chapter by capturing a screen from each exercise, then printing the captured screen in a document to which you add your name. Figure 1.17, for example, occurs after step 3 in exercise 1 (and corresponds to Figure 1.3d) and proves that Julie Rubin did her homework.

   The instructions below show you how to create a document similar to the one in Figure 1.17. They require you to use the Paint accessory, which is covered in Chapter 2, but we think you can handle it now. To create the document in Figure 1.17:

   a. Do the hands-on exercise as it is described in the text until you come to the screen you want to capture. Press the Print Screen key to copy the screen to the clipboard (an area of memory that is available to every Windows application).

   b. Click the Start button, click Programs, click Accessories, then click Paint to open the Paint accessory. If necessary, click the Maximize button so that the Paint window takes the entire desktop.

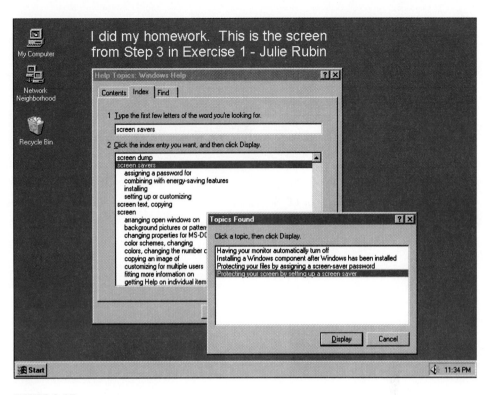

FIGURE 1.17 Practice Exercise 2

    c. Pull down the Edit menu. Click Paste to copy the screen from the clipboard to the drawing area.

    d. Click the text tool (the capital A), then click and drag in the drawing area to create a dotted rectangle that will contain the message to your instructor. Type the text indicating that you did your homework. Click outside the rectangle to deselect it.

    e. Pull down the File menu and click the Page Setup command to display the Page Setup dialog box. Click the Landscape option button. Change the margins to one inch all around. Click OK.

    f. Pull down the File menu a second time. Click Print. Click OK.

    g. Follow the same steps to print screens from the other two exercises. We suggest that you print the screen from exercise 2, step 6 (Figure 1.7e). In addition, print the screen from exercise 3, step 3 (Figure 1.10c), which occurs after vertically tiling the windows.

3. A Look Ahead: Figure 1.18 contains a document that was created using the WordPad program (a simple word processor) that is included in Windows 95. We describe how to use the program in the next chapter, but we think you can do the exercise now.

    a. Double click the My Computer icon on the desktop to display the contents of your configuration. Pull down the View menu and switch to the Details view. Size the windows as necessary.

    b. Press Alt+Print Screen to copy just the My Computer window (as opposed to the entire screen) to the Windows clipboard.

    c. Click the Start menu, click Programs, click Accessories, then click WordPad to open the word processor. Maximize the window.

    d. Pull down the Edit menu. Click the Paste command to copy the contents of the clipboard to the document you are about to create. The My Computer window should be pasted into your document.

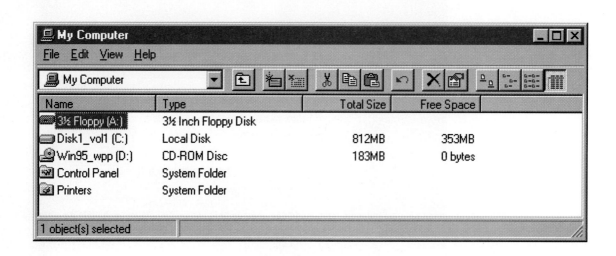

Dear Professor,

Enclosed please find the contents of My Computer as it exists on my computer system. As you can see, I have one floppy drive labeled drive A. I also have one hard drive, labeled drive C, with a total disk capacity of 812 MB. There are 353 MB remaining on my hard drive, so I still have a lot of space left. I also have a CD-ROM, which is drive D.

I enjoyed reading the introductory chapter and I look forward to learning more about Windows 95.

Sincerely,

Heather Bond

FIGURE 1.18   Practice Exercise 3

e. Press Ctrl+End to move to the end of your document. Press the enter key three times (to leave three blank lines).
f. Type a modified form of the memo in Figure 1.18 so that it conforms to your configuration. Type just as you would on a regular typewriter except do *not* press the enter key at the end of a line as the program will automatically wrap from one line to the next. If you make a mistake, just press the backspace key to erase the last character, and continue typing.
g. Finish the memo and sign your name. Pull down the File menu, click the Print command, then click OK in the dialog box to print the document. Submit the completed document to your instructor.

Case Studies

Your Own Reference Manual

Use the online Help facility to browse the suggested "tips and tricks," then select five tips that you think will be most helpful to you in this class. Use the Print command button to print each screen, create a cover page using the WordPad accessory (described in Chapter 2), then submit the completed assignment to your instructor.

You can improve on the appearance of your manual by capturing each Help screen to the clipboard, pasting the captured screen into a WordPad document, then formatting the captured text. It sounds complicated, but it is really very easy as you will see in the next chapter. All you need to do is click and drag the text you want to capture, press Ctrl+C to capture the text to the clipboard, switch to WordPad, then press Ctrl+V to paste the contents of the clipboard into the WordPad document. Be sure to indicate that the information in your document comes from the Windows 95 Help facility.

The Upgrade

Windows 95 is likely to be bundled with the computer you purchase today, but what if you purchased a machine prior to the availability of the new operating system? Do you need to upgrade, and if so, how much will it cost you as an individual user? The decision is more difficult for organizations with large numbers of existing computers, such as a school or university.

Put yourself in the position of the Director of Information Systems in a medium-sized installation with 100 computers and answer the following questions: What is the direct cost of the upgrade (i.e., the cost of 100 licenses of Windows 95)? What are the hidden costs (e.g., additional hardware and/or training)? What are the benefits to the upgrade? What are the drawbacks?

The president of the company has called a meeting for next Friday, at which point you are to present your findings as well as the proposed schedule for the upgrade (if that is your recommendation).

Under the Hood

The Director of Information Systems has asked for your help in assessing whether or not to upgrade. She read that Windows 95 does much more than provide an improved user interface and that Microsoft completely overhauled the operating system to add many features that are transparent to the typical end-user. Plug and Play compatibility, for example, simplifies the installation of new hardware (e.g., a CD-ROM and sound card). The 32-bit architecture enables preemptive multitasking, which means that one does not have to wait for the completion of one task (e.g., downloading a file or formatting a disk) to begin another. Contact Microsoft and ask for information on the benefits of Windows 95 so that you can provide information to the Director of Information Systems.

The Director of Training

After much debate, your organization has made the decision to upgrade to Windows 95 and has asked you to prepare a two-hour class to help existing users convert to the new operating system. The class is to focus entirely on the new interface and how it differs from its predecessor. We don't expect you to prepare the entire class, but we would like written evidence that you have done this assignment. Two or three pages will suffice. Use the information in Appendix A (pages 191–206) as the basis for this assignment.

THE COMMON USER INTERFACE: THE WORDPAD AND PAINT ACCESSORIES

OBJECTIVES

After reading this chapter you will be able to:

1. Use the WordPad accessory to create, save, edit, and print a simple document.
2. Use the Paint Accessory to create, save, edit, and print a simple graphic.
3. Explain the importance of the common user interface; list several commands that function identically in WordPad and Paint.
4. Use the clipboard to cut, copy, and paste text within a document or graphics within a drawing.
5. Define multitasking; use the Taskbar to switch back and forth between open applications.
6. Create a compound document using the WordPad and Paint accessories.

OVERVIEW

All Windows applications share a common user interface and possess a consistent command structure. This is a critically important concept and it is one of the major benefits of the Windows environment. There is a sense of familiarity in going from one Windows application to the next because all applications work basically the same way. Thus, once you know how to use one Windows application, you can apply that knowledge to any other Windows application.

This chapter focuses on the common user interface in conjunction with the WordPad and Paint accessories that are included in Windows 95. WordPad is a simple word processor. Paint is an effective drawing program. The applications have very different functions, yet they follow a consistent menu structure. Once you learn WordPad, it will be that much easier to learn Paint, because both applications follow the same conventions and use the same basic techniques.

The chapter also shows you how to use the multitasking capability that is built into Windows. Multitasking enables you to run multiple applications at the same time and to switch back and forth between those applications.

Throughout the book we emphasize learning by doing. The three hands-on exercises in this chapter are very important as they enable you to apply the conceptual material at the computer. Exercises 1 and 2 demonstrate the basics of WordPad and Paint, respectively. The third exercise opens both applications simultaneously and demonstrates the use of multitasking.

THE COMMON USER INTERFACE

The *common user interface* is one of the most significant benefits of the Windows environment. Consider, for example, Figures 2.1a and 2.1b, containing maximized windows for the WordPad and Paint accessories, respectively. The application windows are similar in appearance despite the fact that they accomplish very different tasks.

Each window in Figure 2.1 contains a control menu box, a menu bar, a title bar, and a Minimize, Maximize or Restore, and a Close button. The *Taskbar* is displayed at the bottom of each window and shows the open application(s). The status bar appears above the Taskbar and displays information relevant to the window or selected object.

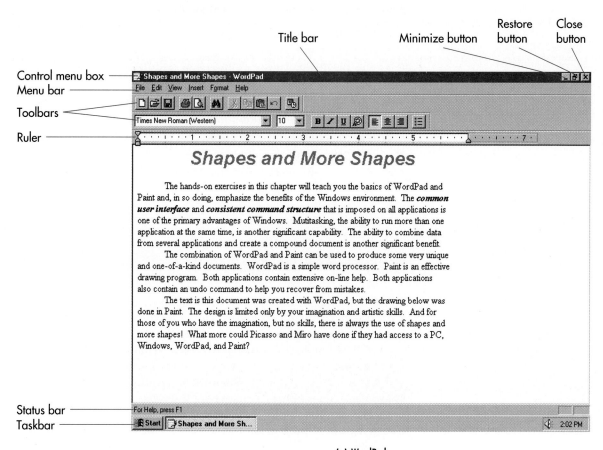

(a) WordPad

FIGURE 2.1   The Advantages of Windows

WHAT YOU SEE IS WHAT YOU GET

All Windows applications are **WYSIWYG** (pronounced "wizzywig") in nature, meaning that What You See Is What You Get. All text appears on the screen exactly the same way it will appear in print. You can use larger or smaller type sizes, boldface or italics, even color (provided that you have a color printer).

There are, of course, differences between the applications. The WordPad accessory displays two toolbars and a ruler at the top of its window. The Paint accessory has a Toolbox at the left of its window, and a color palette at the bottom. Nevertheless, the function of these disparate elements is the same in both applications—to provide a quick and easy way of executing a command within the application.

More significantly, WordPad and Paint share a consistent command structure in which the same menus are found in both applications. The menu bar is displayed immediately under the title bar in each application. The File, Edit, View, and Help menus are present in both WordPad and Paint. (These menus are also found in almost every other Windows application.)

The same commands are also found in the same menus. The Save, Open, Print, and Exit commands, for example, are contained in the File menu for both

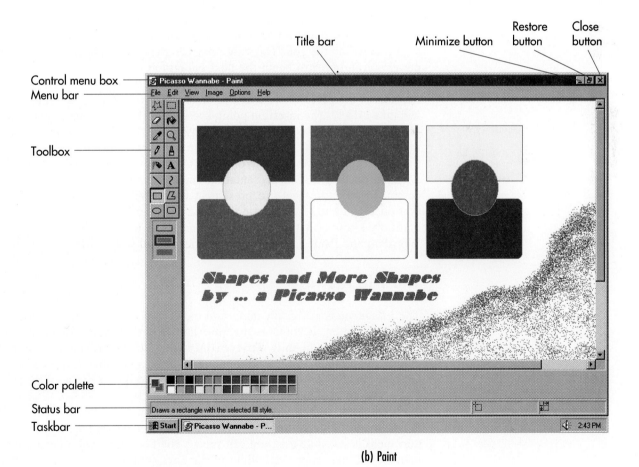

(b) Paint

FIGURE 2.1   The Advantages of Windows (continued)

WordPad and Paint. The Cut, Copy, Paste, and Undo commands are in the Edit menu for both applications. You may not know what these commands do now, but once you learn how they work in one application, you will intuitively know how they work in the other.

It doesn't matter whether you use WordPad or Paint as in this chapter, whether you use Word, WordPerfect, or WordPro as a full-featured word processor, or whether you use Lotus, Excel, or Quattro Pro as a spreadsheet. Each of these applications has the common user interface and consistent command structure that are found in every Windows application.

THE WORDPAD ACCESSORY

The *WordPad accessory* is a simple, yet effective, word processor. It does not have a spell-checker or thesaurus, but is otherwise capable of performing the basic operations common to any word processor. These include the ability to create a document and save it on disk, the ability to retrieve a previously saved document and make changes in it, and of course, the ability to print the completed document. WordPad supports basic formatting such as boldface or italics, changing fonts, or changing margins and alignment. It also lets you move or copy text within a document.

A newcomer to word processing has one major transition to make from a typewriter. With a typewriter, you press the carriage return at the end of every line. With a word processor, however, you type continually *without* pressing the enter key at the end of a line because the word processor will automatically wrap the text from one line to the next as you reach the right margin. In other words, when the word being typed is too long to fit on the current line, WordPad will start a new line for you. The only time you press the enter key is at the end of a paragraph in order to begin the next paragraph on a new line.

Another key concept is that of the *insertion point,* the flashing vertical line that marks the place where text will be entered (or the point at which a command will take effect). The insertion point is always at the beginning of a new document, but it can be moved anywhere within an existing document simply by clicking the mouse at the desired location.

We do not cover all of WordPad, just the essentials to create, edit, and print a simple document. Our presentation emphasizes the basic menus and consistent command structure that are present in every Windows application. This means that once you know how to use the basic commands in one application, you automatically know how to use those commands in every other application. Indeed, WordPad and Paint have many similarities as you will see throughout the chapter.

The File Menu

The *File menu* is a critically important menu that is present in virtually every Windows application. It contains the Save and Open commands to save a document on disk, then subsequently retrieve (open) that document at a later time. The File menu also contains the Print command to print a document, the Close command to close the current document but continue working in the application, and the Exit command to quit the application altogether.

The *Save command* copies the document that is currently being edited (the document in memory) to disk. The Save As dialog box appears the first time a document is saved so that you can specify the file name and other required information. All subsequent executions of the Save command save the document under the assigned name, replacing the previously saved version with the new version.

Drive to which
file will be saved

File name

File type

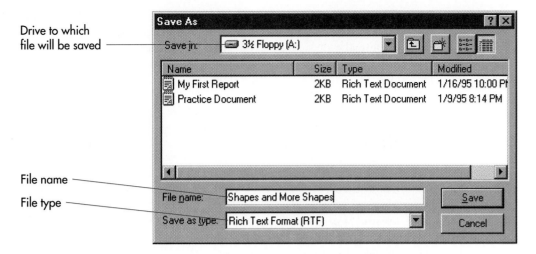

(a) Save As Dialog Box

Drive from which
file will be retrieved

Selected file

File name

File type

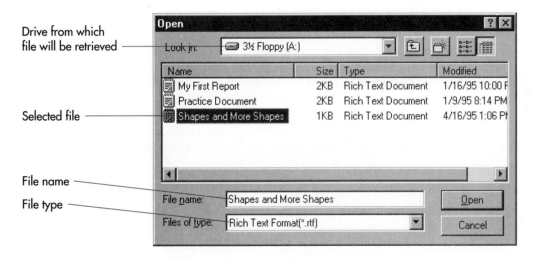

(b) Open Dialog Box

FIGURE 2.2 Save and Open Commands

The Save As dialog box requires a file name (e.g., Shapes and More Shapes in Figure 2.2a), which can be up to 255 characters in length. It also requires the drive (and optionally a folder) in which the file is to be saved. And finally, it requires the file type (format), which determines how the file is actually saved on disk.

WordPad is typical of many applications in that it can save a file in different formats (file types). WordPad can save a file as a Word 6.0 document, or in the more general Rich Text File (RTF) format, which can be read by a variety of word processors. The RTF format is useful if you do not have Word for Windows installed on your system, and/or if you want to exchange documents between different word processors.

The ***Open command*** brings a copy of a previously saved document into memory, enabling you to work with that document. The Open command displays the Open dialog box in which you specify the file to retrieve. You indicate the drive (and optionally the folder) that contains the file, as well as the type of file you want to retrieve. WordPad will then list all files of that type on the designated drive (and folder), enabling you to open the file you want.

The Save and Open commands work in conjunction with one another. The Save As dialog box in Figure 2.2a, for example, saves the file Shapes and More Shapes onto the disk in drive A. The Open dialog box in Figure 2.2b brings that file back into memory so that you can work with the file, after which you can save the revised file for use at a later time.

LONG FILE NAMES

Windows 95 allows file names of up to 255 characters (spaces and commas are permitted). Anyone using Windows 95 for the first time will take descriptive names such as *Shapes and More Shapes* for granted, but veterans of MS-DOS and Windows 3.1 will appreciate the improvement over the earlier 8.3 naming convention (an eight-character name followed by a three-letter extension to indicate the file type).

The Edit Menu

The *Edit menu* is another basic menu that is found in virtually every Windows application. It contains the *Cut, Copy,* and *Paste commands* to move or copy text within a document or between documents. It also contains the *Undo command* to reverse (undo) the last command that was executed.

Text is moved or copied using the *clipboard,* a temporary storage area available to all Windows programs. Selected text is cut or copied from a document into the clipboard from where it can be pasted to a new location(s). A move requires that you select the desired text, execute a Cut command to remove the text from its current location and place it in the clipboard, move the insertion point to the new location, and finally paste the text from the clipboard into the new location. A copy operation necessitates the same steps except that the selected text is copied rather than cut, which leaves the text in its original location and also duplicates it at the new location.

The Cut, Copy, and Paste commands are found in the Edit menu for Word-Pad as they are for virtually all Windows applications. The contents of the clipboard are replaced by each subsequent Cut or Copy command, but are unaffected by the Paste command; that is, the contents of the clipboard can be pasted into multiple locations in a document.

The Format Menu

The *Format menu* enables you to change the appearance of a document. Most formatting is done within the context of *select-then-do.* You select the text to format by dragging the mouse over the text to highlight it, then you execute the appropriate command. The selected text may be a character, a word, a sentence, a paragraph, or even the entire document. Various formatting commands let you change the alignment in a paragraph or create a bulleted list.

The Font command in the Format menu lets you change the appearance of selected text as shown in Figure 2.3. A *font* (or *typeface*) is a complete set of characters (upper- and lowercase letters, numbers, punctuation marks, and special symbols) of a specific design. There are literally thousands of fonts, with Times New Roman and Arial two of the most common. A *type style* is a variation in appearance—for example, **bold**, *italic*, or ***bold italic.***

The size of the font—the *type size*—is measured in points where one point equals $\frac{1}{72}$ of an inch; a typical document, this book for example, is set in 10 point

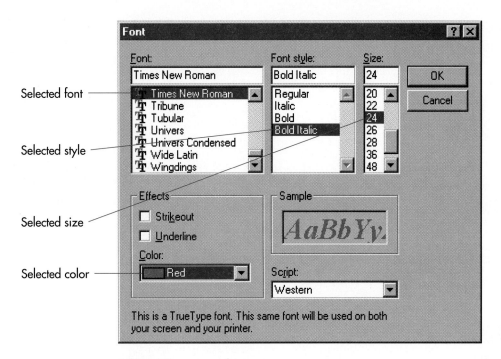

Selected font

Selected style

Selected size

Selected color

FIGURE 2.3 The Font Command

type. The Font command also enables you to apply special effects such as <u>under-lining</u> or ~~strikeout~~. You can even change the color, but you will need a color printer to reap the benefits of this command.

USE RESTRAINT

More is not necessarily better, especially in the case of too many fonts, which result in cluttered documents that impress no one. Limit yourself to a maximum of two fonts per document, and then use different sizes and/or styles for emphasis. Use the different styles (e.g., boldface or italics) in moderation, because if you emphasize too many elements the effect is lost.

Toolbars

Toolbars provide immediate access to common commands and offer an alternative to the pull-down menus. The picture on each button is indicative of its function and in addition, a ToolTip (containing the name of the button) appears if you point to the tool.

The toolbar contains buttons for the most basic commands, such as opening and closing a file, printing a document, and so on. It contains tools to cut, copy, and paste text and to undo the last command. The Formatting toolbar provides access to formatting operations such as boldface, italics, and underlining. It also lets you change the alignment in a paragraph and create a bulleted list.

The toolbars may appear overwhelming initially, but there is absolutely no need to memorize what the individual buttons do. That will come with time. We suggest, however, that you will have a better appreciation for the various buttons if you consider them in groups according to their general function as shown in Figure 2.4.

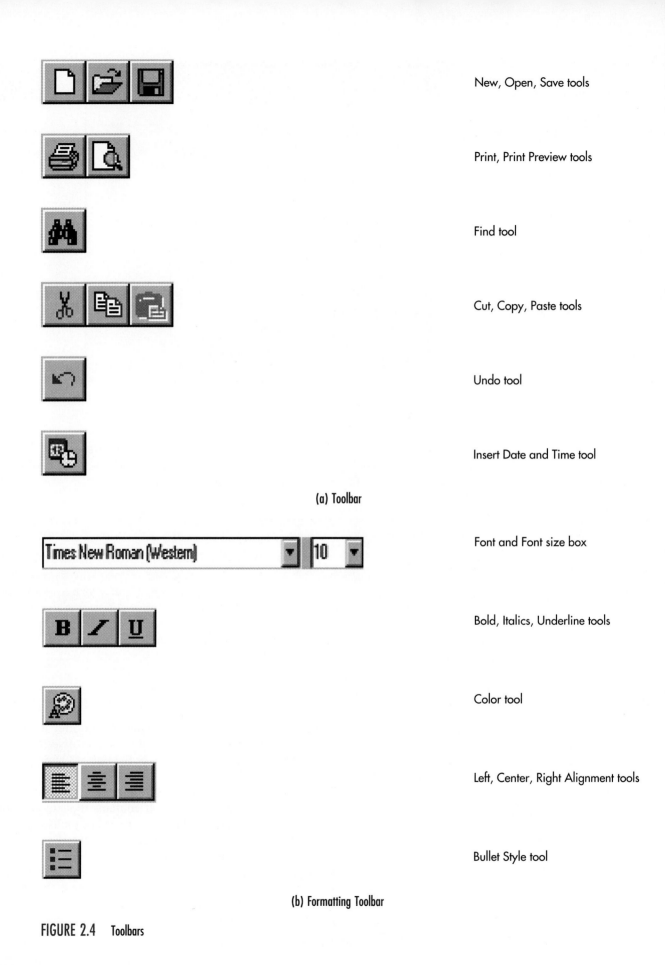

New, Open, Save tools

Print, Print Preview tools

Find tool

Cut, Copy, Paste tools

Undo tool

Insert Date and Time tool

(a) Toolbar

Font and Font size box

Bold, Italics, Underline tools

Color tool

Left, Center, Right Alignment tools

Bullet Style tool

(b) Formatting Toolbar

FIGURE 2.4   Toolbars

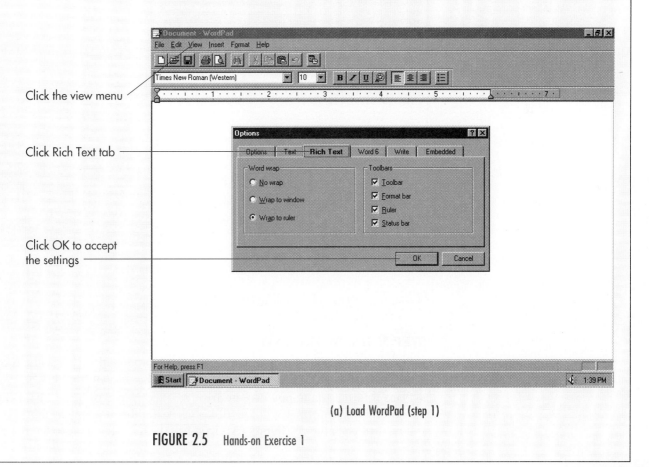

HANDS-ON EXERCISE 1

The WordPad Accessory

Objective: To create, save, edit, and print a simple document; to cut, copy, and paste text within a document; to change fonts, styles, and type sizes. The exercise requires a formatted disk. Use Figure 2.5 as a guide in the exercise.

STEP 1: Open WordPad

➤ Click the **Start Button** to display the Start menu. Click (or point to) the **Programs menu,** click (or point to) the **Accessories submenu,** then click **WordPad** to open the WordPad program.

➤ If necessary, click the **Maximize button** in the WordPad window so that it takes the entire desktop.

➤ Pull down the **View menu.** Click **Options** to display the Options dialog box in Figure 2.5a.

➤ Click the **Rich Text tab** since that is the type of document you will create in this exercise. Set the options to match those in Figure 2.5a.

➤ Click **OK** to accept the settings and close the Options dialog box.

STEP 2: Create the Document

➤ Do not worry about formatting until after you have entered the entire document in Figure 2.5b. Type the title, **Shapes and More Shapes.** Press the **enter key** twice in a row—once to indicate the end of the paragraph, and once to place a blank line between the title and the next paragraph.

Click the view menu

Click Rich Text tab

Click OK to accept the settings

(a) Load WordPad (step 1)

FIGURE 2.5   Hands-on Exercise 1

➤ Type the text in Figure 2.5b just as you would on a regular typewriter with one exception—do *not* press the enter key at the end of a line, because WordPad will automatically begin a new line as necessary.

➤ Proofread the document and correct any errors.

WORD WRAP

WordPad will automatically start a new line when the word being typed is too long to fit on the current line. You have the option, however, of specifying when the "word wrap" is to take place—at the end of the ruler or the end of the window. We suggest the ruler rather than the window, so that the printed document will match the document on the screen. Pull down the View menu, click Options, click the Rich Text tab (because this is the type of document you are creating), then click the Wrap to Ruler option button. Click OK to exit the Options dialog box.

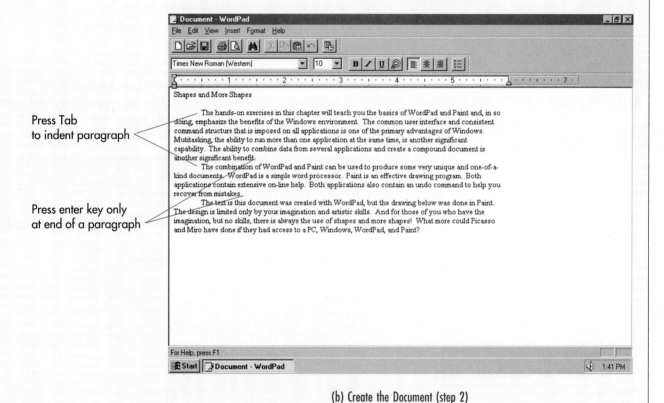

Press Tab
to indent paragraph

Press enter key only
at end of a paragraph

(b) Create the Document (step 2)

FIGURE 2.5   Hands-on Exercise 1 (continued)

STEP 3: Save the Document

➤ Pull down the **File menu** and click the **Save command** (or click the **Save icon** on the toolbar). You will see the Save As dialog box in Figure 2.5c.

➤ Place a formatted floppy disk in drive A. (See step 5 on page 21 for information on how to format a floppy disk.) Click the **down arrow** in the **Save in** list box, then click the **3½ floppy (A:) icon** to save the document to the floppy disk.

> Click the **File name** text box. Click and drag to select the name of the default document (Document or Document.doc. See boxed tip on file extensions). Type **Shapes and More Shapes** as the new name.

> Click the **down arrow** in the **Save As Type** list box. Click **Rich Text Format (RTF)** as the file type.

> Click the **Save command button** to save the file.

FILE EXTENSIONS

Veterans of MS-DOS will recognize the three character extension at the end of a file name to indicate the application associated with a file. RTF and DOC, for example, denote a WordPad and Word for Windows document, respectively. The extensions are displayed (hidden) according to the option specified in the View menu of My Computer. To display (hide) the extension, open My Computer, pull down the View menu, and click the Options command. Click the View tab, then clear (check) the box to hide the MS-DOS file extensions.

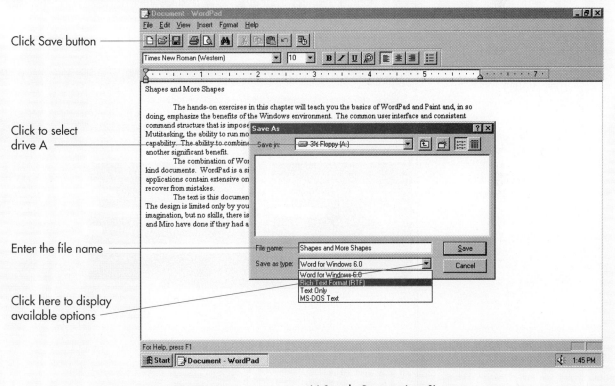

Click Save button

Click to select drive A

Enter the file name

Click here to display available options

(c) Save the Document (step 3)

FIGURE 2.5 Hands-on Exercise 1 (continued)

STEP 4: Select Then Do

> Press and hold the **left mouse button** as you drag the mouse over the entire document. Release the mouse. The entire document should be highlighted (selected) as in Figure 2.5d.

➤ Click the **down arrow** on the Font Size list box to display the various point sizes as shown in Figure 2.5d. Click **12** to change the point size of the selected text.

➤ Click anywhere in the document to deselect the document, then click and drag to select just the title.

➤ Click the **down arrow** on the Font list box to display the available fonts. If necessary, scroll until you can select **Arial** (or Arial Western) to change the font of the selected text. Click the **down arrow** on the Font Size list box, then click **24** to change the size of the title.

➤ Experiment with different selections and effects until you are satisfied with the appearance of the title within your document.

➤ Click the **Save button** on the toolbar to save the modified document.

SELECTING TEXT

The *selection area,* the unmarked column at the far left of the window, makes it easy to select a line, paragraph, or the entire document. To select a line, point to the line and click the selection area; to select a paragraph, point to any line in the paragraph and double click the selection area; and to select the entire document, click the selection area while you press the Ctrl key. To select a single word, double click anywhere within the word. Click anywhere in the document to cancel a selection.

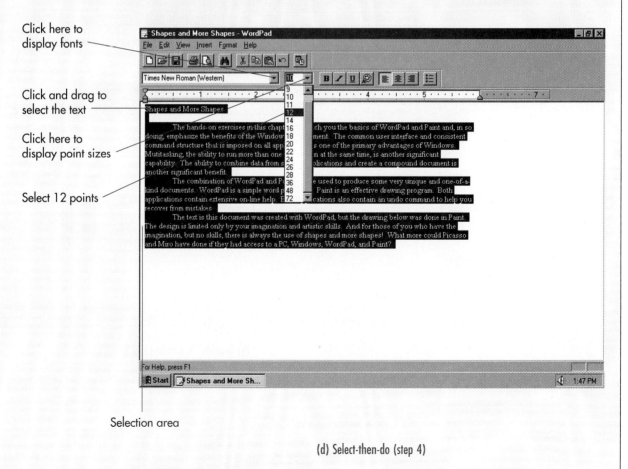

(d) Select-then-do (step 4)

FIGURE 2.5 Hands-on Exercise 1 (continued)

ONLINE HELP

Online Help is available for WordPad just as it is for any Windows application. Pull down the Help menu and click Help Topics (or press the F1 key) at any time. Search through the index until you find the desired information, then click the Display command button to open a popup window with detailed instructions. Click the Print button (or right click in the Help window) to print the displayed topic.

STEP 5: The Undo Command

➤ If the title is not selected, click and drag to reselect the title. Click the **Center button** on the toolbar to center the title as shown in Figure 2.5e.

➤ Pull down the **Edit menu** and click **Undo** (or click the **Undo icon** on the toolbar). The title returns to its original alignment.

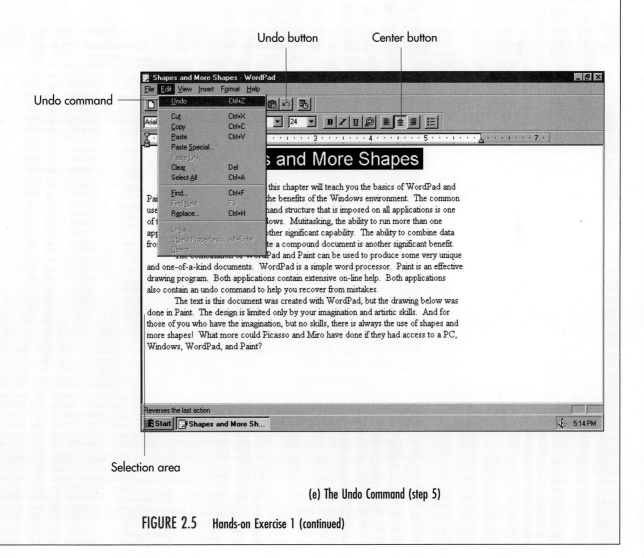

(e) The Undo Command (step 5)

FIGURE 2.5   Hands-on Exercise 1 (continued)

- ➤ Click the **Center button** to again center the title, or alternatively, click the **Undo button** to cancel the previous Undo command (which will restore the centered title).
- ➤ Save the document.

THE UNDO COMMAND

The Undo command reverses the effect of the preceding command and enables you to recover from mistakes. The command is invaluable at any time, but especially when you are learning. Pull down the Edit menu and click Undo (or click the Undo button on the toolbar). You must, however, use the command immediately after the action you wish to undo. Some commands (e.g., the Save command) cannot be undone, in which case the Undo command will be unavailable (dim) on the Edit menu.

STEP 6: Boldface, Italics, and Color

- ➤ Check that the title is still selected, then click the **Italics button** to italicize the title. The title should remain highlighted. Click the **Boldface button** to boldface the selected text. The title is now in boldface and italics.
- ➤ The Italics and Boldface buttons function as toggle switches. Click either button when the style is in effect to cancel the effect and return to normal text.
- ➤ The title should still be selected. Click the **Color button** as shown in Figure 2.5f to pull down the list of available colors. Click **Red.** Click anywhere in the document to deselect the text.
- ➤ Boldface and/or italicize these phrases: **common user interface** and **consistent command structure.**
- ➤ Click the **Save button** to save the modified document.

KEYBOARD SHORTCUTS

Most people begin with the mouse, but add keyboard shortcuts as they become more proficient. Ctrl+B, Ctrl+I, and Ctrl+U are shortcuts to boldface, italicize, and underline, respectively. Ctrl+Home and Ctrl+End move to the beginning and end of a document. These shortcuts are recognized not just in WordPad, but in virtually every Windows application.

STEP 7: Cut, Copy, and Paste

- ➤ This step will move and copy text using a combination of the Cut, Copy, and Paste commands. To move the last paragraph to the beginning of the document:
  - • Click and drag to select the last paragraph as shown in Figure 2.5g. Pull down the **Edit menu** and click the **Cut command** (or click the **Cut button** on the toolbar) to remove the paragraph from the document and place it in the clipboard.

Bold button   Italics button   Color button

Save button

The title is still selected

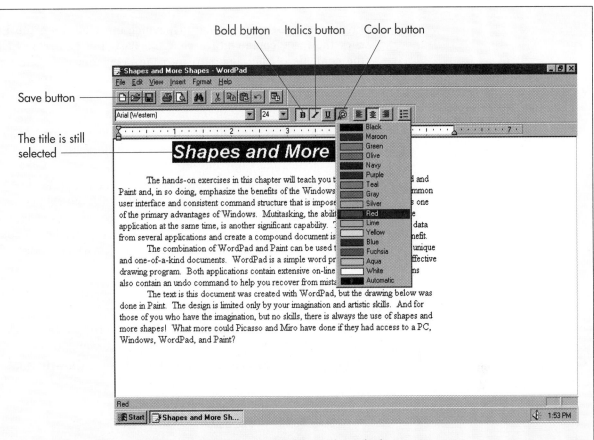

(f) Boldface, Italics, and Color (step 6)

Cut command

Click and drag to select the paragraph

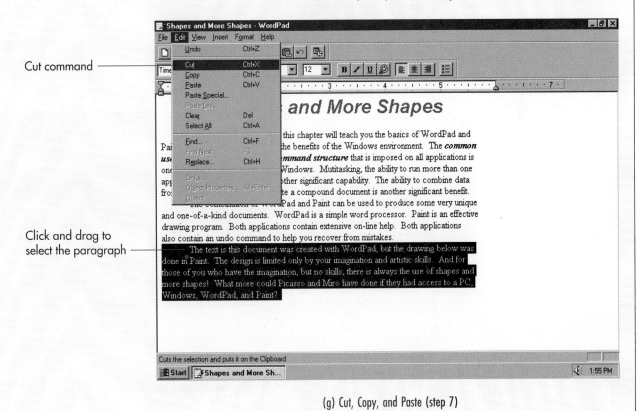

(g) Cut, Copy, and Paste (step 7)

FIGURE 2.5   Hands-on Exercise 1 (continued)

- Click at the beginning of the first paragraph. Pull down the **Edit menu** and click the **Paste command** (or click the **Paste button** on the toolbar) to paste the contents of the clipboard into the document. The paragraph has been moved to the beginning of the document. Press the **Tab key** (if necessary) to indent the first paragraph.

➤ To copy the last sentence in the first paragraph to the end of the document:

- Click and drag to select the last sentence in the first paragraph containing the names of Picasso and Miro. Pull down the **Edit menu** and click the **Copy command** (or click the **Copy button**).

- Press **Ctrl+End** to move to the end of the document. Press the **enter key** (if necessary) to begin a new paragraph. Pull down the **Edit menu** and click the **Paste command** (or click the **Paste button**) to paste the contents of the clipboard into the document. The selected sentence has been copied to the end of the document. Press the **Tab key** (if necessary) to indent the new paragraph.

➤ Save the modified document.

STEP 8: Print the Completed Document

➤ Pull down the **File menu.** Then click **Print** to produce the Print dialog box of Figure 2.5h. Click **OK** to print the completed document.

➤ Pull down the **File menu** and click **Exit** (or click the **Close button**) to quit Word-Pad.

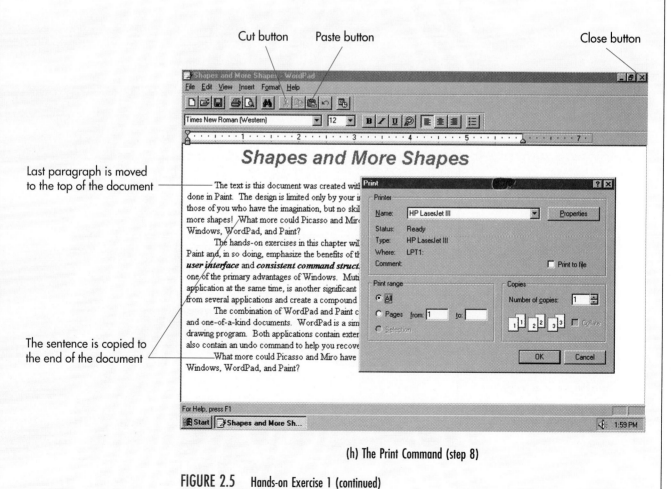

(h) The Print Command (step 8)

FIGURE 2.5   Hands-on Exercise 1 (continued)

THE PAINT ACCESSORY

The *Paint accessory* enables you to create simple or (depending on your ability) elaborate drawings. You already have an intuitive understanding of how Paint works because of your knowledge of Windows in general, and WordPad in particular. Thus, there is a sense of familiarity in the maximized Paint window in Figure 2.6, which contains several familiar elements. Can you identify the control menu box, the title bar, the menu bar, the Minimize, Restore, and Close buttons, and the vertical and horizontal scroll bars?

The menu bar is especially important as it provides access to the File, Edit, View, and Help menus that are present in virtually every Windows application. The consistent menu structure implies that common commands will be found in

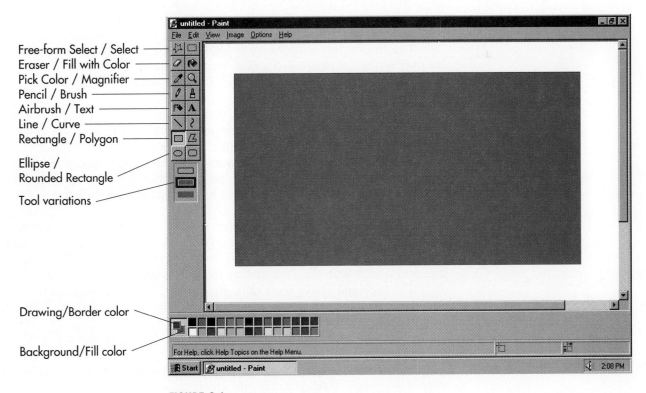

FIGURE 2.6   The Paint Accessory

familiar menus. For example, the File menu for both Paint and WordPad will contain the Save, Open, Print, Close, and Exit commands. The Edit menu will hold the Cut, Copy, Paste, and Undo commands. On-line Help also functions identically in both applications.

Nevertheless, Paint is a significantly different application from WordPad and has its unique elements. The ***Toolbox*** at the left of the window contains the various drawing tools that are explained shortly. The ***Color box*** at the bottom of the window determines the drawing and background color for the selected tool. The ***drawing color*** is used for straight or curved lines, for the border of shapes such as a rectangle or ellipse, and for text. The ***background color*** is used for the fill inside enclosed shapes, and for erasing. The basic principles are very simple:

1. Select a tool (e.g., the rectangle in Figure 2.6) by clicking on a tool.
2. Select the variation (if any) for the tool. The rectangle has three variations: a border only, a filled rectangle with a border, or a filled rectangle with no border.
3. Select the drawing and background colors by pointing to the color in the Color box, then clicking the left and right mouse button, respectively. The drawing (border) color appears on top (red in Figure 2.6) and the background (fill) color on the bottom (light blue in Figure 2.6).
4. Click in the drawing area where you want the shape to begin, then click and drag to create the shape.

The individual tools are labeled in Figure 2.6 and described briefly below. Do not be concerned if you do not appreciate all of the tools at this time, because you will be introduced to them in greater detail in the hands-on exercise, which follows shortly.

The Free-form Select and Select tools are used to define part of the drawing so that it can be cut or copied to the clipboard. The Free-form tool selects an irregularly shaped area. The Select tool defines a rectangular area.

The Eraser does what its name implies and erases any portion of the drawing over which it is dragged. You can increase (decrease) the size of the eraser to erase more (less) of the drawing as you drag the mouse.

The Fill with Color tool (a bucket spilling paint) fills in a bounded area with the drawing color. Selecting the tool, then clicking inside a closed shape fills the shape with the designated color. If, however, the border is somehow broken, the color will leak through and fill the entire drawing area.

The Brush and Airbrush tools draw using the selected size of the brush and airbrush, respectively. The Brush tool can be used for free-form writing or to create a special shape. The Airbrush tool is an effective way to enhance the background of a drawing.

The Pick Color tool lets you select a color from the drawing, as opposed to the Color box. The Magnifier tool enlarges a portion of the drawing so that you can modify the drawing on a bit-by-bit basis. The Text tool inserts text into a picture and is used with the Text toolbar to select a specific font, style, or size.

The Line and Curve tools draw straight and curved lines, respectively. The Pencil is used for free-form drawing. The Rectangle, Polygon, Ellipse, and Rounded Rectangle create the indicated shapes.

Best of all, you don't have to be an artist to use Paint, and you will get better with practice. The Undo command is invaluable, as is the on-line Help. Even with limited knowledge and ability you can create a reasonable drawing. And, even if you can't draw, you can still create a variety of shapes in all sizes and colors.

The Paint Accessory

Objective: To create, save, edit, and print a simple drawing; to experiment with different colors and drawing tools; to cut, copy, and paste parts of a drawing. Use Figure 2.7 as a guide in the exercise.

STEP 1: Open Paint

➤ Click the **Start Button** to display the Start menu. Click (or point to) the **Programs menu,** click (or point to) the **Accessories submenu,** then click the **Paint icon** to open the Paint accessory. If necessary, click the **Maximize button** so that Paint takes the entire desktop.

➤ The Toolbox and the Color box should both be displayed (see Figure 2.7a). If either element is missing, pull down the View menu in order to check the appropriate command and display the item.

POINT AND SLIDE

Click the Start button, then slowly slide the mouse pointer over the various menu options. Notice that each time you point to a submenu its items are displayed. Point to (don't click) the Programs menu, point to (don't click) the Accessories submenu, then click the Paint icon to open the accessory. You don't have to click a submenu—you can just point and slide!

STEP 2: Draw a Rectangle

➤ Chose the color(s) for the rectangle. Point to the desired color, then click the **left mouse button** to choose the drawing color (red in Figure 2.7a).

➤ Point to the desired color, then click the **right mouse button** to choose the background color (blue in Figure 2.7a).

➤ Click the **Rectangle tool,** which in turn displays three types of rectangles from which to choose. Click the **middle rectangle** to draw a blue (background color) rectangle with a red (drawing color) border.

➤ Click in the drawing area at the place where the rectangle is to begin, then drag the mouse diagonally to draw the rectangle. Release the mouse to complete the rectangle in Figure 2.7a.

PICK UP THE MOUSE

It seems that you always run out of room on your real desk just when you need to move the mouse a little further. The solution is to pick up the mouse and move it closer to you—the pointer will stay in its present position on the screen, but when you put the mouse down, you will have more room on your desk in which to work.

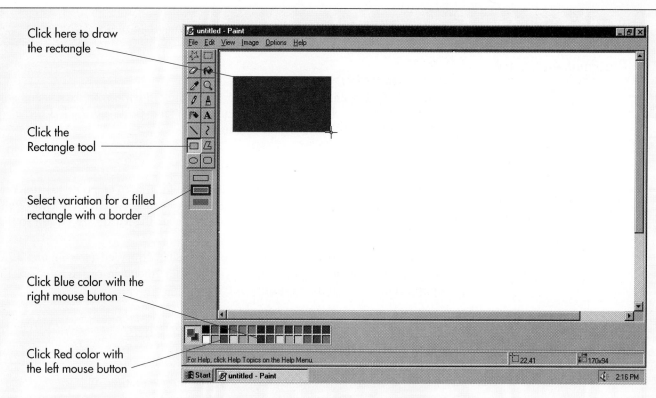

Click here to draw
the rectangle

Click the
Rectangle tool

Select variation for a filled
rectangle with a border

Click Blue color with the
right mouse button

Click Red color with
the left mouse button

(a) Draw a Rectangle (step 2)

FIGURE 2.7   Hands-on Exercise 2

STEP 3: The Eraser and the Undo Command

➤ Click the **Rounded Rectangle tool.** Click and drag in the drawing area underneath the existing rectangle to draw the rounded rectangle as shown in Figure 2.7b.

➤ Click the **Eraser tool.** Click and drag in the drawing area to (attempt to) erase the rounded rectangle. You are not, however, erasing but instead are "painting" in blue, which corresponds to the current background color.

➤ Pull down the **Edit menu** and click **Undo** (or press **Ctrl+Z**) to undo the effects of the Erase command.

THREE LEVELS OF UNDO

The Undo command in the Paint accessory is superior to its counterpart in WordPad in that you can undo up to three commands (as opposed to only one in WordPad). In other words, you can execute the Undo command three times in a row to reverse (undo) the preceding three commands. Since successive Undo commands are permitted, Paint also provides a Repeat command (in the Edit menu) to reverse the effect of the Undo command; for example, execute the Repeat command twice in a row to cancel the last two Undo commands.

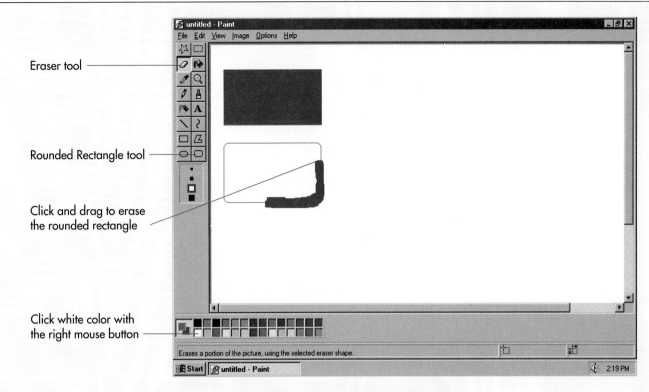

Eraser tool

Rounded Rectangle tool

Click and drag to erase
the rounded rectangle

Click white color with
the right mouse button

(b) The Eraser (step 3)

FIGURE 2.7 Hands-on Exercise 2 (continued)

➤ Point to color **white** within the **Color box,** then click the **right mouse button** so that background color matches the background in the drawing area.

➤ The Eraser is still selected. Click the largest eraser size, then click and drag in the drawing to erase the rounded rectangle.

➤ Click the **Undo** button or press **Ctrl+Z** to cancel the Erase command and restore the rounded rectangle.

STEP 4: Draw a Shape, Any Shape

➤ Use the left and right mouse button to select a different color combination for the drawing and background colors, respectively.

➤ Select the **Ellipse tool** and select (click) the middle shape to draw a filled ellipse. Click and drag in the drawing area to draw an ellipse or a circle (see boxed tip on the Shift key).

➤ Draw several different shapes in several different colors until you are content with your drawing.

THE SHIFT KEY

The Shift key has a special effect in combination with various tools. Press and hold the Shift key while you drag the ellipse or rectangle to produce a circle or square, respectively. Press and hold the Shift key in conjunction with the line tool to draw a horizontal or vertical line, or a line at a 45-degree angle.

STEP 5: Save the Drawing

➤ Pull down the **File menu.** Click the **Save command.** You will see the Save As dialog box in Figure 2.7c.

➤ Place the formatted floppy disk from the first exercise in drive A. Click the **down arrow** in the **Save in** list box. Click the **3½ floppy (A:) icon** to save the document to the floppy disk.

➤ Click the **File Name** text box, then click and drag over the default name, untitled or untitled.bmp (See tip on file extensions on page 55). Type **Picasso Wannabe** as the name of the drawing.

➤ Click the **Save command button** to save the file.

CHANGE THE FILE TYPE

Even simple bit map images create large files. The rectangles drawing, for example, takes over 400KB if saved in the default 256-color format. You can save considerable space, without affecting the drawing itself, by changing to a 16-color bit map. You will also speed up the Open and Save commands since Windows will be reading and writing smaller files.

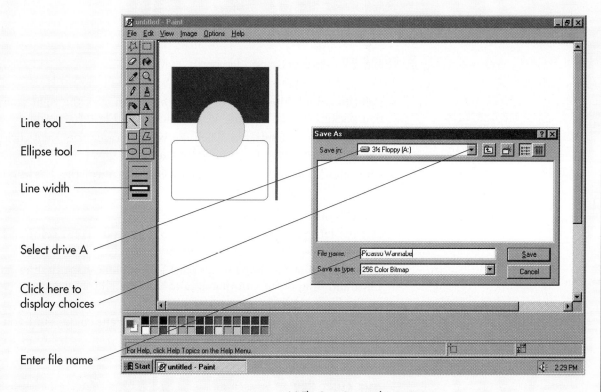

Line tool

Ellipse tool

Line width

Select drive A

Click here to display choices

Enter file name

(c) The Save Command (step 5)

FIGURE 2.7   Hands-on Exercise 2 (continued)

STEP 6: The Text tool

➤ Click the **Text tool** (the mouse pointer changes to a tiny cross). Click and drag in the drawing where you want the title to go. You will see a dotted line outline a text frame as shown in Figure 2.7d.

➤ Type the title of your drawing, **Shapes and More Shapes,** as shown in Figure 2.7d. Press the **backspace key** to erase the last letter(s) you typed if you make a mistake.

➤ Press the **enter key** to start a new line, then type your name as the artist.

➤ Use the **Text toolbar** to change the font, size, or apply boldface, italics, or underlining. (Pull down the **View menu** and click **Text toolbar** if you do not see the toolbar. If necessary, click and drag the title bar of the Text (fonts) toolbar to move the toolbar within the drawing area.)

➤ Change the color of the text by clicking a different color in the Color box.

➤ Save the drawing.

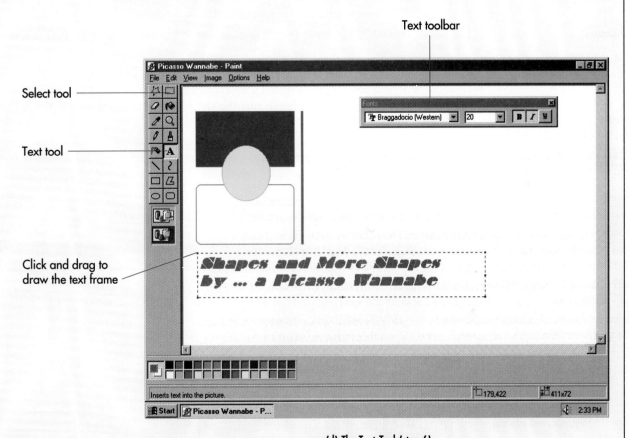

Text toolbar

Select tool

Text tool

Click and drag to
draw the text frame

(d) The Text Tool (step 6)

FIGURE 2.7   Hands-on Exercise 2 (continued)

ONLINE HELP

Online Help is available for Paint just as it is for any other Windows application. Pull down the Help menu and click Help Topics (or press the F1 key) at any time. Search through the index until you find the desired information, then click the Display command button to open a popup window with detailed instructions. Click the Print button (or right click in the Help window) to print the displayed topic.

STEP 7: Copy and Paste

➤ Click the **Select tool** (the cursor changes to a cross hair). Click and drag in the drawing area to select the portion of the drawing to copy. Release the mouse to complete the selection.

➤ You will see a dashed line outlining the selection as shown in Figure 2.7e. If you make a mistake, click outside the selected area to cancel the selection and start over.

➤ You can change the size of the selection, which also changes the size of its contents:

 • To change the height or width, click and drag a sizing handle on the appropriate border and drag in the direction you want to go: inward to make the selection smaller or outward to make it larger.

 • To change both dimensions at the same time, click and drag a sizing handle on the corner.

➤ Pull down the **Edit menu.** Click **Copy** to copy the selection to the clipboard.

➤ Pull down the **Edit menu** a second time. Click **Paste.** The contents of the clipboard have been pasted into the drawing and appear within the selection box in the upper-left corner of the drawing area.

➤ Click inside the selection area (the mouse pointer changes to a heavy cross), then drag the selection to another part of the drawing. Release the mouse button to complete the paste operation. Click outside the selection area to cancel the selection.

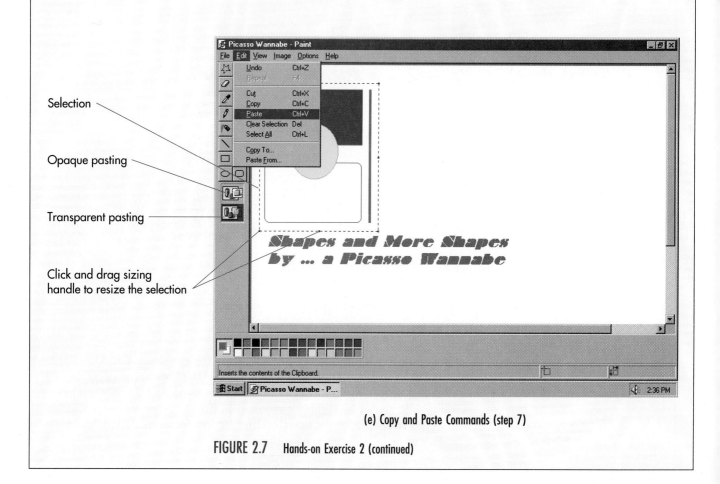

(e) Copy and Paste Commands (step 7)

FIGURE 2.7   Hands-on Exercise 2 (continued)

➤ You can paste the selected part of the drawing as many times as you like by pulling down the Edit menu, selecting Paste, and dragging the cutout to another location. Experiment with Copy and Paste commands until you are satisfied with your drawing.

➤ Save the drawing.

TRANSPARENT VERSUS OPAQUE PASTING

The contents of the clipboard are inserted (pasted) into a document in one of two ways, opaquely or transparently, according to the selected icon in the Toolbox. If you paste opaquely (the top icon), the pasted object will cover the underlying drawing. If you paste transparently (the bottom icon), the underlying drawing will show through.

STEP 8: The other tools

➤ Click the **Airbrush tool** as shown in Figure 2.7f. Click the **left mouse button** to choose a drawing color from the Color box, then click and drag in the drawing to create the airbrush effect.

➤ Click the **Fill with Color tool.** The effect of the tool depends on where you click in the drawing. Click within a closed shape and you change only the color of that shape. Click outside of a closed shape—for example, in the background of the drawing—and you change the entire background.

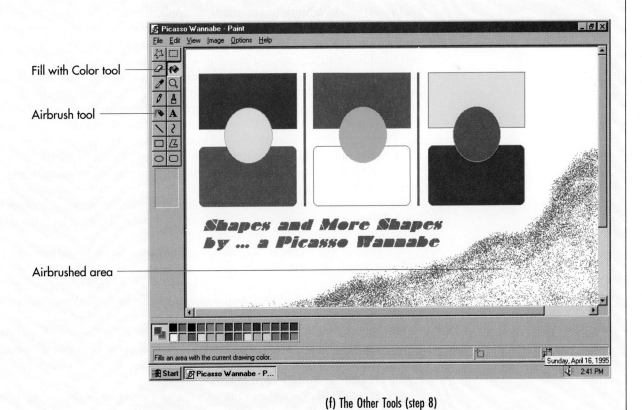

Fill with Color tool

Airbrush tool

Airbrushed area

(f) The Other Tools (step 8)

FIGURE 2.7   Hands-on Exercise 2 (continued)

➤ Experiment with all the tools to put the finishing touches on your drawing. Remember, you can use the **Undo command** to reverse the effects of the three most recent commands.

ERASING A LARGE AREA

The Eraser tool is adequate to erase small areas in a drawing but tedious for larger areas. Click either the Free-form or regular Select tool, then click and drag in the drawing to select the area you wish to erase. Check that the background color is set properly (if necessary, right click the appropriate color), then press the Del key to erase the selected area. You can also use this technique to paint the selected area a different color. Use the Undo command if the effect is different from what you intended.

STEP 9: Print the completed drawing

➤ Save the drawing a final time. Pull down the **File menu**. Click **Print** to produce the Print dialog box. Click **OK** to print the completed document.

➤ Pull down the **File menu** and click **Exit** (or click the **Close button**) to quit Paint.

MULTITASKING

Multitasking, the ability to run multiple applications at the same time, is another major benefit of the Windows environment. It enables you to run a word processor (e.g., WordPad) in one window and a drawing program (e.g., Paint) in a second window. You can open a game in a third window, communicate on-line in a fourth window, and so on. You can work in one application as long as you like, then you can switch to a different window and work on another application.

Each open application has a corresponding button on the Taskbar that appears automatically when the application is opened and disappears upon closing. To change to a different task, all you do is click the corresponding button on the Taskbar, and Windows automatically switches to that application.

The application windows can be displayed simultaneously as in Figure 2.8a. Alternatively, one application can be maximized, as in Figure 2.8b, to allow a larger work area for that application (while temporarily hiding the other application). Either way you can do several things "at once" by switching from one task to the other.

Consider, for example, Figure 2.8a, which displays tiled windows for Word-Pad and Paint. WordPad is the active application because its title bar is highlighted. You can switch to Paint by clicking anywhere in its window, or by clicking its button on the Taskbar. And you can switch back to WordPad at any time, by clicking in its window or by clicking its button on the Taskbar.

Figure 2.8b displays a maximized window for WordPad and is our preferred way of working. Note, however, that Paint is also open in Figure 2.8b and that it is in memory even though its window is not visible. You can switch to Paint simply by clicking its button on the Taskbar.

Figure 2.8b also illustrates the concept of a *compound document,* which contains data from multiple applications. The text in the document was created using WordPad. The drawing was created in Paint, copied to the clipboard, then pasted into the WordPad document.

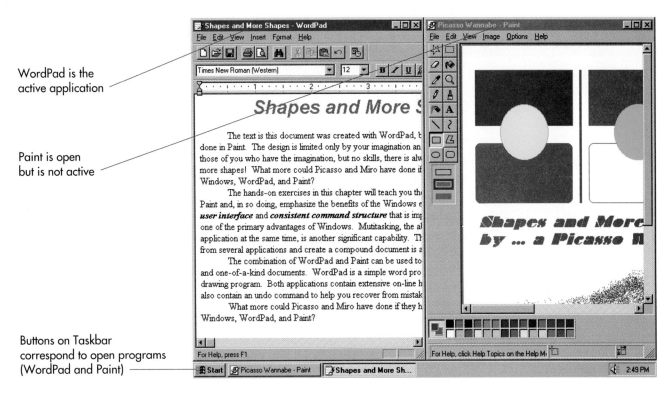

WordPad is the
active application

Paint is open
but is not active

Buttons on Taskbar
correspond to open programs
(WordPad and Paint)

(a) Tiled Windows

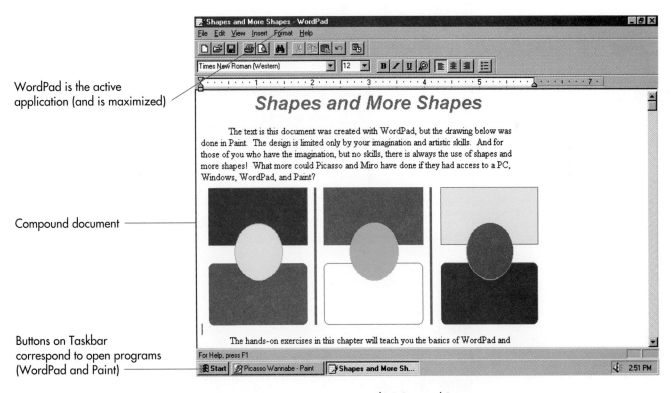

WordPad is the active
application (and is maximized)

Compound document

Buttons on Taskbar
correspond to open programs
(WordPad and Paint)

(b) A Compound Document

FIGURE 2.8   Multitasking

Multitasking

Objective: Create a compound document using the WordPad and Paint accessories. Use the Taskbar to switch between open applications. Use Figure 2.9 as a guide in the exercise.

STEP 1: Open WordPad

➤ Open **WordPad** as you did in the first hands-on exercise. Check the Taskbar to see the open application(s), which now includes the WordPad accessory.

➤ If necessary, click the **maximize button** so that WordPad takes the entire desktop, as shown in Figure 2.9a.

➤ Place the disk from the previous exercise in drive A. Pull down the **File menu** and click the **Open command** (or click the **Open button** on the toolbar) to display the Open dialog box in Figure 2.9a:

• Click the **down arrow** in the Look in box and select drive A.

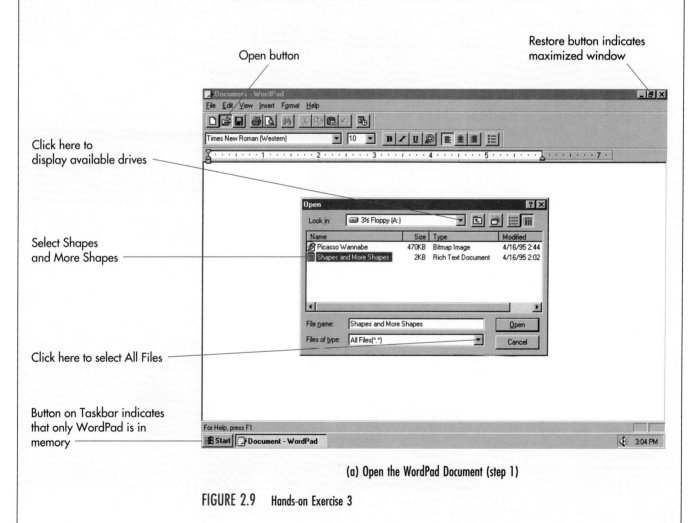

(a) Open the WordPad Document (step 1)

FIGURE 2.9 Hands-on Exercise 3

- Click the **down arrow** on the File type box and select All Files (*.*).
- Click the **Details button** within the Open box to display the file details (file name, size, type, and date last modified).

➤ You should see two files on drive A, corresponding to the drawing and document you created in the previous two exercises. (You may or may not see the extensions as described in the tip on page 55.)

➤ Select (click) the **Shapes and More Shapes** document. Click the **Open button** to open the document.

THE MOST RECENTLY OPENED FILE LIST

The easiest way to open a recently used document is to select the document directly from the File menu. Pull down the File menu, but instead of clicking the Open command, check to see if the document appears on the list of the most recently opened documents. If so, you can click the document name rather than having to make the appropriate selections through the Open dialog box.

STEP 2: Open Paint

➤ Click the **Start button,** then open **Paint** as you did in the previous exercise. The Taskbar now contains two buttons, indicating that WordPad and Paint are both open.

➤ If necessary, click the **Maximize button** so that Paint takes the entire desktop.

➤ Pull down the **File menu** as shown in Figure 2.9b. Open the Picasso Wannabe drawing by:
- Clicking the **Open command** to display the Open dialog box, then following the same procedure as described in step 1, *or*
- Clicking the **Picasso Wannabe drawing** from the list (of most recently opened documents) at the bottom of the pull-down menu.

The drawing from the previous exercise should be visible on your screen.

STEP 3: Copy the Drawing

➤ Select (click) the rectangular **Select tool.** Click and drag within the drawing to select the part of the drawing you wish to copy as shown in Figure 2.9c.

➤ Pull down the **Edit menu.** Click the **Copy command** to copy the selection to the clipboard.

KEYBOARD SHORTCUTS

Ctrl+X (the X is supposed to remind you of a pair of scissors), Ctrl+C, and Ctrl+V are shortcuts to cut, copy, and paste, respectively. The shortcuts pertain not just to WordPad or Paint, but to virtually every Windows application. The shortcuts are easier to remember when you realize that the letters, X, C, and V, are next to each other on the bottom row of the keyboard.

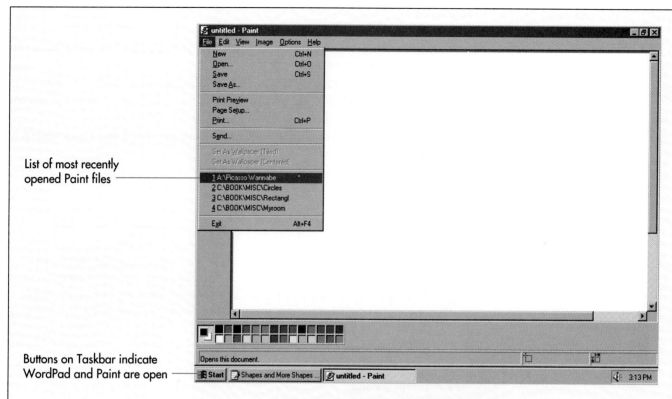

List of most recently
opened Paint files

Buttons on Taskbar indicate
WordPad and Paint are open

(b) Open the Paint Drawing (step 2)

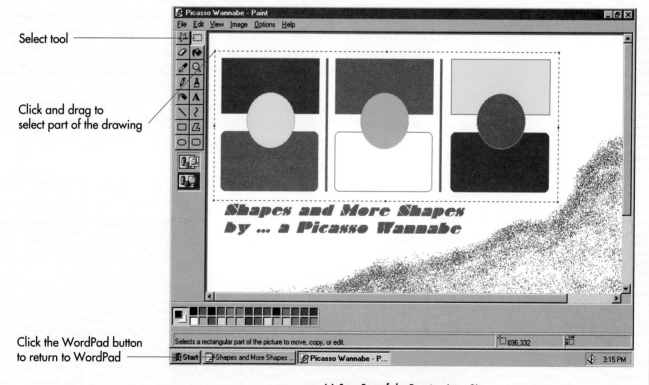

Select tool

Click and drag to
select part of the drawing

Click the WordPad button
to return to WordPad

(c) Copy Part of the Drawing (step 3)

FIGURE 2.9   Hands-on Exercise 3 (continued)

STEP 4: Create the Compound Document

➤ Click the **WordPad button** on the Taskbar to return to the WordPad document. (The Paint drawing remains open in memory but is no longer visible.)

➤ Click at the end of the first paragraph as shown in Figure 2.9d. Press the **enter key** to insert a blank line.

➤ Pull down the **Edit menu** and click the **Paste command** to paste the drawing into the document. (You can click the Paste icon on the Toolbar or you can use the Ctrl+V keyboard shortcut.)

➤ Click anywhere in the drawing to (select the drawing and) display the sizing handles shown in Figure 2.9d.

 • To change one dimension (the length *or* the width) click and drag a border handle in the direction you want to go.

 • To change both dimensions simultaneously (and maintain the proportion of the drawing) click and drag a corner handle.

 • Once the drawing object is selected, you can use the Cut or Copy commands to move or copy the drawing elsewhere in the document. You can also press the Del key to delete the object.

➤ Save the modified document.

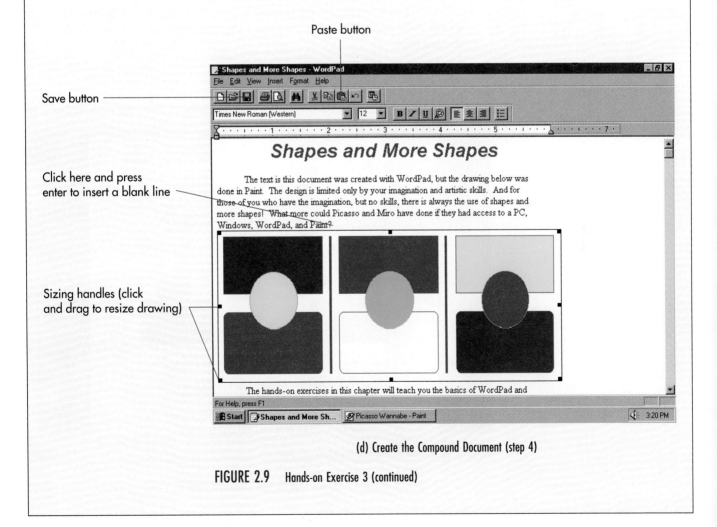

(d) Create the Compound Document (step 4)

FIGURE 2.9   Hands-on Exercise 3 (continued)

THE SAVE AS COMMAND

The Save As command saves a document under a different name and enables you to retain a copy of the original document (prior to making any changes). Pull down the File menu, click Save As to produce the Save As dialog box, then enter the name of the new document together with any other required information. All subsequent changes will be saved under the new name. The original document is retained under the original name.

STEP 5: The Print Preview Command

➤ Pull down the **File menu** and click the **Print Preview command** (or click the Print Preview button on the Toolbar) to preview the document prior to printing as shown in Figure 2.9e.

➤ Click the **Zoom In** and/or **Zoom Out** buttons to vary the amount of the document that you can see.

- If you are satisfied with the document, click the **Print button**, then click the **OK command button** in the Print dialog box.

- If you are not satisfied with the document, click the **Close button** to return to the document. Make the necessary changes, then preview the document a second time.

➤ Save the completed document.

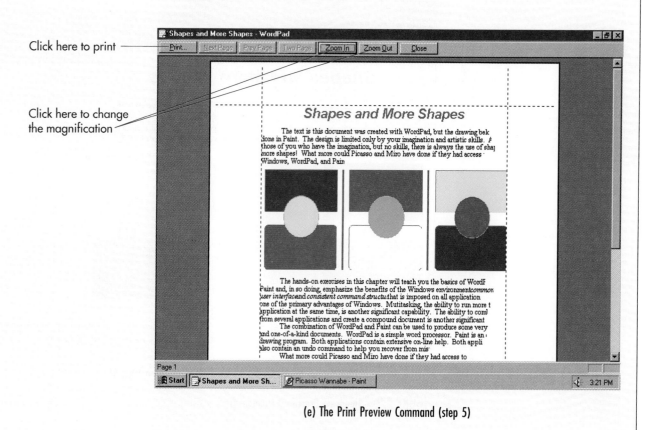

(e) The Print Preview Command (step 5)

FIGURE 2.9   Hands-on Exercise 3 (continued)

THE PAGE SETUP COMMAND

The Page Setup command lets you change the margins and/or orientation (Portrait or Landscape) of a document. Pull down the File menu, click Page Setup, then enter the desired settings. Click OK to accept the settings and exit the Page Setup dialog box. Pull down the File menu and click the Print command to print the document with the new settings.

STEP 6: Exit Windows

➤ Pull down the **File menu** and click **Exit** (or click the **Close button**) to exit Word-Pad. The WordPad window closes and the WordPad button disappears from the Taskbar.

➤ Pull down the **File menu** and click **Exit** (or click the **Close button**) to exit Paint. The Paint window closes and the Paint button disappears from the Taskbar.

➤ Click the **Start button,** then click the **Shut Down command.** The option button to shut down the computer is already selected. Click **Yes,** then wait as Windows gets ready to shut down the system. Wait until you see the screen indicating that it is OK to turn off the computer.

➤ Congratulations on a job well done.

MINIMIZE THE APPLICATION

Minimize (rather than close) an application if you intend to use it continually during a session. The application remains in memory, which saves you from having to reload the application when you need it. Click the minimize button to reduce the application to a button on the Taskbar, then click its button on the Taskbar whenever you want to return to the application.

SUMMARY

The common user interface with its consistent command structure is one of the primary advantages of the Windows environment. This provides a sense of familiarity from one application to the next in that all applications follow the same conventions and work basically the same way.

The WordPad accessory is a simple, yet effective, word processor. It does not have a spell-checker or thesaurus, but is otherwise capable of performing the basic operations common to any word processor. The Paint accessory enables you to create simple or (depending on your ability) elaborate drawings.

The common user interface ensures that all Windows applications have a consistent command structure. The File menu contains the Save and Open commands, the Print command, and the Close and Exit commands. The Edit menu contains the Cut, Copy, and Paste commands, and the Undo command. The Help menu is also found in every Windows application.

The clipboard is a temporary storage location available to any Windows application. Data is cut or copied onto the clipboard, from where it can be pasted to another location in the same document, or to another document.

Multitasking, the ability to run multiple applications simultaneously, is one of the primary advantages of Windows. The Taskbar contains a button for each open application and lets you switch back and forth between these programs by clicking the appropriate button.

KEY WORDS AND CONCEPTS

Background color	Font	Sizing handles
Clipboard	Format menu	Taskbar
Color box	Insertion point	Toolbox
Common user interface	Multitasking	Typeface
Compound document	Open command	Type size
Copy command	Paint accessory	Type style
Cut command	Paste command	Undo command
Drawing color	Save command	WordPad accessory
Edit menu	Selection area	WYSIWYG
File menu	Select-then-do	

MULTIPLE CHOICE

1. Which of the following operations does *not* place data onto the clipboard?
   (a) Cut
   (b) Copy
   (c) Paste
   (d) All of the above

2. Which commands are found in both WordPad and Paint?
   (a) Cut, Copy, and Paste
   (b) Save and Open
   (c) Undo and Exit
   (d) All of the above

3. What happens if you select a block of text, copy it, move to the beginning of the document, paste it, move to the end of the document, and paste the text again?
   (a) The selected text will appear in three places: at the original location, and at the beginning and end of the document
   (b) The selected text will appear in two places: at the beginning and end of the document
   (c) The selected text will appear in just the original location
   (d) The situation is not possible; that is, you cannot paste twice in a row without an intervening cut or copy operation

4. How do you change the font for *existing* text within a WordPad document?
- (a) Select the text, then choose the new font
- (b) Choose the new font, then select the text
- (c) Either (a) or (b)
- (d) Neither (a) nor (b)

5. What happens if you select a block of text, cut it, move to the beginning of the document, paste it, move to the end of the document, and paste the text again?
- (a) The selected text will appear in three places: at the original location, and at the beginning and end of the document
- (b) The selected text will appear at the beginning and end of the document
- (c) The selected text will appear in just the original location
- (d) The situation is not possible; that is, you cannot paste twice in a row without an intervening cut or copy operation

6. What is the effect of executing two successive Undo commands, one right after the other, in the WordPad accessory?
- (a) The situation is not possible because the Undo command is not available
- (b) The situation is not possible because the Undo command cannot be executed twice in a row
- (c) The Undo commands cancel each other out; that is, the document is the same as it was prior to the first Undo command
- (d) The last two commands prior to the first Undo command are reversed

7. What is the effect of executing two successive Undo commands, one right after the other, in the Paint accessory?
- (a) The situation is not possible because the Undo command is not available
- (b) The situation is not possible because the Undo command cannot be executed twice in a row
- (c) The Undo commands cancel each other out; that is, the document is the same as it was prior to the first Undo command
- (d) The last two commands prior to the first Undo command are reversed

8. The Save command:
- (a) Brings a document from disk into memory
- (b) Brings a document from disk into memory, then erases the document on disk
- (c) Stores the document in memory on disk
- (d) Stores the document in memory on disk, then erases the document in memory

9. The Open command:
- (a) Brings a document from disk into memory
- (b) Brings a document from disk into memory, then erases the document on disk
- (c) Stores the document in memory on disk
- (d) Stores the document in memory on disk, then erases the document in memory

10. Which menu contains the commands to print and save the current document, open a previously saved document, and exit the application?
    (a) File menu
    (b) Edit menu
    (c) Text menu
    (d) Print menu

11. Which of the following is true regarding the selection of colors in Paint?
    (a) Click the left mouse button to select the Drawing color
    (b) Click the right mouse button to select the Background color
    (c) Both (a) and (b)
    (d) Neither (a) nor (b)

12. How do you switch from WordPad to Paint, given that both applications are open and that their windows are cascaded one on top of the other?
    (a) Click the Paint button on the Taskbar
    (b) Click anywhere within the Paint window
    (c) Both (a) and (b)
    (d) Neither (a) nor (b)

13. How do you change the size of an object so that it maintains the original proportion between height and width?
    (a) Drag a handle on the left or right side of the object to change its width, then drag a handle on the top or bottom edge to change the height
    (b) Drag a sizing handle on any of the corners
    (c) Both (a) and (b)
    (d) Neither (a) nor (b)

14. Assume that the WordPad application has been opened and that its window has been maximized. Which of the following is true?
    (a) Clicking the Close button will remove WordPad from the Taskbar
    (b) Clicking the Minimize button will remove WordPad from the Taskbar
    (c) Both (a) and (b)
    (d) Neither (a) nor (b)

15. Assume that WordPad is opened, its window is maximized, Paint is opened, and its window is also maximized. Which of the following is true?
    (a) The Taskbar contains a button for both WordPad and Paint
    (b) The WordPad window is no longer visible and WordPad has been removed from memory
    (c) The Paint window is no longer visible and Paint has been removed from memory
    (d) All of the above

ANSWERS

1. c	**6.** c	**11.** c
2. d	**7.** d	**12.** c
3. a	**8.** c	**13.** b
4. a	**9.** a	**14.** a
5. b	**10.** a	**15.** a

Exploring Windows 95

1. Use Figure 2.10 to match each action with its result; a given action may be used more than once or not at all.

Action

a. Click at 1
b. Click at 12, then click at 2
c. Click at 3
d. Click at 4
e. Click at 5
f. Click at 9, then click at 6
g. Click at 9, click at 7, then click and drag at 10
h. Click at 9, then click at 8
i. Click at 9, then right click at 11
j. Click and drag at 13

Result

____ Boldface the selected text in WordPad
____ Change the font of the selected text in WordPad
____ Change the drawing color in Paint
____ Copy the selected Paint image to the clipboard
____ Print the WordPad document
____ Change the size of the font for the selected text
____ Paste the contents of the clipboard at the end of the WordPad document
____ Select the Text tool in Paint
____ Select the title of the Paint picture
____ Select the title of the WordPad document

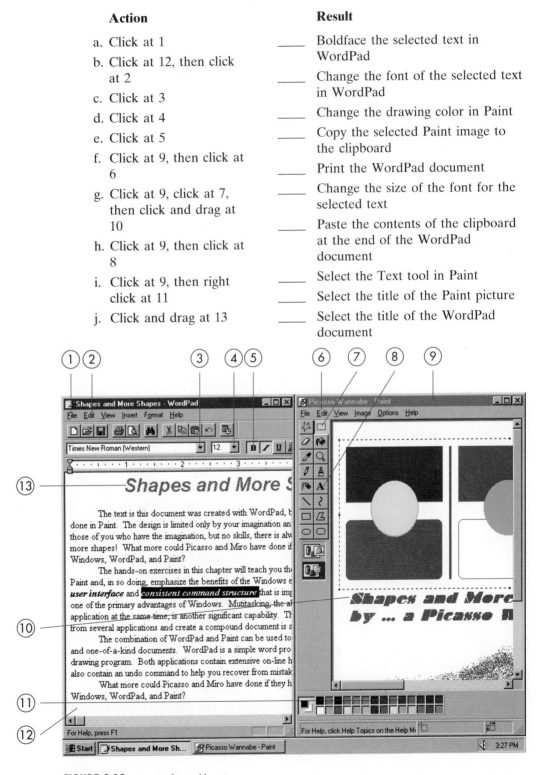

FIGURE 2.10   Screen for Problem 1

2. The Common User Interface: Use Figures 2.1a and 2.1b, which appeared at the beginning of the chapter, together with the appropriate pull-down menus, to answer the following questions regarding the WordPad and Paint accessories:

   a. Which application window (WordPad, Paint, or both) contains a title bar? A menu bar? Minimize, Restore, and Close buttons?

   b. Which pull-down menus are common to both WordPad and Paint?

   c. How do you access the Help menu in WordPad? in Paint?

   d. Which menu in WordPad contains the commands to cut, copy, and paste? Which menu in Paint?

   e. What are the keyboard shortcuts for the Cut, Copy, and Paste commands in the WordPad accessory? What are the corresponding shortcuts in Paint?

   f. Which application (WordPad, Paint, or both) has an Undo command? In which menu is it found?

   g. Which menu(s) in WordPad contain the commands to open and save a file? To print a document? To exit? Which menu(s) contain the comparable commands in Paint?

   h. What are the keyboard shortcuts to boldface, italicize, and underline text in WordPad? What are the corresponding shortcuts in Paint?

   i. What do your answers to parts (a) through (h) tell you about the advantages of a common user interface?

3. Exploring WordPad: Use the tips in the chapter, the on-line Help facility, and/or explore the pull-down menus to answer the following:

   a. How do you change justification within a document? What different types of justification are available? Does the justification command affect a word, a paragraph, or the entire document?

   b. What are the default margins (left, right, top, and bottom)? How do you change these values?

   c. How do you find all occurrences of a specific character string within a document? How do you substitute one character string for another?

   d. How do you center the title of a document? How do you boldface the title? How do you display the title in a larger type size than the rest of the document?

   e. How do you insert the current date and time into a document?

   f. What is meant by a bulleted style? How do you implement this style within a document?

   g. What are the default tab settings? How do you change these values?

   h. What is a hanging indent? How do you create a hanging indent in WordPad?

4. Exploring Paint: Use the tips in the chapter, the on-line Help facility, and/or explore the pull-down menus to answer the following:

   a. How do you draw a square rather than a rectangle? A circle rather than an ellipse?

   b. How do you draw a perfectly horizontal line? A perfectly vertical line? A line at a 45-degree angle?

   c. How do you use the curve tool to draw an S-shaped curve?

   d. What is the effect of clicking on a color using the left mouse button? What happens if you click on a color using the right mouse button?

e. How do you draw a red rectangular box with a blue border around it?

f. How do you create a custom color? What color is produced if red and blue are both set to 255 and green is set to 0? What color is produced if red and green are both set to 255 and blue is set to 0?

Practice with Windows 95

1. Use the Preamble to the Constitution as the basis for the following exercise, which you are to complete and submit to your instructor. Enter the text as shown below:

   We, the people of the United States, in order to form a more perfect Union, establish justice, insure domestic tranquility, provide for the common defense, promote the general welfare, and secure the blessings of liberty to ourselves and our posterity, do ordain and establish this Constitution for the United States of America.

   a. Choose any font you like, but specify italic as the style, and 10 points as the size. Use left justification.

   b. Copy the preamble to a new page, then change the specifications for the copied text to center the entire preamble. Use the same font as before, but choose regular rather than italic for the style.

   c. Create a title page for your assignment, containing your name, course name, and appropriate title. Choose a different font for the title page than for the rest of the document, and set the title in at least 24 points. Submit all three pages to your instructor.

2. Use the document in Figure 2.11 as the basis for the following exercise:

   a. Use WordPad to create a document containing the written message to your roommate. Save the message in a file called Proposed Room Layout.

   b. Use Paint to draw the room layout. Save the drawing in a file called Room Design. Copy the drawing to the clipboard.

   c. Switch back to the WordPad document containing the note to your roommate. Use the Paste command to bring the drawing into this document.

   d. Use WordPad to create a second document in the form of a note to your parents describing the room layout. Save this message in a file called Note To Parents.

   e. If necessary, copy the room layout into the clipboard, then use the Paste command to bring the drawing into the message to your parents.

3. Exploring Fonts: The Font folder within the Control Panel displays the names of all available fonts on a system and enables you to obtain a printed sample of any specific font.

   a. Open My Computer. Double click the Control Panel within My Computer, then double click the shortcut to the Fonts folder. You should see a list of the fonts available on your system.

   b. Pull down the View menu and (if necessary) check the Hide Variations command so that you see just the font names. Pull down the View menu a second time (or click the toolbar) to switch to the List view.

Jessica,

I have been racking my brain trying to come up with a way to arrange the furniture in our room to give us a roomier feel. I think that I have come up with a pretty decent arrangement, and I have laid it out with Paint so that we can think about it before we actually start to move the furniture around. What do you think? If you want to try different layouts before you decide, the Paint file is on my computer and is named Room Layout.

See you when I get back Sunday night!

Carol

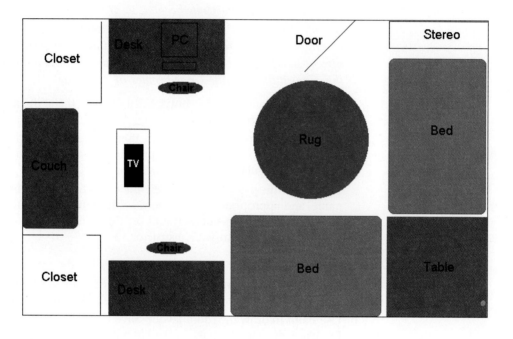

FIGURE 2.11   Practice Exercise 2

  c. Double click (open) the name of any font you wish to examine (e.g., Desdemona in Figure 2.12). Click the Print button in the Fonts window to print a sample of the selected font.

  d. Click the Fonts button on the Taskbar to return to the Fonts window and open a different font. Print a sample page of this font as well. Print a sample page of a third font in similar fashion.

  e. Click the Start button, click Programs, click Accessories, then open the WordPad accessory. Create a title page containing your name, class, and date, and the title of this assignment (Exploring Fonts). Center the title. Use boldface or italics as you see fit. Be sure to use a suitable type size.

  f. Staple the four pages together (the title page and three font samples), then submit them to your instructor.

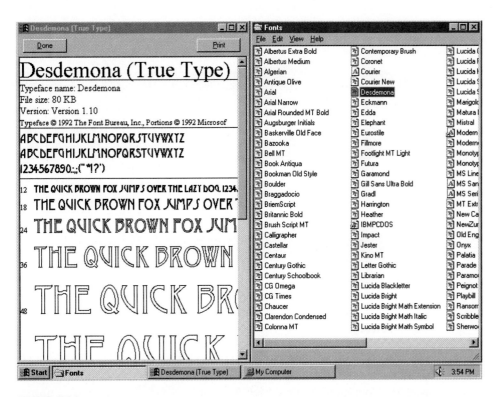

FIGURE 2.12 Practice Exercise 3

4. **Return to My Computer:** The document in Figure 2.13 was created by capturing a window from within My Computer, then including that window in a compound document created by the WordPad accessory. Do the following to create the document in Figure 2.13.

a. Place the floppy disk you have used throughout the chapter in drive A. Double click the My Computer icon, then double click the icon for drive A within the My Computer window.

b. If necessary, pull down the View menu to display the toolbar, then change to the Details view. Size the window so that you can see contents of all four columns as shown in Figure 2.13. The floppy disk contains the files that were created in the hands-on exercises. The entries in the modified column reflect the date and time that you did the exercises.

c. Press Alt+Print Screen to capture the window as opposed to the entire desktop.

d. Click the Start menu, click Programs, click Accessories, then click Word-Pad to open the word processor.

e. Pull down the Edit menu. Click the Paste command to copy the contents of the clipboard to the document you are about to create. The window for drive A should be pasted into your document.

f. Press Ctrl+End to move to the end of your document. Press the enter key three times (to leave three blank lines).

g. Type a modified form of the memo in Figure 2.13 so that it conforms to your configuration. Finish the memo and sign your name. Pull down the File menu, click the Print command, then click OK in the dialog box to print the document. Submit the completed document to your instructor.

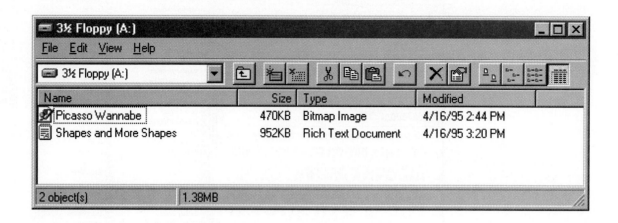

Dear Professor,

This is further proof that I did the Hands-on Exercises in the chapter. I followed the instructions for all of the exercises, saving the files on the floppy disk in drive A. Then, I used My Computer to open drive A, pressed Alt+Print Screen to capture the window, switched to WordPad, and pasted the window into the document. So here I am, and as you can see, I am becoming rather proficient with basic Windows operations.

Sincerely,

Shea Davis

FIGURE 2.13   Practice Exercise 4

CASE STUDIES

The Cover Page

Use WordPad to create a cover page for the assignments you will do this semester. The cover page should include the title of the assignment, your name, course information, and date. The title of the assignment should be formatted in a different font, size, and color than the personal information (name, course, date). The title is to be centered approximately two inches from the top of the page, whereas the personal information should appear in the lower right-hand corner of the page. Print the cover page and submit it to your instructor for inclusion in a class contest for the most innovative design.

Plans for the Future

Use WordPad to write a three-paragraph essay about what you intend to do when you graduate from college. Include both your long-range and short-range goals, as well as personal and professional goals. When you have finished the essay, emphasize two different phrases by italicizing one and boldfacing the other. Print the essay at this time.

Be sure you have printed the essay in its present form. Copy the first paragraph to the bottom of the document, then move the second paragraph to the top of the document. (The essay need not make sense in its revised form, as these steps are just to provide practice moving and copying text.) Print the document in its revised form; then submit both copies of your essay together with a cover page.

Modern Art

Use the Paint accessory to create a drawing that will reflect what you want to be doing five years from now. Let your imagination be your guide in using the various Paint tools to create a thought-provoking picture. Be creative in your use of color and shading, and do not let the fact that you are not artistic inhibit you in any way. You will be amazed at what you can do with the simple tools and palette provided. Print the completed drawing, and submit it with your cover page to your instructor.

A Compound Document

Use the drawing from the previous exercise to illustrate the essay that you wrote. Use the Windows 95 multitasking capabilities and the clipboard to copy the picture and paste it into the WordPad document. Add a sentence or two to reference the illustration. Print out the compound document and submit it to your instructor as proof you did the exercise.

MANAGING FILES AND FOLDERS: MY COMPUTER AND THE EXPLORER

OBJECTIVES

After reading this chapter you will be able to:

1. Use My Computer to locate a specific file or folder; describe the different views available for My Computer.
2. Describe how folders are used to organize a disk; create a new folder; copy and/or move a file from one folder to another.
3. Delete a file, then recover the deleted file from the Recycle Bin.
4. Discuss the importance of regular backup; list several factors to consider in developing an appropriate backup strategy.
5. Describe the document orientation of Windows 95; use the New command to create a document without explicitly opening the associated application.
6. Explain the differences in browsing with My Computer versus browsing with the Windows Explorer.
7. Use the Find command to locate a specific file; explain how a wild card can be used to locate files of a specific type.
8. Explain the different types of shortcuts that are available, then create one or more shortcuts.

OVERVIEW

A hard disk contains hundreds (indeed thousands) of files, which are stored in folders, the electronic equivalent of manila folders in a filing cabinet. The ability to manage those files is one of the most important skills you can acquire and the focus of this entire chapter.

We begin by discussing My Computer, which lets you search the drives on your computer for a specific file or folder. We show you how to create a new folder and how to move or copy a file from one folder to another. We show you how to rename a file, how to delete a file, and how to recover a deleted file from the Recycle Bin.

All of these operations can be done through My Computer or through the more powerful Windows Explorer. My Computer is intuitive and geared for the novice, as it opens a new window for each folder you open. Explorer, on the other hand, is more sophisticated and provides a hierarchical view of the entire system in a single window. A beginner will prefer My Computer, whereas a more experienced user will most likely opt for the Explorer. This is the same sequence in which we present the material. We start with My Computer, then show you how to accomplish the same result more quickly through the Explorer.

The chapter ends with presentation of two powerful techniques that you will appreciate as you gain experience with Windows. We show you how to use the Find command to locate a misplaced file and/or identify a file(s) containing specific text. We also show you how to create shortcuts that let you open a document or application through a desktop icon, as opposed to browsing the system or going through a series of menus.

MY COMPUTER

My Computer enables you to browse all of the drives (floppy disks, hard disks, and CD-ROM drive) that are attached to your computer. It is present on every desktop, but its contents will vary depending on the specific configuration. Our system, for example, has one floppy drive, one hard disk, and a CD-ROM as shown in Figure 3.1. Each drive is represented by an icon and is assigned a letter.

The first (often only) floppy drive is designated as drive A, regardless of whether it is a 3½ inch drive or the older, and now nearly obsolete, 5¼ inch drive. A second floppy drive, if it exists, is drive B. Our system contains a single 3½ floppy drive (note the icon in Figure 3.1a) and is typical of systems purchased in today's environment.

The first (often only) hard disk on a system is always drive C, whether or not there are one or two floppy drives. A system with one floppy drive and one hard disk (today's most common configuration) will contain icons for drive A and drive C. Additional hard drives (if any) and/or the CD-ROM are labeled from D on.

In addition to an icon for each drive on your system, My Computer also contains two additional folders. (Folders are discussed in the next section.) The *Control Panel* enables you to configure (set up) all of the devices (mouse, sound, and so on) on your system and was discussed in Chapter 1. The *Printers folder* lets you add a new printer and/or view the progress of a printed document.

The contents of My Computer can be displayed in different views (Large Icons, Small Icons, Details, and List) according to your preference or need. You can switch from one view to the next by choosing the appropriate command from the View menu or by clicking the corresponding button on the toolbar.

The *Large Icons view* and *Small Icons view* in Figure 3.1a and 3.1b, respectively, display each object as a large or small icon. The choice between the two depends on your personal preference. You might, for example, choose large icons if there are only a few objects in the window. Small icons would be preferable if there were many objects and you wanted to see them all. The *Details view* in Figure 3.1c displays additional information about each object. You see the type of object, the total size of the disk, and the remaining space on the disk. (A List view is also available and displays the objects with small icons but without the file details.)

Large icons button

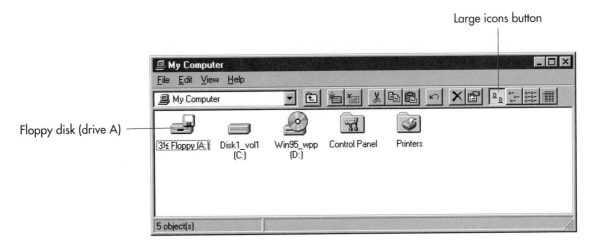

Floppy disk (drive A)

(a) Large Icons

Small icons button

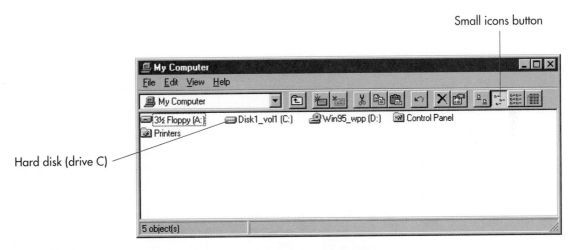

Hard disk (drive C)

(b) Small Icons

Details button

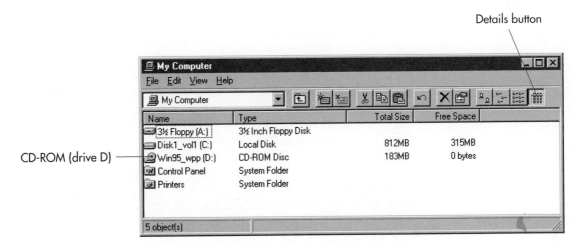

CD-ROM (drive D)

(c) Details View

FIGURE 3.1   My Computer

A *file* is any data or set of instructions that have been given a name and stored on disk. There are, in general, two types of files, ***program files*** and ***data files.*** Microsoft Word and Microsoft Excel are program files. The documents and spreadsheets created by these programs are data files. A ***program file*** is executable because it contains instructions that tell the computer what to do. A ***data file*** is not executable and can be used only in conjunction with a specific program.

A file must have a name by which it can be identified. The ***file name*** can contain up to 255 characters and may include spaces and other punctuation. (This is very different from the rules that existed under MS-DOS that limited file names to eight characters followed by an optional three-character extension.) Long file names permit descriptive entries, such as *Term Paper for Western Civilization* (as opposed to a more cryptic *TPWESCIV* that would be required under MS-DOS).

Files are stored in ***folders*** to better organize the hundreds (often thousands) of files on a hard disk. A Windows folder is similar in concept to a manila folder in a filing cabinet and contains one or more documents (files) that are somehow related to each other. An office worker stores his or her documents in manila folders. In Windows you store your data files (documents) in electronic folders on disk.

Folders are the key to the Windows storage system. You can create any number of folders to hold your work just as you can place any number of manila folders into a filing cabinet. You can create one folder for your word processing documents and a different folder for your spreadsheets. Alternatively, you can create a folder to hold all of your work for a specific class; this may contain a combination of word processing documents and spreadsheets. The choice is entirely up to you and you can use any system that makes sense to you. Anything at all can go into a folder—program files, data files, even other folders.

Figure 3.2 displays two different views of a folder containing six documents. The name of the folder (Homework) appears in the title bar next to the icon of an open folder. The minimize, maximize, and close buttons appear at the right of the title bar. A toolbar appears below the menu bar in each view.

The Details view in Figure 3.2a displays the name of each file in the folder (note the descriptive file name), the file size, the type of file, and the date and time the file was last modified. Figure 3.2b shows the Large Icons view, which displays only the file name and an icon representing the application that created the file. The choice between views depends on your personal preference. (A Small Icons view and List view are also available.)

File Type

Every data file has a specific ***file type*** that is determined by the application that created the file initially. One way to recognize the file type is to examine the Type column in the Details view as shown in Figure 3.2a. The History Term Paper, for example, is a Microsoft Word 6.0 document, and the Student Gradebook is an Excel 5.0 worksheet.

You can also determine the file type (or associated application) from any view (not just the Details view) by examining the application icon displayed next to the file name. Look carefully at the icon next to the History Term Paper in Figure 3.2a, for example, and you will recognize the icon for Microsoft Word. The application icon is recognized more easily in the Large icons view in Figure 3.2b.

Still another way to determine the file type is through the three-character extension displayed after the file name. (A period separates the file name from the extension.) Each application has a unique extension, which is automatically assigned to the file name when the file is created. DOC and XLS, for example,

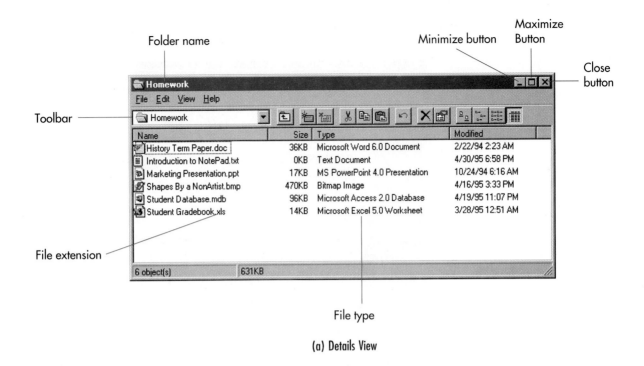

(a) Details View

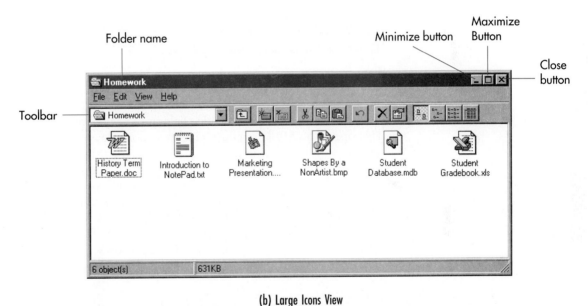

(b) Large Icons View

FIGURE 3.2   The Homework Folder

are the extensions for Microsoft Word and Excel, respectively. The extension may be suppressed or displayed according to an option in the View menu of My Computer. See step 2 of the hands-on exercise on page 95.

Browsing My Computer

You need to be able to locate a folder and/or its documents quickly so that you can retrieve the documents and go to work. There are several ways to do this, the easiest of which is to browse My Computer. Assume, for example, that you are looking for the Homework folder in Figure 3.3 in order to work on your term paper for history. Figure 3.3 shows how easy it is to locate the Homework folder.

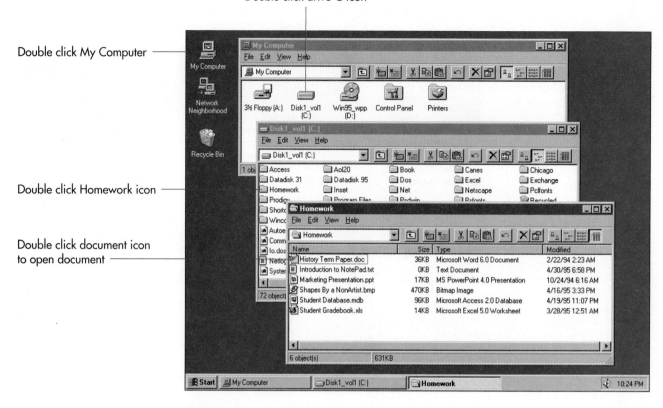

Double click drive C icon

Double click My Computer

Double click Homework icon

Double click document icon to open document

FIGURE 3.3   Browsing My Computer

You would start by double clicking the My Computer icon on the desktop. This opens the My Computer window and displays all of the drives on your system. Next you would double click the icon for drive C because this is the drive that contains the folder you are looking for. This opens a second window, which displays all of the folders on drive C. And finally you would double click the icon for the Homework folder to open a third window containing the documents in the Homework folder. Once you are in the Homework folder, you would double click the icon of any existing document (which loads the associated application and opens the document), enabling you to begin work.

LEARNING BY DOING

The exercise that follows has you create a new folder on drive C, then create various files in that folder. The files are created using Notepad and Paint, two accessories that are included in Windows 95. We chose to create the files using these simple accessories, rather than more powerful applications such as Word or Excel, because we wanted to create the files quickly and easily. We also wanted to avoid reliance on specific applications that are not part of Windows 95. The emphasis throughout this chapter is on the ability to manipulate files within the Windows environment after they have been created.

The exercise also illustrates the document orientation of Windows 95, which enables you to think in terms of the document rather than the application that created it. You simply point to an open folder, click the right mouse button to display a shortcut menu, then select the New command. You will be presented with a list of objects (file types) that are recognized by Windows 95 because the associated applications have been previously installed. Choose the file type that you want, and the associated application will be opened automatically. (See step 4 in the following hands-on exercise.)

THE DOCUMENT, NOT THE APPLICATION

Windows 95 is document oriented, meaning that you are able to think in terms of the document rather than the application that created it. You can still open a document in traditional fashion, by loading the program that created the document, then using the File Open command in that program to retrieve the document. It's much easier, however, to browse through My Computer to find the folder containing the document, then double click the document. Windows loads the associated program and opens the requested data file. In other words, you can open a document without even knowing the associated application.

HANDS-ON EXERCISE 1

My Computer

Objective: Open My Computer and create a new folder on drive C. Use the New command to create a Notepad document and a Paint drawing. Use Figure 3.4 as a guide in the exercise.

STEP 1: Create a Folder

➤ Double click the **My Computer icon** to open My Computer. Double click the icon for **drive C** to open a second window as shown in Figure 3.4a. The size and/or position of your windows will probably be different from ours.

➤ Make or verify the following selections in each window. (You have to pull down the View menu each time you choose a different command.)

- The **Toolbar command** should be checked.
- The **Status Bar command** should be checked.
- **Large Icons** should be selected.

➤ If necessary, click anywhere within the window for **drive C** to make it the active window. (The title bar reflects the internal label of your disk, which was assigned when the disk was formatted. Your label will be different from ours.)

➤ Pull down the **File menu,** click (or point to) **New** to display the submenu, then click **Folder** as shown in Figure 3.4a.

STEP 2: The View Menu

➤ A new folder has been created within the window for drive C with the name of the folder (New Folder) highlighted. Type **Homework** to change the name of the folder as shown in Figure 3.4b. Press **enter.**

➤ Pull down the **View menu** and click the **Arrange Icons command.** Click **By Name** to arrange the folders alphabetically within the window for drive C.

➤ Pull down the **View menu** a second time. Click **Options,** then click the **View tab** in the Options dialog box. Check the box (if necessary) to **Hide MS-DOS file extensions.** Click **OK.**

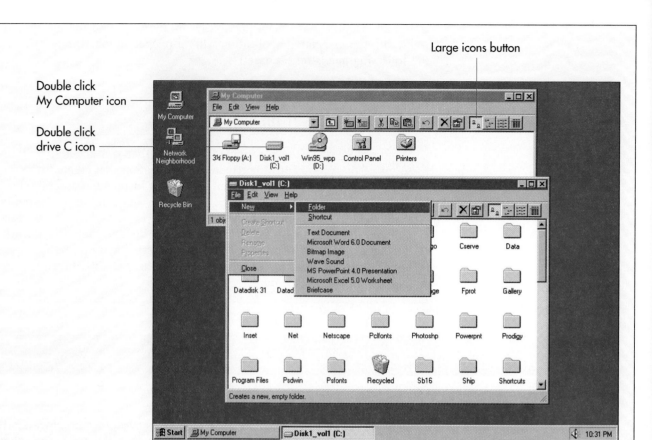

Double click
My Computer icon

Double click
drive C icon

Large icons button

(a) Create a Folder (step 1)

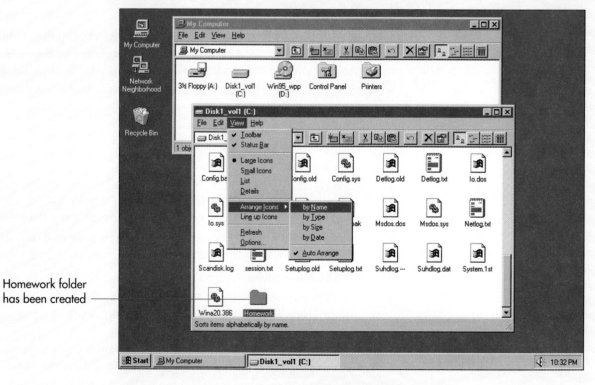

Homework folder
has been created

(b) View Menu (step 2)

FIGURE 3.4   Hands-on Exercise 1

HOMEWORK FOLDER ALREADY EXISTS

If you are working on a LAN with other students, you may see the error message "Cannot Rename New Folder. A folder with the name you specified already exists." This means that another student has already created the homework folder on this machine, and hence you must delete that student's folder in order to create a homework folder of your own. Press Esc (or click OK) to close the Error Renaming File dialog box. Press Esc a second time to deselect the folder name (homework). Select (click) the existing homework folder and press the Del key, then create a homework folder of your own.

STEP 3: Open the Homework Folder

➤ Click the **Homework folder** to select it. Pull down the **File menu** and click **Open** (or double click the folder) to open the Homework folder.

➤ The Homework folder opens into a window as shown in Figure 3.4c. The window is empty because the folder does not contain any documents. If necessary, pull down the **View menu** and check the **Toolbar command** to display the toolbar.

➤ **Right click** a blank position on the Taskbar to display the menu in Figure 3.4c. Click **Tile Vertically** to tile the three open windows.

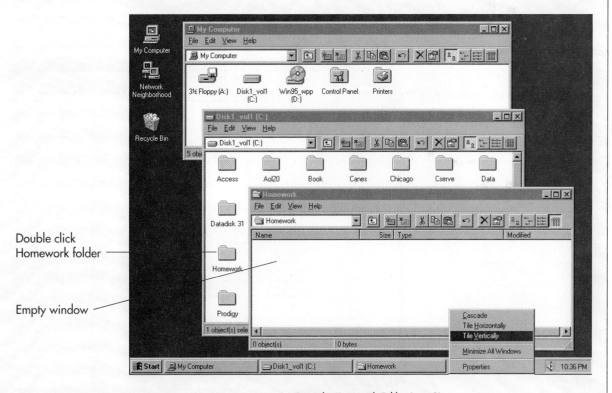

Double click Homework folder

Empty window

(c) Open the Homework Folder (step 3)

FIGURE 3.4   Hands-on Exercise 1 (continued)

STEP 4: The New Command

➤ The windows on your desktop should be tiled vertically. Click in the **Homework window.** The title bar for the Homework window should be highlighted.

➤ Pull down the **File menu** (or point to an empty area in the window and click the **right mouse button**).

➤ Click (or point to) the **New command** to display a submenu. The document types depend on the installed applications:

• You may (or may not) see Microsoft Word Document or Microsoft Excel Worksheet, depending on whether or not you have installed these applications.

• You will see Text Document and Bitmap Image corresponding to the Notepad and Paint accessories that are installed with Windows 95.

➤ Select (click) **Text Document** as the type of file to create as shown in Figure 3.4d. The icon for a new document will appear with the name of the document, New Text Document, highlighted. Type **Files and Folders** to change the name of the document. Press **enter.**

THE RIGHT MOUSE BUTTON

The right mouse button is the fastest way to access a menu or a properties sheet. Point to any object (e.g., the Taskbar, a folder, a file, or even the desktop itself), then click the right mouse button to display a menu or a properties sheet for that object.

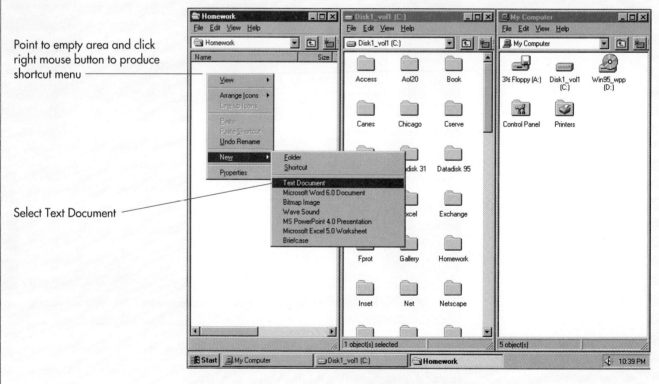

(d) The New Command (step 4)

FIGURE 3.4   Hands-on Exercise 1 (continued)

THE NOTEPAD ACCESSORY

The Notepad accessory is ideal to create "quick and dirty" files that require no formatting and that are smaller than 64K. Notepad opens and saves files in ASCII (text) format only. Use a different editor, such as WordPad or a full-fledged word processor such as Microsoft Word, to create larger files or files that require formatting.

STEP 5: Create the Document

➤ If necessary, pull down the **View menu** and change to the **Large Icons view** so that the view in your Homework folder matches the view in Figure 3.4e.

➤ Select (click) the **Files and Folders document.** Pull down the **File menu.** Click **Open** (or double click the **Files and Folders icon** without pulling down the File menu) to load Notepad and open a Notepad window. The window is empty because the text of the document has not yet been entered.

➤ Pull down the **Edit menu:**

• If there is no check mark next to Word Wrap, click the **Word Wrap command** to enable this feature.

• If there is a check mark next to Word Wrap, click outside the menu to close the menu without changing any settings.

Double click Files and Folders icon

Click here to close Notepad

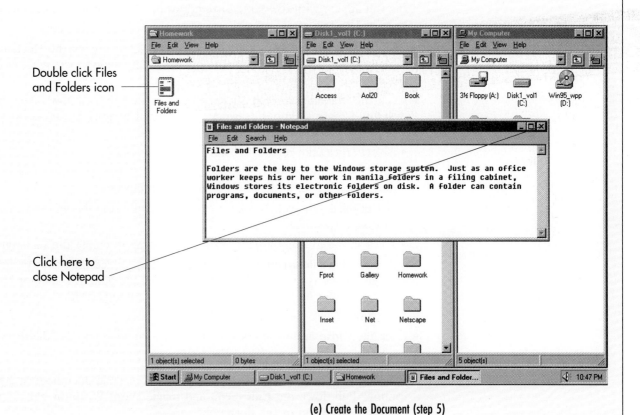

(e) Create the Document (step 5)

FIGURE 3.4   Hands-on Exercise 1 (continued)

➤ Type the text of the document as shown in Figure 3.4e. Type just as you would on a regular typewriter with one exception—press the enter key only at the end of a paragraph, not at the end of every line. Since word wrap is in effect, Notepad will automatically start a new line when the word you are typing does not fit at the end of the current line.

➤ Pull down the **File menu** and click **Save** to save the document when you are finished. Click the **Close button** to close the Notepad accessory.

FILE EXTENSIONS

Longtime DOS users will recognize a three-character extension at the end of a file name to indicate the file type—for example, TXT to indicate a text (ASCII) file. The extensions are displayed or hidden according to the option you establish through the View menu of My Computer. Open My Computer, pull down the View menu, and click the Options command. Click the View tab, then check (clear) the box to hide (show) MS-DOS file extensions. Click OK to accept the setting and exit the dialog box.

STEP 6: Create a Drawing

➤ **Right click** within the Homework folder, click (or point to) the **New command,** then click **Bitmap Image** as the type of file to create. The icon for a new drawing will appear with the name of the drawing (New Bitmap Image) highlighted.

➤ Type **Rectangles** to change the name of the drawing. Press **enter.**

➤ Pull down the **File menu,** and click **Open** (or double click the **Rectangles icon** without pulling down the menu) to open a Paint window. The window is empty because the drawing has not yet been created.

➤ Click the **Maximize button** (if necessary) so that the window takes the entire desktop. Create a simple drawing consisting of various rectangles as shown in Figure 3.4f. To draw a rectangle:

- Select (click) the rectangle tool.
- Select (click) the type of rectangle you want (a border only, a filled rectangle with a border, or a filled rectangle with no border).
- Select (click) the colors for the border and fill using the left and right mouse button, respectively.
- Click in the drawing area, then click and drag to create the rectangle.

➤ Pull down the **File menu** and click **Save As** to produce the Save As dialog box. Change the file type to **16-Color Bitmap** (from the default 256-color bitmap) to create a smaller file and conserve space on the floppy disk.

➤ Click **Save.** Click **Yes** to replace the file.

➤ Click the **Close button** to close Paint when you have finished the drawing.

STEP 7: Edit the Document

➤ Double click the **Files and Folders icon** to reopen the document in a Notepad window. Pull down the **Edit menu** and toggle Word Wrap on. Press **Ctrl+End** to move to the end of the document.

➤ Add the additional text as shown in Figure 3.4g. Do *not* save the document at this time.

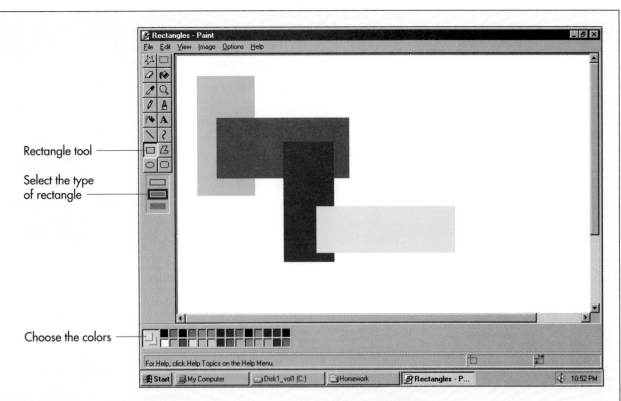

Rectangle tool

Select the type of rectangle

Choose the colors

(f) Create the Drawing (step 6)

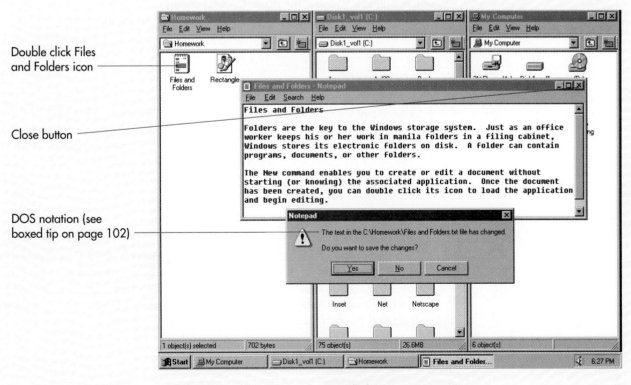

Double click Files and Folders icon

Close button

DOS notation (see boxed tip on page 102)

(g) Edit the Document (step 7)

FIGURE 3.4   Hands-on Exercise 1 (continued)

➤ Click the **Close button** to exit Notepad. You will see the informational message in Figure 3.4g, which indicates you have forgotten to save the changes. Click **Yes** to save the changes and exit.

THE NEW COMMAND

The easiest way to create a new document is to select the folder that is to contain the document, pull down the File menu, click New (or right click an empty space within a folder); then choose the type of document you want to create. Once the document has been created, double click its icon to load the associated application and begin editing the document. In other words, you can think about the document and not the application.

STEP 8: Change the View

➤ Right click an empty space on the Taskbar, then click the **Tile Horizontally command** to tile the windows as shown in Figure 3.4h. (The order of your windows may be different from ours.)

➤ Click in the window for the **Homework folder,** then click the **Details button** on the toolbar to display the Details view.

➤ Press the **F5 key** to refresh the window and update the file properties (the file size, type, and the date and time of the last modification).

➤ Click in the window for **drive C,** then click the **List view** or **Small Icons button** on the toolbar to display small icons as shown in Figure 3.4h.

DOS NOTATION

The visually oriented storage system within Windows 95 makes it easy to identify folders and the documents within those folders. DOS, however, was not so simple and used a text-based notation to indicate the drive, folder, and file. For example, C:\HOMEWORK\FILES AND FOLDERS, specifies the file FILES AND FOLDERS, in the HOMEWORK folder, on drive C.

STEP 9: Continue with the Next Exercise

➤ You have created a folder and several documents on drive C that you will need in the next exercise. Hence, if you are working at school and cannot be guaranteed the same machine the next time you enter the lab, it is important that you continue with the next exercise at this time. Otherwise, you will have to re-create all of the files in this exercise.

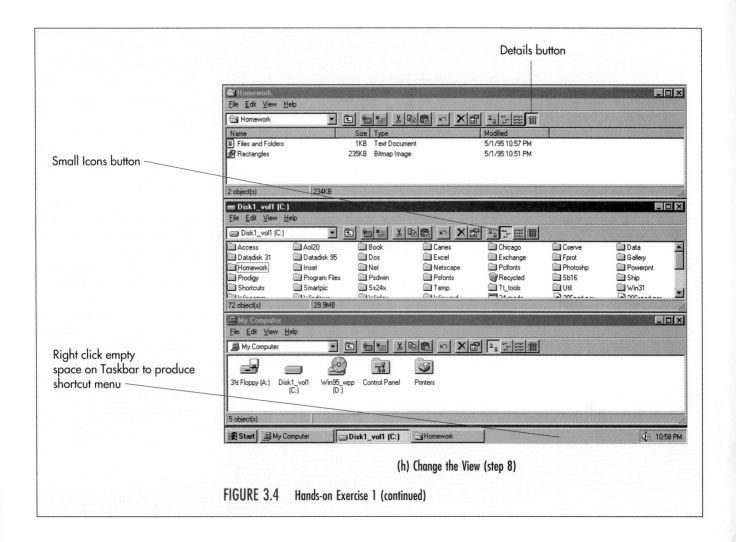

Details button

Small Icons button

Right click empty
space on Taskbar to produce
shortcut menu

(h) Change the View (step 8)

FIGURE 3.4   Hands-on Exercise 1 (continued)

FILE OPERATIONS

The exercise just completed had you create a folder and place documents in that folder. As you continue to work on the computer, you will create additional folders, as well as files within those folders. Learning how to manage those files is one of the most important skills you can acquire. This section describes the different types of file operations that you will perform on a daily basis.

Moving and Copying a File

There are two general ways to move or copy a file from one location to another. You can use the Cut, Copy, and Paste commands, or you can simply drag and drop the files from one location to the other. Both techniques require you to open the disk or folder containing the source file (the file you are moving or copying) in order to select the file you will move or copy. This is typically done by opening successive windows through My Computer.

Assume, for example, that you want to copy a file from the Homework folder on drive C to a floppy disk in drive A. You would begin by double clicking the My Computer icon to open the My Computer window. Then you would double click the icon for drive C because that is the drive containing the file you want to copy. And then you would double click the icon for the Homework folder (opening a third window) because that is the folder containing the file to be copied.

To copy the file (after the Homework folder has been opened), select the file by clicking its icon, then drag the icon to the drive A icon in the My Computer window. (Alternatively, you could select the file, pull down the Edit menu, and click the Copy command, then click the icon for drive A, pull down the Edit menu, and click the Paste command.) It sounds complicated, but it's not, and you will get a chance to practice in the hands-on exercise.

Backup

It's not a question of *if* it will happen, but *when*—hard disks die, files are lost, or viruses may infect a system. It has happened to us and it will happen to you, but you can prepare for the inevitable by creating adequate backup *before* the problem occurs. The essence of a **backup strategy** is to decide which files to back up, how often to do the backup, and where to keep the backup. Once you decide on a strategy, follow it, and follow it faithfully!

Our strategy is very simple—backup what you can't afford to lose, do so on a daily basis, and store the backup away from your computer. You need not copy every file, every day. Instead copy just the files that changed during the current session. Realize, too, that it is much more important to backup your data files, rather than your program files. You can always reinstall the application from the original disks, or if necessary, go to the vendor for another copy of an application. You, however, are the only one who has a copy of the term paper that is due tomorrow.

Deleting files

The **Delete command** deletes (removes) a file from a disk. If, however, the file was deleted from a hard disk, it is not really gone, but moved instead to the Recycle Bin from where it can be subsequently recovered.

The **Recycle Bin** is a special folder that contains all of the files that were previously deleted from any hard disk on your system. Think of the Recycle Bin as similar to the wastebasket in your room. You throw out (delete) a report by tossing it into a wastebasket. The report is gone (deleted) from your desk, but you can still get it back by taking it out of the wastebasket as long as the basket wasn't emptied. The Recycle Bin works the same way. Files are not deleted from the hard disk per se, but are moved instead to the Recycle Bin from where they can be recovered. The Recycle Bin should be emptied periodically, however, or else you will run out of space on the disk. Once a file is removed from the Recycle Bin, it can no longer be recovered.

WRITE-PROTECT YOUR BACKUP DISKS

You can write-protect a floppy disk to ensure that its contents are not accidentally altered or erased. A 3½-inch disk is write-protected by sliding the built-in tab so that the write-protect notch is open. The disk is write-enabled when the notch is covered. The procedure is reversed for a 5¼-inch disk; that is, the disk is write-protected when the notch is covered and write-enabled when the notch is open.

File Operations

Objective: Copy a file from drive C to drive A, and from drive A back to drive C. Delete a file from drive C, then restore the file using the Recycle Bin. Demonstrate the effects of write-protecting a disk. Use Figure 3.5 as a guide in the exercise.

STEP 1: Open the Homework Folder

➤ Double click the icon for **My Computer** to open My Computer. Double click the icon for **drive C** to open a second window showing the contents of drive C. Double click the **Homework folder** to open a third window showing the contents of the Homework folder.

➤ Right click the **Taskbar** to tile the windows vertically as shown in Figure 3.5a. Your windows may appear in a different order from those in the figure.

➤ Make or verify the following selections in each window. (You have to pull down the View menu each time you choose a different command.)

  • The **Toolbar command** should be checked.

  • The **Status Bar command** should be checked.

  • Choose the **Details view** in the Homework window and the **Large Icons view** in the other windows.

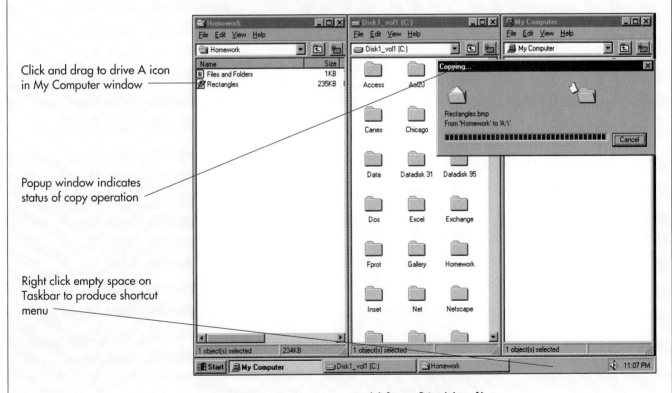

Click and drag to drive A icon in My Computer window

Popup window indicates status of copy operation

Right click empty space on Taskbar to produce shortcut menu

(a) Copy to Drive A (step 1)

FIGURE 3.5   Hands-on Exercise 2

➤ Pull down the **View menu** in any open window. Click **Options,** then click the **View tab** in the Options dialog box.

➤ Check the box (if necessary) to **Hide MS-DOS file extensions.** Click **OK** to exit the dialog box.

QUICK VIEW

If you forget what is in a particular document, you can use the Quick View command to preview the document without having to open it. Select (click) the file you want to preview, then pull down the File menu and click Quick View (or right click the file and select the Quick View command) to display the file in a preview window. If you decide to edit the file, pull down the File menu and click Open File for Editing, otherwise click the close button to close the preview window.

STEP 2: Backup the Homework Folder

➤ Place a freshly formatted disk in drive A. Be sure the disk is not write-protected, or else you will not be able to copy files to the disk.

➤ Click and drag the icon for the **Rectangles file** from the Homework folder to the icon for **drive A** in the My Computer window.

  • You will see the ⊘ symbol as you drag the file until you reach a suitable destination (e.g., until you point to the icon for drive A). The ⊘ symbol will change to a plus sign when the icon for drive A is highlighted, indicating that the file can be successfully copied.

  • Release the mouse to complete the copy operation. You will see a popup window as shown in Figure 3.5a, indicating the progress of the copy operation. This takes several seconds since Rectangles is a large file (235KB).

➤ Click and drag the icon for the **Files and Folders file** from the Homework folder to the icon for drive A.

➤ You may or may not see a popup window showing the copy operation since Files and Folders is a small file (1KB) and copies quickly.

USE THE RIGHT MOUSE BUTTON TO MOVE OR COPY A FILE

The result of dragging a file with the left mouse button depends on whether the source and destination folders are on the same or different drives. Dragging a file to a folder on a different drive copies the file. Dragging the file to a folder on the same drive moves the file. If you find this hard to remember, and most people do, click and drag with the right mouse button to produce a shortcut menu asking whether you want to copy or move the file. This simple tip can save you from making a careless (and potentially serious) error. Use it!

STEP 3: View the Contents of Drive A

➤ Double click the icon for **drive A** in the My Computer window to open a fourth window.

➤ Right click a blank area on the Taskbar. Tile the windows vertically or horizontally (it doesn't matter which command you select) to display the windows as in Figure 3.5b.

➤ Click in the window for drive A. If necessary, pull down the **View menu,** display the Toolbar, and change to the **Details view.**

➤ Compare the file details for each file in the Homework folder and drive A; the details are identical, reflecting the fact that the files have been copied.

CHANGE THE COLUMN WIDTH

Drag the right border of a column heading to the right (left) to increase (decrease) the width of the column in order to see more (less) information in that column. Double click the right border of a column heading to automatically adjust the column width to accommodate the widest entry in that column.

File details are identical

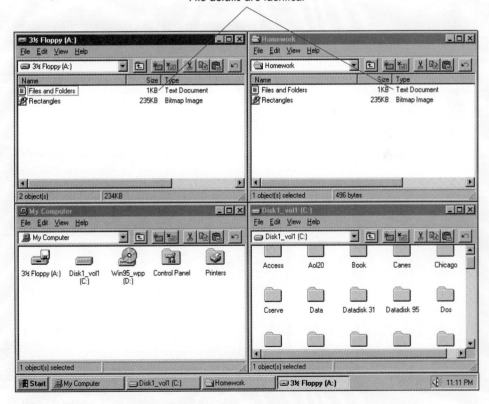

(b) View the Contents of Drive A (step 3)

FIGURE 3.5 Hands-on Exercise 2 (continued)

STEP 4: Delete a File

➤ Select (click) the **Files and Folders icon** in the Homework folder. Pull down the **File menu.** Click **Delete.**

➤ You will see the dialog box in Figure 3.5c, asking whether you want to delete the file. Click **Yes** to delete the file.

➤ Right click the **Rectangles icon** in the Homework folder to display a shortcut menu. Click **Delete.** Click **Yes** when asked whether to delete the Rectangles file. The Homework folder is now empty.

THE UNDO COMMAND

The Undo command pertains not just to application programs such as Notepad or Paint, but to file operations as well. It will, for example, undelete a file if it is executed immediately after the Delete command. Pull down the Edit menu and click Undo to reverse (undo) the last command. Some operations cannot be undone (in which case the command will be dimmed out), but Undo is always worth a try.

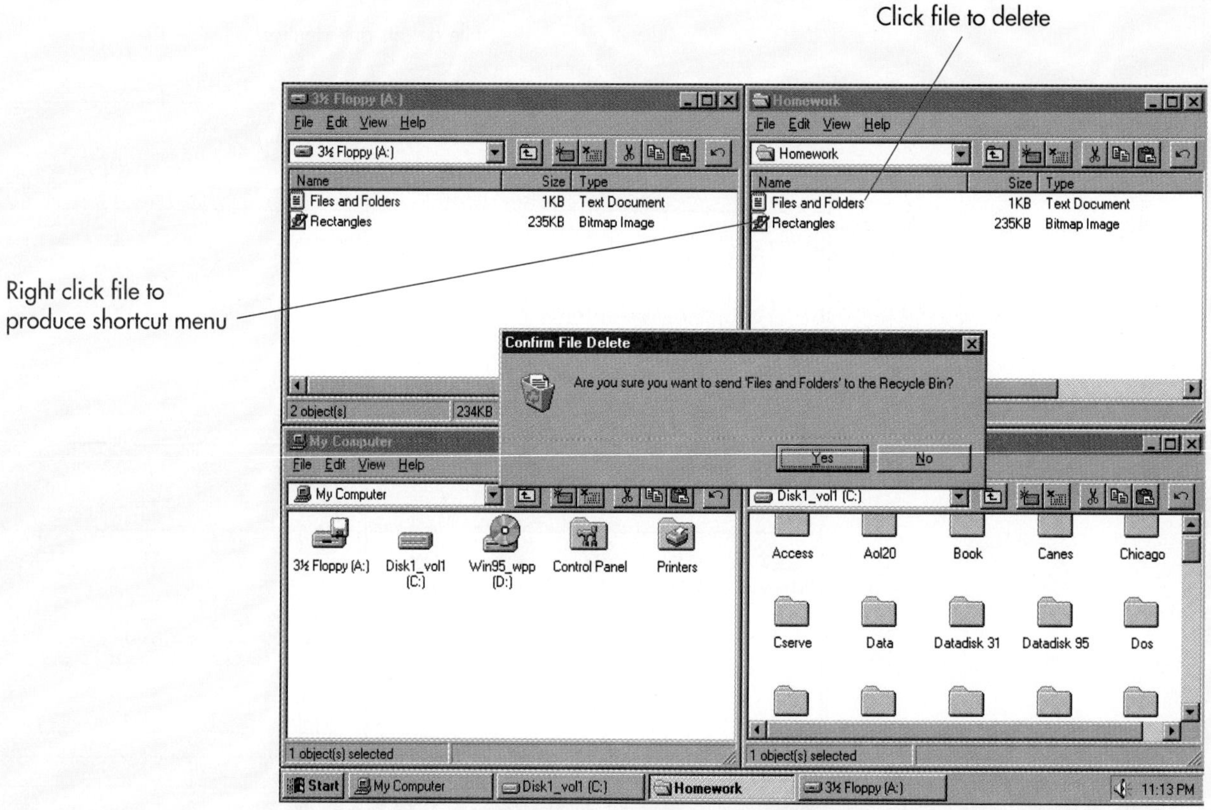

Click file to delete

Right click file to produce shortcut menu

(c) Delete a File (step 4)

FIGURE 3.5   Hands-on Exercise 2 (continued)

STEP 5: Copy from Drive A to Drive C

➤ The backup you did in step 2 enables you to copy (restore) the Files and Folders file from drive A to drive C. You can do this in one of two ways:

- Select (click) the **Files and Folders icon** in the window for drive A. Pull down the **Edit menu.** Click **Copy.** Click in the **Homework folder.** Pull down the **Edit menu.** Click **Paste** as shown in Figure 3.5d.
- Click and drag the icon for the **Files and Folders** file from drive A to the Homework folder.

➤ Either way, you will see a popup window showing the Files and Folders file being copied from drive A to drive C.

➤ Use whichever technique you prefer to copy the Rectangles file from drive A to drive C.

BACK UP IMPORTANT FILES

We cannot overemphasize the importance of adequate backup and urge you to copy your data files to floppy disks and store those disks away from your computer. It takes only a few minutes, but you will thank us, when (not if) you lose an important file and wish you had another copy.

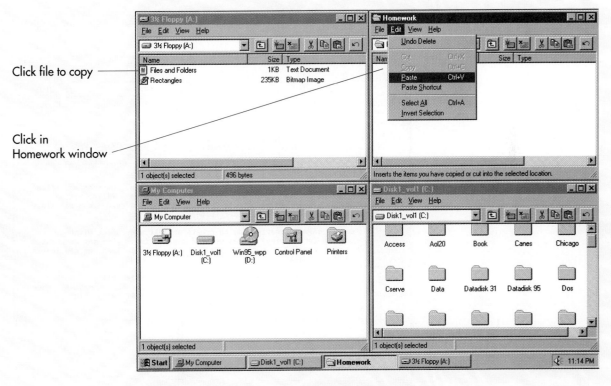

Click file to copy

Click in
Homework window

(d) Copy to Drive C (step 5)

FIGURE 3.5   Hands-on Exercise 2 (continued)

STEP 6: Modify a File

➤ Double click the **Files and Folders icon** in the Homework folder to reopen the file as shown in Figure 3.5e. Pull down the **Edit menu** and toggle Word Wrap on.

➤ Press **Ctrl+End** to move to the end of the document. Add the paragraph shown in Figure 3.5e.

➤ Pull down the **File menu** and click **Save** to save the modified file. Click the **Close button** to close the file.

➤ The Files and Folders document has been modified and should once again be backed up to drive A. Click and drag the icon for **Files and Folders** from the Homework folder to the drive A window.

➤ You will see a message indicating that the folder (drive A) already contains a file called Files and Folders (which was previously copied in step 2) and asking whether you want to replace the existing file with the new file. Click **Yes.**

THE SEND TO COMMAND

The Send To command is an alternative way to copy a file to a floppy disk and has the advantage that the floppy disk icon need not be visible. Select (click) the file to copy, then pull down the File menu (or simply right click the file). Click the Send To command, then select the appropriate floppy drive from the resulting submenu.

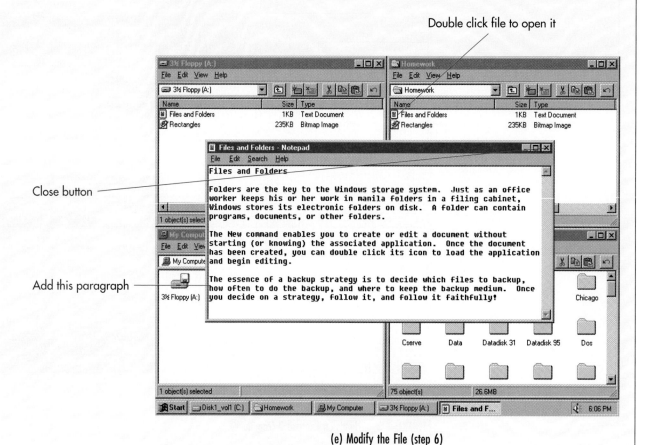

(e) Modify the File (step 6)

FIGURE 3.5 Hands-on Exercise 2 (continued)

STEP 7: Write-protect a Disk

➤ You can write-protect a floppy disk so that its contents cannot be changed; that is, existing files cannot be modified or erased nor can new files be added.

➤ Remove the floppy disk from drive A and follow the appropriate procedure:
  - To write-protect a 3½ disk, move the built-in tab so that the write-protect notch is open.
  - To write-protect a 5¼ disk, cover the write-protect notch with a piece of opaque tape.

➤ Return the write-protected disk to the floppy drive.

➤ Click the icon for the **Rectangles file** on drive A, then press the **Del key** to delete the file.

➤ You will see a warning message, asking whether you are sure you want to delete the file. Click **Yes.**

➤ You will see the error message in Figure 3.5f, indicating that the file cannot be deleted because the disk is write-protected. Click **OK.**

➤ Remove the write-protection by reversing the procedure you followed earlier. Select the **Rectangles file** a second time and delete the file. Click **Yes** in response to the confirmation message, after which the file will be deleted from drive A.

➤ You have just deleted the Rectangles file, but we want it back on drive A for the next exercise. Accordingly, click and drag the **Rectangles icon** in the Homework folder to the icon for **drive A** in the My Computer window.

➤ Click the **Close button** in the window for drive A.

Click file to delete, press Del key

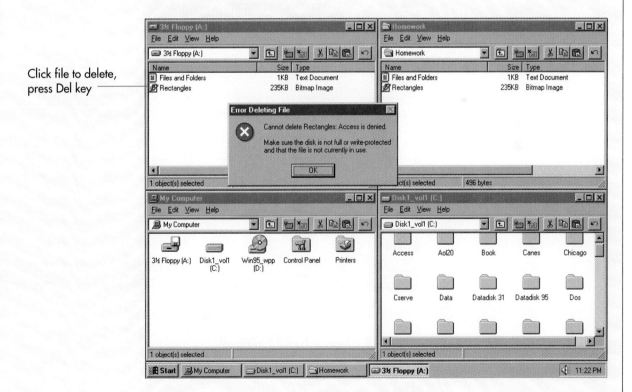

(f) Write-protect a Disk (step 7)

FIGURE 3.5   Hands-on Exercise 2 (continued)

STEP 8: The Recycle Bin

➤ Select (click) the **Files and Folders icon** in the Homework folder. Pull down the **File menu** and click **Delete.** Click **Yes** in the dialog box asking whether you want to delete the file.

➤ To restore a file, you need to open the Recycle Bin:
  • Double click the **Recycle Bin icon** if you can see the icon on the desktop *or*
  • Double click the **Recycle icon** within the window for drive C. (You may have to scroll in order to see the icon.)

➤ Right click a blank area on the **Taskbar,** then tile the open windows as shown in Figure 3.5g. The position of your windows may be different from ours. The view in the Recycle Bin may also be different.

➤ Your Recycle Bin contains all files that were previously deleted from drive C, and hence you may see a different number of files than those displayed in Figure 3.5g.

➤ Scroll until you can select the (most recent) **Files and Folders icon.** Pull down the **File menu** and click the **Restore command.** The Files and Folders file is returned to the Homework folder.

Recycle Bin

Select file to restore

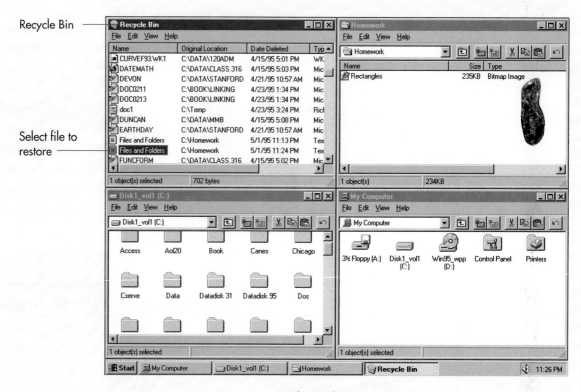

(g) The Recycle Bin (step 8)

FIGURE 3.5   Hands-on Exercise 2 (continued)

STEP 9: Exit Windows

➤ Click the **Close button** in each of the four open windows (The Recycle Bin, My Computer, drive C, and Homework) to close each window.

➤ Exit Windows if you do not want to continue with the next exercise at this time.

WINDOWS EXPLORER

The *Windows Explorer* enables you to browse through all of the drives, folders, and files on your system. It does not do anything that could not be accomplished through successive windows via My Computer. The Explorer does, however, let you perform a given task more quickly and for that reason is preferred by more experienced users.

Assume, for example, that you are taking five classes this semester and that you are using the computer in each course. You've created a separate folder to hold the work for each class and have stored the contents of all five folders on a single floppy disk. Assume further that you need to retrieve your third English assignment so that you can modify the assignment.

You can use My Computer to browse the system as shown in Figure 3.6a. You would start by opening My Computer, double clicking the icon for drive A to open a second window, then double clicking the icon for the English folder to display its documents. The process is intuitive, but it can quickly lead to a desktop cluttered with open windows. And what if you next needed to work on a paper for Art History? That would require you to open the Art History folder, which produces yet another open window on the desktop.

The Explorer window in Figure 3.6b offers a more sophisticated way to browse the system as it shows both the hierarchy of folders as well as the contents of the selected folder. The Explorer window is divided into two panes. The left pane contains a tree diagram of the entire system, showing all drives and optionally the folders in each drive. One (and only one) object is always selected in the left pane and its contents are displayed automatically in the right pane.

Look carefully at the tree diagram in Figure 3.6b and note that the English folder is currently selected. The icon for the selected folder is an open folder to differentiate it from the other folders, which are closed and are not currently selected. The right pane displays the contents of the selected folder (English in Figure 3.6b) and is seen to contain three documents, Assignments 1, 2, and 3. The right pane is displayed in the Details view, but could just as easily have been displayed in another view (e.g., Large or Small Icons) by clicking the appropriate button on the toolbar.

As indicated, only one folder can be selected (open) at a time in the left pane, and its contents are displayed in the right pane. To see the contents of a different folder (e.g., Accounting), you would select (click) the Accounting folder, which will automatically close the English folder.

Double click
drive A icon

Double click
English folder

English folder

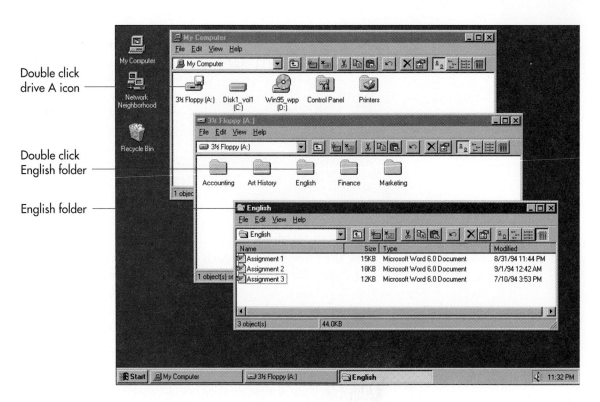

(a) My Computer

Tree diagram   Contents of selected folder

Minus sign indicates My
Computer is expanded
(subordinates are visible)

Selected folder

No subordinates exist

Plus sign indicates drive is
collapsed (subordinates
are not visible)

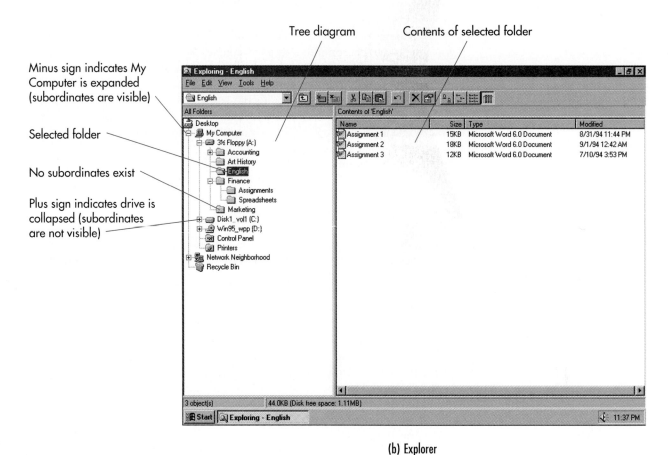

(b) Explorer

FIGURE 3.6   Browsing a System

The tree diagram in the left pane displays the drives and their folders in hierarchical fashion. The desktop is always at the top of the hierarchy and contains My Computer, which in turn contains various drives, each of which contains folders, which in turn contain documents and/or additional folders. Each object may be expanded or collapsed to display or hide its subordinates.

Look again at the icon next to My Computer in Figure 3.6b and you see a minus sign, indicating that My Computer has been expanded to show the various drives on the system. There is also a minus sign next to the icon for drive A to indicate that it too has been expanded to show the folders on the disk. Note, however, the plus sign next to drives C and D, indicating that these parts of the tree are currently collapsed and thus their subordinates are not visible.

A folder may contain additional folders and thus individual folders may also be expanded or collapsed. The minus sign next to the Finance folder shown in Figure 3.6b, for example, shows that the folder has been expanded and contains two additional folders, for Assignments and Spreadsheets, respectively. The plus sign next to the Accounting folder, however, indicates the opposite; that is, the folder is collapsed and its folders are not currently visible. A folder with neither a plus nor a minus sign, such as Art History or Marketing, means that the folder does not contain additional folders and cannot be expanded or collapsed.

The advantage of the Windows Explorer over My Computer is the uncluttered screen and ease with which you switch from one folder to the next. If, for example, you wanted to see the contents of the Art History folder, all you would do would be to click its icon in the left pane, which automatically changes the right pane to show the documents in Art History. The Explorer also makes it easy to move or copy a file from one folder or drive to another as you will see in the hands-on exercise that follows shortly.

ORGANIZE YOUR WORK

A folder may contain anything at all—program files, document files, or even other folders. Organize your folders in ways that make sense to you, such as a separate folder for every class you are taking. You can also create folders within a folder; for example, a correspondence folder may contain two folders of its own, one for business correspondence, and one for personal letters.

LEARNING BY DOING

The Explorer is especially useful for moving or copying files from one folder or drive to another. You simply open the folder that contains the file, use the scroll bar in the left pane (if necessary) so that the destination folder is visible, then drag the file from the right pane to the destination folder. The Explorer is a powerful tool, but it takes practice to master.

The next exercise illustrates the procedure for moving and copying files and uses the floppy disk from the previous exercise. The disk already contains two files: one Notepad document and one Paint drawing. The exercise has you create an additional document of each type so that there are a total of four files on the floppy disk. You then create two folders on the floppy disk, one for drawings and one for documents, and move the respective files into each folder. And finally, you copy the contents of each folder from drive A to a different folder on drive C. By the end of the exercise you will have had considerable practice in both moving and copying files.

Windows Explorer

Objective: Use the Windows Explorer to copy and move a file from one folder to another. Use Figure 3.7 as a guide in the exercise.

STEP 1: Open the Windows Explorer

➤ Click the **Start Button.** Click (or point to) the **Programs command** to display the Programs menu. Click **Windows Explorer.**

➤ Click the **Maximize button** so that the Explorer takes the entire desktop as shown in Figure 3.7a. Do not be concerned if your screen is different from ours.

➤ Make or verify the following selections using the **View menu.** (You have to pull down the View menu each time you choose a different command.)

• The **Toolbar command** should be checked.

• The **Status Bar command** should be checked.

• The **Details view** should be selected.

➤ Pull down the **View menu** a second time. Click **Options,** then click the **View tab** in the Options dialog box. Check the box (if necessary) to **Hide MS-DOS file extensions.** Click **OK.**

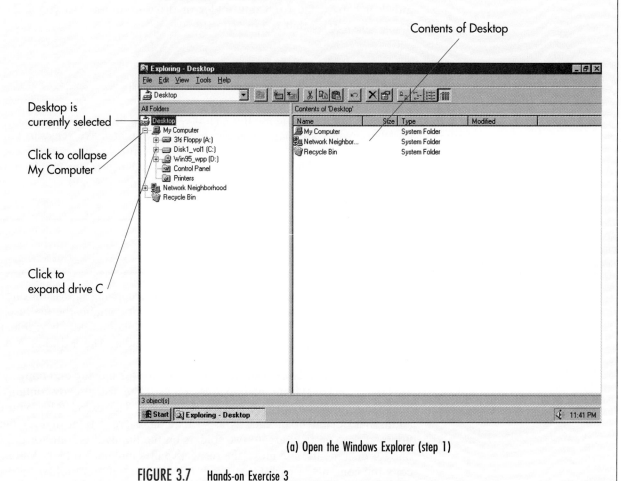

(a) Open the Windows Explorer (step 1)

FIGURE 3.7   Hands-on Exercise 3

STEP 2: Collapse and Expand My Computer

➤ Click (select) the **Desktop icon** in the left pane to display the contents of the desktop in the right pane. Our desktop contains only the icons for My Computer, Network Neighborhood, and the Recycle Bin. Your desktop may have different icons.

➤ Toggle back and forth between expanding and collapsing My Computer by clicking the plus or minus sign that appears next to the icon for My Computer. Clicking a plus sign expands My Computer, after which a minus sign is displayed. Clicking the minus sign collapses My Computer and changes the minus sign to a plus sign. End with My Computer expanded as shown in Figure 3.7a.

➤ Place the disk from the previous exercise in drive A. Expand and collapse each drive within My Computer. End with a **plus sign** next to drive C so that the hard drive is collapsed as shown in Figure 3.7a.

STEP 3: Create a Notepad Document

➤ Click the icon for **drive A** in the left pane to view the contents of the disk in the right pane. You should see the Files and Folders and Rectangles files that were created in the previous exercise.

➤ Pull down the **File menu.** Click (or point to) **New** to display the submenu. Click **Text Document** as the type of file to create.

➤ The icon for a new document will appear with the name of the document (New Text Document) highlighted. Type **About Explorer** to change the name of the document. Press **enter.** Double click the **File icon** to open the Notepad accessory and create the document.

➤ Move and/or size the Notepad window to your preference. You can also maximize the window so that you have more room in which to work.

➤ Pull down the **Edit menu** and toggle Word Wrap on. Enter the text of the document as shown in Figure 3.7b.

➤ Pull down the **File menu** and click **Save** to save the document when you are finished. Click the **Close button** to close Notepad and return to the Explorer.

STEP 4: Create a Paint Drawing

➤ Click the icon for **drive A** in the Explorer window, then pull down the **File menu.** (Alternatively, you can click the **right mouse button** in the right pane of the Explorer window when drive A is selected in the left pane.)

➤ Click (or point to) the **New command** to display the submenu. Click **Bitmap Image** as the type of file to create.

➤ The icon for a new drawing will appear with the name of the file (New Bitmap Image) highlighted. Type **Circles** to change the name of the file. Press **enter.** Double click the **File icon** to open the Paint accessory and create the drawing.

➤ Move and/or size the Paint window to your preference. You can also maximize the window so that you have more room in which to work.

➤ Create a simple drawing consisting of various circles and ellipses as shown in Figure 3.7c.

➤ Pull down the **File menu.** Click **Save As** to produce the Save As dialog box. Change the file type to **16-Color Bitmap** (from the default 256-color bitmap) to create a smaller file and conserve space on the floppy disk. Click **Save.** Click **Yes** to replace the file.

➤ Click the **Close button** to close Paint and return to the Explorer.

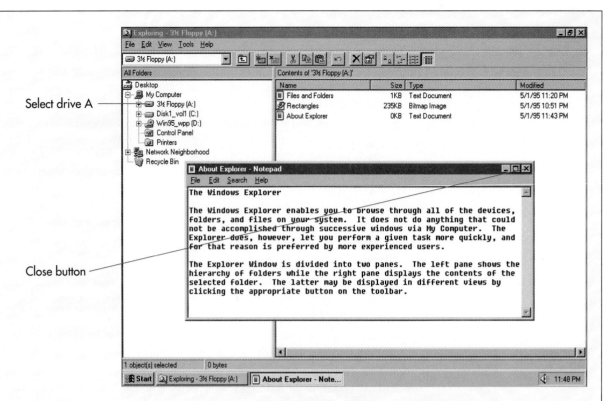

Select drive A

Close button

(b) Create a Notepad Document (step 2)

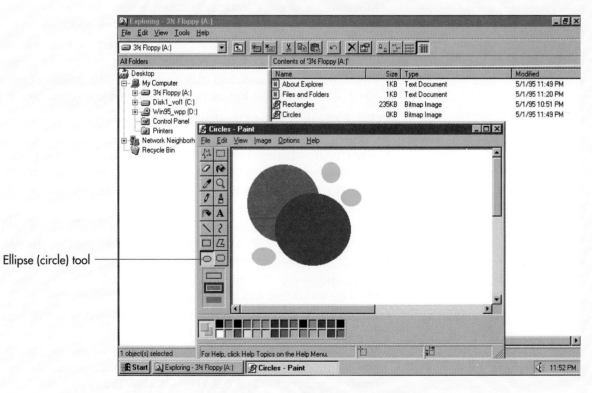

Ellipse (circle) tool

(c) Create a Drawing (step 4)

FIGURE 3.7   Hands-on Exercise 3 (continued)

STEP 5: Create the Folders

➤ If necessary, click the icon for **drive A** in the left pane of the Explorer window. Drive A should contain four files as shown in Figure 3.7d (the folders have not yet been created).

➤ Pull down the **File menu,** click (or point to) the **New command,** then click **Folder** as the type of object to create.

➤ The icon for a new folder will appear with the name of the folder (New Folder) highlighted. Type **Documents** to change the name of the folder. Press **enter.**

➤ Click the icon for **drive A** in the left pane. Pull down the **File menu.** Click (or point to) the **New command.** Click **Folder** as the type of object to create.

➤ The icon for a new folder will appear with the name of the folder (New Folder) highlighted. Type **Drawings** to change the name of the folder. Press **enter.** The right pane should now contain four documents and two folders.

➤ Pull down the **View menu.** Click (or point to) the **Arrange icons** command to display a submenu, then click the **By Name** command.

➤ Click the **plus sign** next to drive A to expand the drive. Your screen should match Figure 3.7d.

  • The left pane shows the subordinate folders on drive A.

  • The right pane displays the contents of drive A (the selected object in the left pane). The folders are shown first and appear in alphabetical order. The document names are displayed after the folders and are also in alphabetical order.

STEP 6: Move the Files

➤ This step has you move the Notepad documents and Paint drawings to the Documents and Drawings folders, respectively.

➤ To move the About Explorer document:

  • Point to the icon for **About Explorer** in the right pane. Use the **right mouse button** to click and drag the icon to the Documents folder in the left pane.

  • Release the mouse to display the menu shown in Figure 3.7e. Click **Move Here** to move the file. A popup window will appear briefly as the file is being moved.

➤ To prove that the file has been moved, you can view the contents of the Documents folder:

  • Click the **Documents folder** in the left pane to select the folder. The icon for the Documents folder changes to an open folder, and its contents (About Explorer) are displayed in the right pane.

➤ Move the Files and Folders document to the Documents folder:

  • Click the icon for **drive A** to select the drive and display its contents in the right pane.

  • Point to the icon for **Files and Folders.** Use the **right mouse button** to click and drag the icon to the Documents folder in the left pane.

  • Release the mouse to display a menu. Click **Move Here** to move the file.

➤ Use the **right mouse button** to move the Circles and Rectangles files to the Drawings folder.

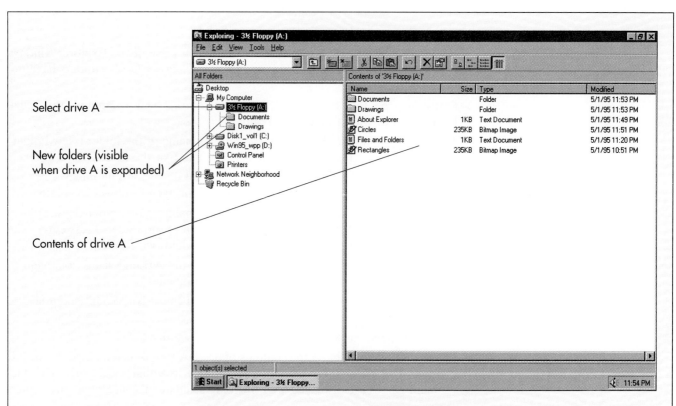

Select drive A ———————

New folders (visible
when drive A is expanded)

Contents of drive A ———————

(d) Create the Folders (step 5)

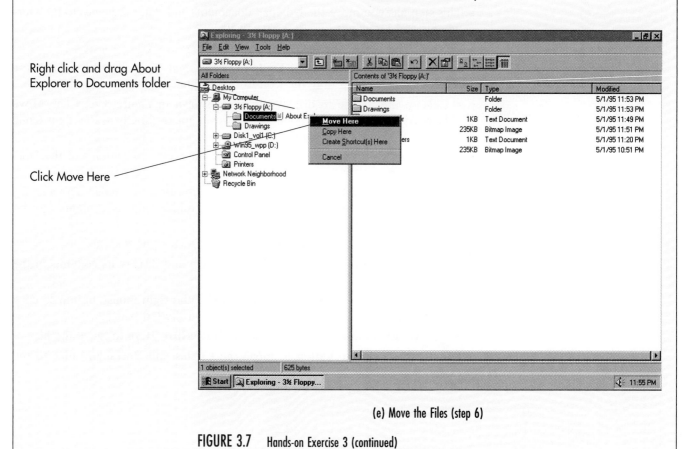

Right click and drag About
Explorer to Documents folder

Click Move Here

(e) Move the Files (step 6)

FIGURE 3.7   Hands-on Exercise 3 (continued)

STEP 7: Copy the Contents of the Documents Folder

➤ This step has you copy the contents of the Documents folder on drive A to the Homework folder on drive C. Click (select) the **Documents folder** on drive A to open the folder and display its contents. You should see the About Explorer and Files and Folders files that were moved in the previous step.

➤ Click the **plus sign** next to the icon for drive C to expand the drive and display its folders. You should see the Homework folder that was created in the first exercise. (Do not click the folder on drive C.)

➤ Point to the **About Explorer** file (in the Documents folder on drive A) as shown in Figure 3.7f. Use the **right mouse button** to click and drag the icon to the Homework folder on drive C. Release the mouse. Click **Copy Here** to copy the file to the Homework folder.

➤ Point to the **Files and Folders** file (in the Documents folder on drive A). Use the **right mouse button** to click and drag the icon to the Homework folder on drive C. Release the mouse. Click **Copy Here.**

➤ You will see a dialog box, asking whether you want to replace the Files and Folders file that is already in the Homework folder (from the previous hands-on exercise). Click **No** since the files are the same.

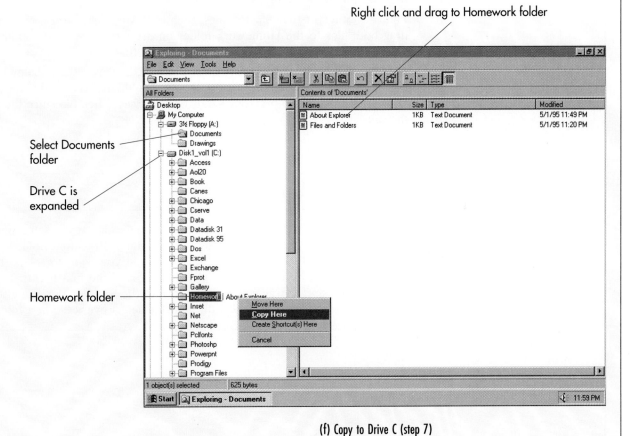

(f) Copy to Drive C (step 7)

FIGURE 3.7   Hands-on Exercise 3 (continued)

STEP 8: Copy the Contents of the Drawings Folder

➤ This step has you copy the contents of the Drawings folder on drive A to the Homework folder on drive C. Click (select) the **Drawings folder** on drive A to open the folder and display its contents. You should see the Circles and Rectangles files that were moved to this folder in the previous step.

➤ Click the icon for the **Circles file,** then press and hold the **Ctrl key** as you click the icon for the Rectangles file to select both files.

➤ Point to either of the selected files, then click the **right mouse button** as you drag both files to the Homework folder on drive C. Release the mouse. Click **Copy Here** to copy the files to the Homework folder.

➤ Explorer will begin to copy both files. You will, however, see a dialog box, asking whether you want to replace the Rectangles file that is already in the Homework folder (from the previous hands-on exercise). Click **No** since the files are the same.

STEP 9: Check Your Work

➤ Select (click) the **Homework folder** on drive C to display its contents. The icon changes to an open folder and you should see the four files in Figure 3.7g.

➤ Click the **Close button** to close Explorer. Click the **Start button** to shut down Windows if you do not want to continue with the next exercise at this time.

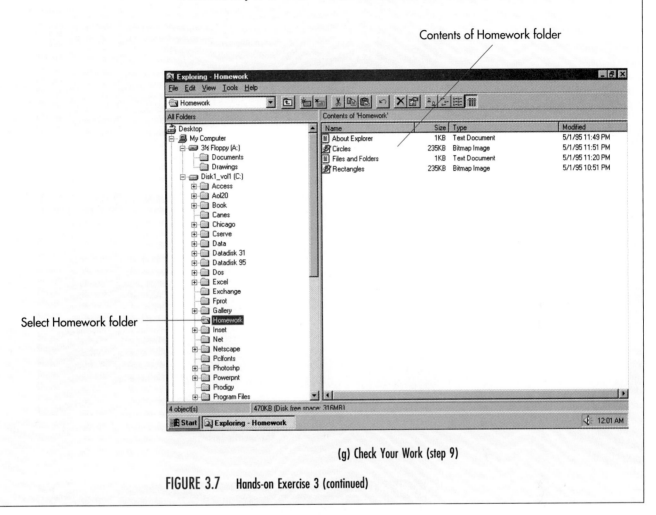

(g) Check Your Work (step 9)

FIGURE 3.7 Hands-on Exercise 3 (continued)

TIPS AND TRICKS

By now you should be comfortable in your ability to browse your system in order to locate a specific file or folder and perform basic file operations. It doesn't matter whether you use My Computer or the Windows Explorer as long as you can accomplish what you set out to do. As you continue to work with Windows, you will be looking for even more powerful techniques, and so we present this final section that will enable you to do your work faster and more efficiently.

The Find Command

Sooner or later you will create a file, then forget where (in which folder) you saved it. Or you may create a document and forget its name, but remember a key word or phrase in the document. Or you may want to locate all files of a certain file type; for example, all of the sound files on your system. The *Find command* can help you to solve each of these problems and is illustrated in Figure 3.8.

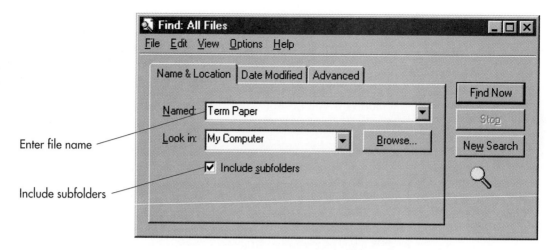

Enter file name

Include subfolders

(a) A Specific File

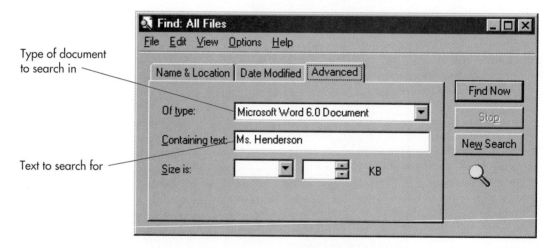

Type of document
to search in

Text to search for

(b) Specific Text

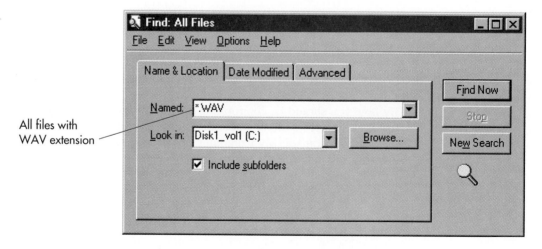

All files with
WAV extension

(c) Wild Card

FIGURE 3.8   The Find Command

The Find command is accessed from the Start menu or from the Tools menu within Explorer. Once you execute the Find command, you are presented with a tabbed dialog box in which you enter the parameters for the search. The dialog box in Figure 3.8a will search the entire system (all drives and all of the folders on each drive) for the file called "Term Paper." It's important to include subfolders in the search, or else you will look only in the first level of the drive and not in any of its folders. If you know the specific drive on which the file is located, you can speed up the search by restricting it to that drive (click the down arrow in the Look in box to select the drive).

The Advanced tab in Figure 3.8b illustrates how to search for a file containing specific text—for example, Ms. Henderson. The Find command will read every document (according to the search parameters specified under the Name & Location tab) and identify the documents containing the specified text. It's important, therefore, to be sure that the Named text box (in the Name & Location tab) is clear, or else the search will look only in the specified file(s), which is not what you intend. If you know the application used to create the document for which you are searching, you can speed up the search by restricting it to files of a specified type—for example, Microsoft Word documents, as is done in the figure.

The search in Figure 3.8c uses a wild card to search for all files with a specified extension. The *wild card* (asterisk) stands for one or more characters in the file name or extension just as a wild card may substitute for any other card in a poker game. For example, to search for all of the sound files on your system (those files with an extension WAV), you would enter *.WAV in the Named list box as is done in Figure 3.8c. To search for all files with the same name (e.g., Assignment) regardless of the extension, you would enter Assignment.*.

All of the searches in Figure 3.8 are initiated by clicking the Find Now button, which returns a window that identifies all files found by Find command. You can then use any of the other capabilities in Explorer to operate on those files. The Find command is illustrated in the exercise on page 127.

Shortcuts

Shortcuts are a powerful tool that let you open a folder, drive, document, or application through a desktop icon, as opposed to going through a series of menus. Consider, for example, the desktop in Figure 3.9, which contains a variety of different shortcuts. Two of the shortcuts are for applications (Excel and Word for Windows), and two are for documents associated with those applications (Modems.doc and 1040.xls). There is also a shortcut to drive A, a shortcut to the Homework folder, and a shortcut to the printer. All shortcuts are distinguished from other icons on the desktop by the *jump arrow* that is part of every shortcut icon.

All of the shortcuts provide a quick way to get to the indicated object. Double click the shortcut to Excel, for example, and you load Excel into memory without having to click the Start button and go through the associated menu(s). Double clicking a document shortcut is even quicker. Double click the shortcut to Modems.doc, for example, and it loads Word for Windows (the associated application), then opens the Modems document.

Double clicking the shortcut for a folder or drive opens the object and displays its contents. Double clicking the shortcut to the printer displays the printer queue (the jobs that are printing or awaiting printing) and lets you see the progress of a document as it is printed. You can also use the printer queue to change the priority of a pending job and/or cancel a job if you change your mind about printing.

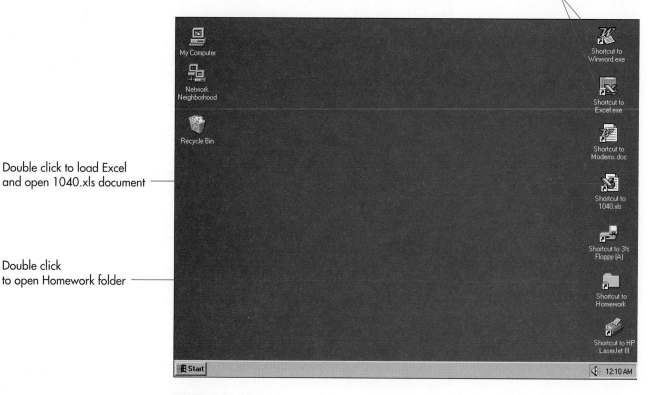

Shortcuts identified by jump arrow

Double click to load Excel and open 1040.xls document

Double click to open Homework folder

FIGURE 3.9 Shortcuts

Creating a shortcut is a two-step process. First you use My Computer or the Windows Explorer to locate the object (the program or data file, the folder, or the icon for the drive or printer) for which you want a shortcut. Then you select the object, pull down the File menu (or use the right mouse button to drag the icon to the desktop), and click the Create Shortcut command. A shortcut icon will appear on the desktop with the phrase "shortcut to" as part of the name.

You can create as many shortcuts as you like, and you can place them anywhere on the desktop. You can change the location of a shortcut at any time by simply dragging its icon. You can also rename a shortcut by selecting its icon and using the Rename command in the File menu. And, as previously indicated, double clicking a shortcut opens the associated object.

FILE EXTENSIONS

MS-DOS uses a three-character extension at the end of a file name to indicate the application associated with the file. XLS and DOC, for example, denote an Excel workbook and Word document, respectively. EXE denotes an executable program. The extensions are displayed (hidden) according to an option set in My Computer or Explorer and carry over to the name of the shortcut at the time the shortcut is created. You can also rename the shortcut at any time to (omit) include the DOS extension.

Deleting a shortcut does not delete the object to which the shortcut refers. Be sure, however, that the object you are deleting is, in fact, a shortcut, and that its icon contains the jump arrow. Deleting an icon without the jump arrow deletes the actual file, which is typically *not* what you intended to do.

HANDS-ON EXERCISE 4

Tips and Tricks

Objective: Use the Find command to locate a designated file and a file containing specific text. Create a shortcut to a document, a folder, and a disk drive. Use Figure 3.10 as a guide in the exercise.

STEP 1: The Find Command

➤ Start Windows. Place the disk from the previous exercise in drive A as we will access the files that you saved on that disk.

➤ You can execute the Find command in two different ways:

• From the desktop: Click the **Start button** to display the Start menu. Click (or point to) the **Find command,** then click **Files or Folders.**

• From the Windows Explorer (which requires that the Explorer be running): Pull down the **Tools menu.** Click (or point to) the **Find command,** then click **Files or Folders.**

➤ You should see the Find Files dialog box in Figure 3.10a (although no files will be listed since the search has not yet taken place). The size and/or position of the dialog box may be different from the one in the figure.

➤ Type **Rectangles** (the file you are searching for) in the Named text box. Click the **down arrow** in the Look in list box. Click **My Computer** to search all of the drives on your system. Be sure the Include subfolders box is checked as shown in Figure 3.10a.

➤ Click the **Find Now command button** to begin the search, then watch the status bar as Windows searches for the designated file.

➤ The search returns two files that satisfy the search parameters and displays their names and locations within the Find Files dialog box of Figure 3.10a. The files are located in the Drawings folder of drive A and in the Homework folder of drive C and correspond to the files that were created in the earlier exercises.

➤ Once a file has been "found," you can perform any file operation on that file by right clicking the file, then choosing the command you want to execute from the menu.

YOU DON'T NEED THE COMPLETE FILE NAME

You can enter only the beginning of a file name and Windows will still find the file(s). If, for example, you're searching for the file "Marketing Homework," you can enter the first several letters—perhaps "Marketing"—and Windows will return all files whose name begins with the letters you've entered, such as "Marketing Homework" and "Marketing Term Paper."

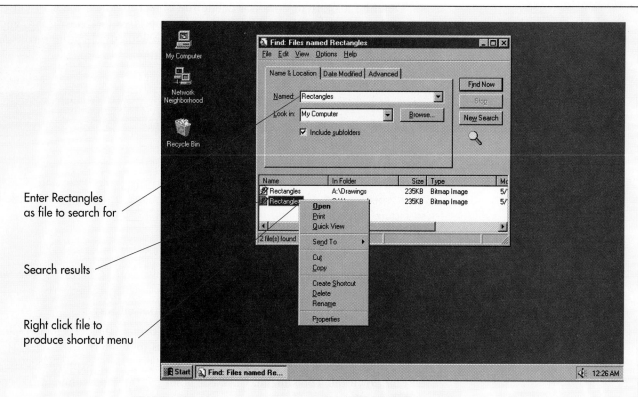

Enter Rectangles
as file to search for

Search results

Right click file to
produce shortcut menu

(a) The Find Command (step 1)

FIGURE 3.10   Hands-on Exercise 4

STEP 2: Search for Specific Text

➤ Click the **New Search command button** to begin a new search. Click **OK** to clear the search and reset the search parameters.

➤ Click the **down arrow** in the Look in list box. Click the **drive A icon** to limit the search to this drive.

➤ Click the **Advanced tab** to produce the dialog box in Figure 3.10b. (The About Explorer file is not yet visible since the search has not taken place.)

➤ Click in the **Containing text** text box. Type **browse** to search for all files that contain the word "browse." (The search is not case-sensitive.)

➤ Click the **Find Now command button** to begin the search, then watch the status bar as Windows searches for the file(s) containing the specified text. The name and location of the file, About Explorer, is displayed in the dialog box as shown in Figure 3.10b.

➤ Click the icon for **About Explorer** and pull down the **File menu** (or simply right click the icon).

➤ Click the **Quick View command** to display the file as shown in Figure 3.10b. The word "browse" is at the end of the first line.

➤ Click the **Close button** to close the Quick View window.

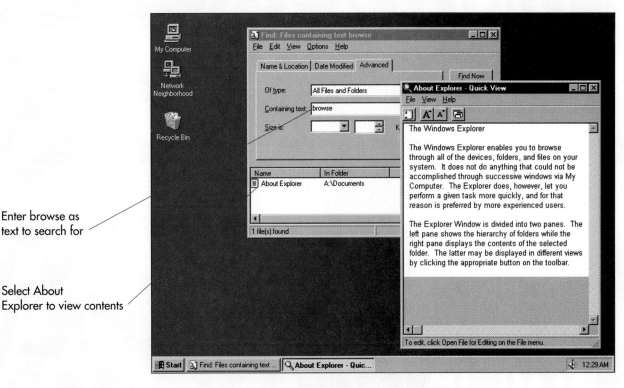

Enter browse as text to search for

Select About Explorer to view contents

(b) Search for Specific Text (step 2)

FIGURE 3.10   Hands-on Exercise 4 (continued)

STEP 3: Create a Shortcut

➤ Point to the **About Explorer icon,** then use the **right mouse button** to click and drag the icon to the desktop. Release the mouse to display the menu in Figure 3.10c. Click the **Create Shortcut(s) Here command** to create the shortcut.

➤ Look for the **jump arrow** to be sure you have created a shortcut for the About Explorer file (as opposed to accidentally moving or copying the file).

➤ You can work with a shortcut icon just as you can with any other icon:

• To move a shortcut, drag its icon to a different location on the desktop.

• To rename a shortcut, **right click** its icon, click the **Rename command,** type the new name, then press the **enter key.**

• To delete a shortcut, **right click** its icon, click the **Delete command,** then click **Yes** in response to the confirming prompt. Do *not* delete the About Explorer shortcut at this time.

➤ Close the Find Files window.

THE UNDO COMMAND

It's very easy to make a mistake and move or copy a file when you intend to create a shortcut. You can, however, use the Undo command to reverse the effect of the last three file operations. Point to a blank area on the desktop, click the right mouse button, then click the Undo command to reverse the operation.

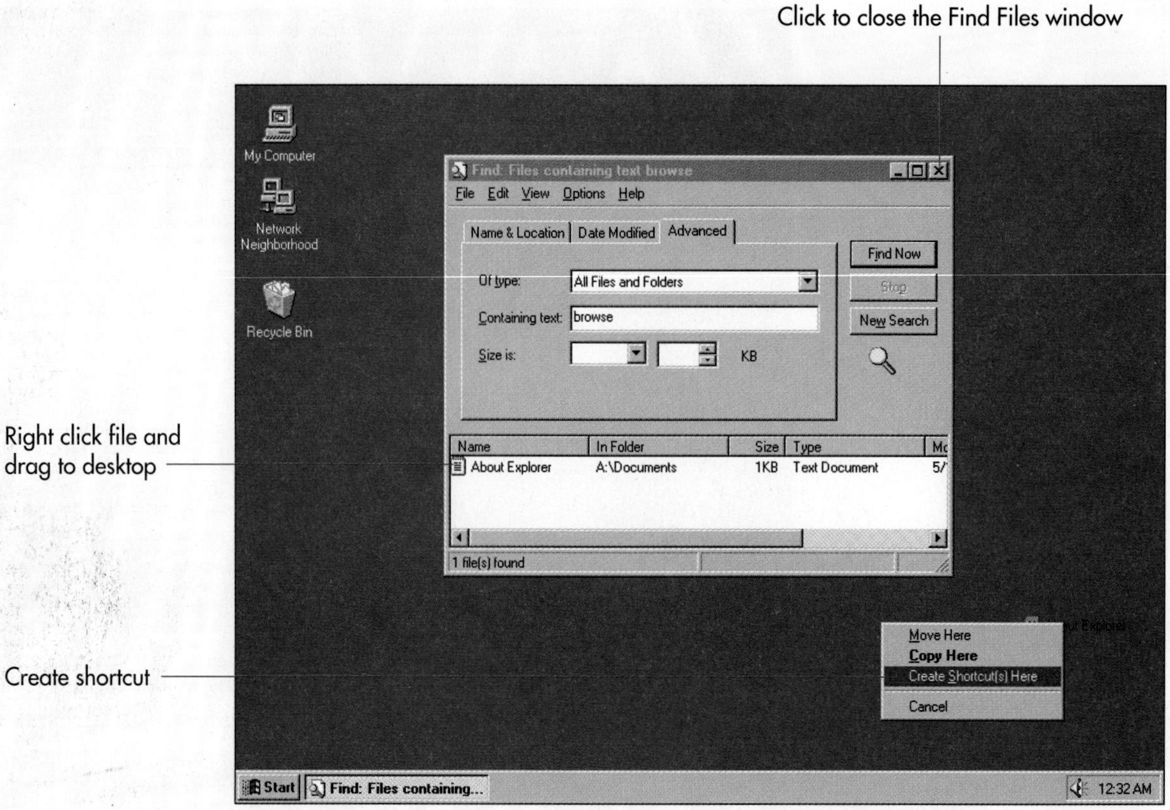

Click to close the Find Files window

Right click file and
drag to desktop

Create shortcut

(c) Create a Shortcut (step 3)

FIGURE 3.10   Hands-on Exercise 4 (continued)

STEP 4: Try the Shortcut

➤ Double click the **Shortcut icon** to open the About Explorer document as shown in Figure 3.10d.

➤ Toggle Word Wrap on. Press **Ctrl+End** to move to the end of the document. Press the **enter key** to begin a new paragraph, then enter the last paragraph shown in Figure 3.10d.

➤ Save the modified file. Click the **Close button** to exit Notepad.

MINIMIZE THE APPLICATION

Minimize (rather than close) an application if you intend to return to the application later in the session. This will save time as you can simply click the corresponding button on the Taskbar, as opposed to having to reload the application.

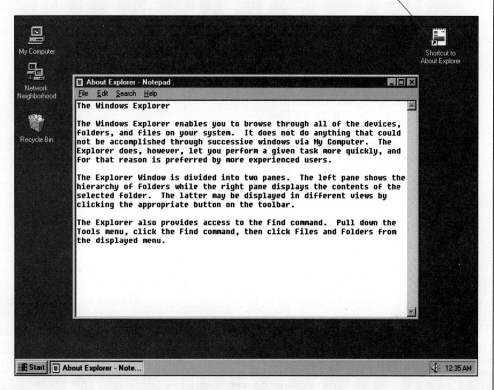

Jump arrow on shortcut icon

(d) Try the Shortcut (step 4)

FIGURE 3.10   Hands-on Exercise 4 (continued)

STEP 5: Create Additional Shortcuts

➤ Click the **Start button.** Point to (or click) the **Programs command** to display the Programs menu. Click **Windows Explorer.**

➤ Move and/or size the Explorer window as in Figure 3.10e so that you have access to the part of the desktop where you want to place the shortcuts.

➤ If necessary, click the **plus sign** to expand My Computer, then click the **plus sign** to expand drive C.

➤ Point to the icon for **drive A,** then use the **right mouse button** to click and drag the icon to the desktop. Release the mouse. Click the **Create Shortcut(s) Here command** to create the shortcut.

➤ Point to the icon for the **Homework folder** on drive C, then use the **right mouse button** to click and drag the icon to the desktop. Release the mouse. Click the **Create Shortcut(s) Here command** to create the shortcut.

➤ Look for the **jump arrow** to be sure you have created shortcuts, as opposed to accidentally moving or copying an object. If you made a mistake, right click a blank area of the desktop, then click the **Undo command** to reverse the unintended move or copy operation.

➤ Close the Explorer window.

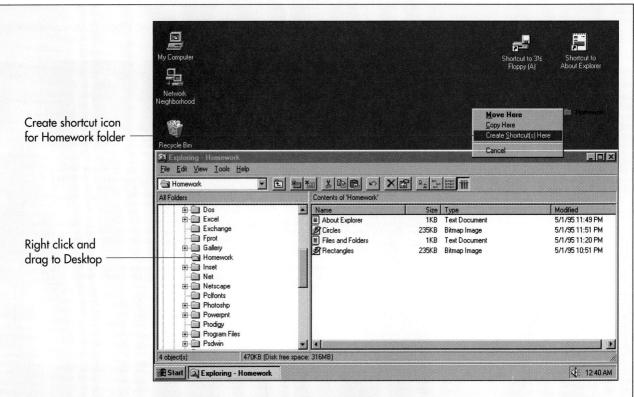

Create shortcut icon for Homework folder

Right click and drag to Desktop

(e) Create Additional Shortcuts (step 5)

FIGURE 3.10   Hands-on Exercise 4 (continued)

STEP 6: Try the Shortcuts

➤ Double click the **Shortcut to Homework folder** to open the folder as shown in Figure 3.10f. Your folder should contain the four documents shown in the figure (as they were created in the previous exercise). The size, position, and/or view of the Homework window may be different from ours.

➤ Double click the **Shortcut to 3½ floppy (A),** which should contain the Documents and Drawings folders created in the previous exercise. However, the size, position, and/or view may be different from ours.

➤ Please delete the Homework folder from drive C if you are working in a lab where other students have access to this machine. Select (click) the **Homework folder** and press the **Del key.** Click **Yes** when asked whether to delete the folder.

➤ Close the open windows. Click the **Start button** to exit Windows.

MODIFY THE START MENU

Click and drag a shortcut icon to the Start button to place the shortcut on the Start menu. It does not appear that anything has happened, but the shortcut will appear at the top of the Start menu. (Click the Start button to display the Start menu, then press the Esc key to exit the menu without executing a command.) To further customize the Start menu, right click the Taskbar, click Properties, then click the Start Menu Programs tab. Click the appropriate command button (Add, Remove, or Advanced), then follow the onscreen instructions.

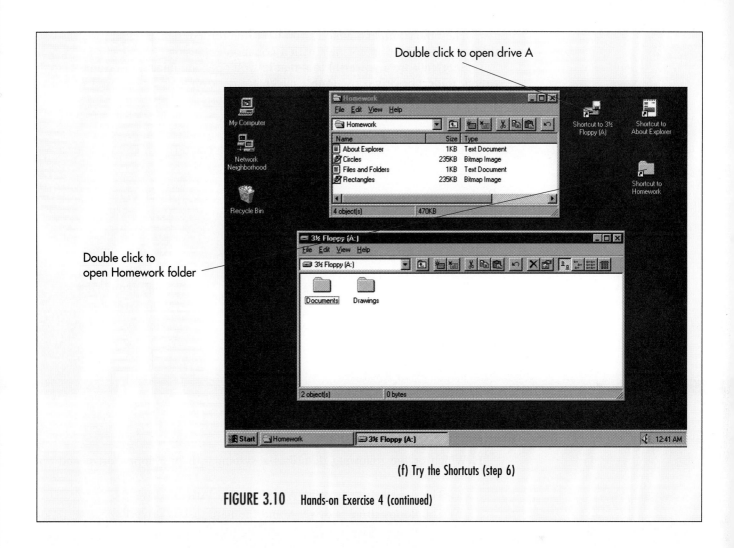

Double click to open drive A

Double click to
open Homework folder

(f) Try the Shortcuts (step 6)

FIGURE 3.10   Hands-on Exercise 4 (continued)

SUMMARY

The first (often only) floppy drive on a system is designated as drive A. The first (often only) hard disk is drive C regardless of whether there are one or two floppy drives. Additional hard drives and/or the CD-ROM drive are labeled from D on.

A file name can contain up to 255 characters and may include spaces and other punctuation. Files are stored in folders to better organize the hundreds (thousands) of files on a disk. A folder may contain program files, data files, and/or other folders.

The most basic way to locate a specific file or folder is to use My Computer, which opens a new window for each successive folder. The Windows Explorer is a more sophisticated tool that displays a hierarchical view of the entire system in a single window.

The Delete command deletes (removes) a file from a disk. If, however, the file was deleted from a hard disk, it is not really gone, but moved instead to the Recycle Bin from where it can be subsequently recovered.

The result of dragging a file icon from one folder to another depends on whether the folders are on the same or different drives. Dragging the file to a folder on the same drive moves the file. Dragging the file to a folder on a different drive copies the file. It's easier, therefore, to click and drag with the right mouse button to produce a menu from which you can select the operation.

The Find command enables you to search for a designated file, for a file containing specific text, or for files with a common extension.

Shortcuts are a powerful tool that let you open an object (a document, application, folder, or drive) by double clicking a desktop icon, as opposed to browsing the system or going through a series of menus.

KEY WORDS AND CONCEPTS

Backup strategy	File name	Printers folder
Control Panel	Find command	Program file
Copy command	Folder	Recycle Bin
Data file	Jump arrow	Restore command
Delete command	Large Icons view	Shortcut
Details view	Move command	Small Icons view
Drag and drop	My Computer	Wild card
Extension	New command	Windows Explorer

MULTIPLE CHOICE

1. Which of the following describes a system with one floppy drive and one hard disk?
   (a) The floppy drive is drive A and the hard disk is drive B
   (b) The floppy drive is drive A and the hard disk is drive C
   (c) The floppy drive is drive B and the hard disk is drive A
   (d) The floppy drive is drive C and the hard disk is drive A

2. The Recycle Bin holds files that were deleted from:
   (a) Drive A
   (b) Drive C
   (c) Both (a) and (b)
   (d) Neither (a) nor (b)

3. How can you determine the file type of a document?
   (a) By examining the application icon displayed next to the file
   (b) From the file extension
   (c) Both (a) and (b)
   (d) Neither (a) nor (b)

4. You load Windows, double click the My Computer icon, double click the icon for drive C, then double click the icon for the Homework folder. How many windows did you open, assuming that you use a separate window for each folder?
   (a) One
   (b) Two
   (c) Three
   (d) Impossible to determine

5. How do you restore a deleted file?
   (a) Select the file in the original folder and execute the Restore command
   (b) Select the file in the Recycle Bin and execute the Restore command
   (c) Both (a) and (b)
   (d) Neither (a) nor (b)

6. How do you create a shortcut for a document?
   (a) Click the left mouse button, then click and drag the document icon from its folder to the desktop
   (b) Click the right mouse button, then click and drag the document icon from its folder to the desktop
   (c) Both (a) and (b)
   (d) Neither (a) nor (b)

7. Which of the following would you use to search for all files that are associated with Microsoft Word, given that these files have the extension DOC?
   (a) *.DOC
   (b) DOC.*
   (c) ?.DOC
   (d) DOC.?

8. A folder may contain:
   (a) Other folders
   (b) Program and/or data files
   (c) Both (a) and (b)
   (d) Neither (a) nor (b)

9. Which of the following will delete a file from drive C?
   (a) Selecting the file, then executing the Delete command
   (b) Dragging the file to the Recycle Bin
   (c) Both (a) and (b)
   (d) Neither (a) nor (b)

10. The left pane of the Explorer window may contain:
    (a) One or more folders with a plus sign
    (b) One or more folders with a minus sign
    (c) Both (a) and (b)
    (d) Neither (a) nor (b)

11. Which of the following was suggested as essential to a backup strategy?
    (a) Backup all program files at the end of every session
    (b) Store backup file(s) at another location
    (c) Both (a) and (b)
    (d) Neither (a) nor (b)

12. Which of the following is true regarding a disk that has been write-protected?
    (a) Existing files cannot be modified or erased
    (b) A new file can be added to the disk
    (c) Both (a) and (b)
    (d) Neither (a) nor (b)

13. Which of the following is true about dragging a file from one folder to another?
    (a) The file will be copied if the folders are on the same drive
    (b) The file will be moved if the folders are on different drives

(c) Both (a) and (b)

(d) Neither (a) nor (b)

14. A shortcut may be created for:

    (a) An application or a document

    (b) A folder or a drive

    (c) Both (a) and (b)

    (d) Neither (a) nor (b)

15. The Find command can search for:

    (a) All files containing a specified phrase

    (b) All files with a designated extension

    (c) Both (a) and (b)

    (d) Neither (a) nor (b)

ANSWERS

1. b	**6.** b	**11.** b
2. b	**7.** a	**12.** a
3. c	**8.** c	**13.** d
4. c	**9.** c	**14.** c
5. b	**10.** c	**15.** c

EXPLORING WINDOWS 95

1. Use Figure 3.11 to match each action with its result; a given action may be used more than once or not at all.

Action	Result
a. Click at 1	_____ Copy the Files and Folders document to drive A
b. Click at 2	
c. Click at 4	_____ Display the contents of the Canes folder
d. Click at 3, drag to 12	
e. Click at 5, Ctrl+click at 7	_____ Expand (show the folders in) the Netscape folder
	_____ Delete the Shapes By a NonArtist document
f. Click at 6, press the Del key	_____ Collapse (suppress the display of the folders on) drive C
g. Click at 8, press the Del key	_____ Display the file extensions with the file names
h. Click at 9	
i. Click at 10	_____ Delete the Prodigy folder
j. Click at 11	_____ Select both the Rectangles and the Student Gradebook files
	_____ Change the view in the right pane to Small Icons
	_____ Create a new folder

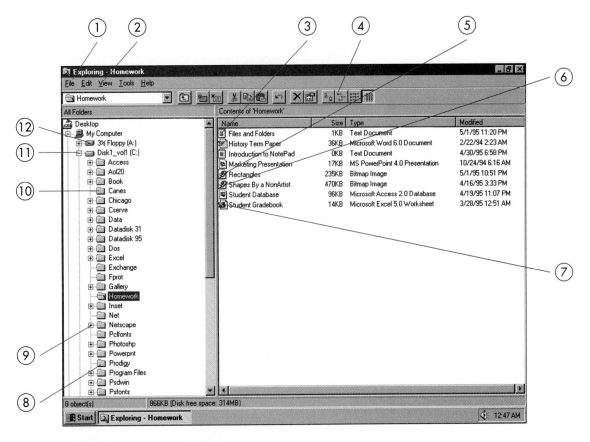

FIGURE 3.11 Screen for Problem 1

2. Each of the messages in Figure 3.12 occurred (or could have occurred) during the various hands-on exercises in the chapter. Indicate the probable cause of each error and the necessary corrective action.

3. My Computer: Answer the following with respect to the screen in Figure 3.13 on page 139:

a. In what sequence were the windows opened?

b. How do you tile the windows? How do you reverse the tiling command?

c. What happens if you drag the About Explorer file to the Recycle Bin on the desktop?

d. What happens if you click and drag the icon for the Circles file to the Canes folder in the window for drive C? To the icon for drive A in the My Computer window?

e. How do you copy the Rectangles file to drive A? How do you move the Rectangles file to drive A?

f. How do you rename a file? How would you cancel the Rename command and restore the original file name?

g. How do you delete the Circles file? How would you undelete the file after it has been deleted?

h. What happens if you click and drag the Rectangles icon to the desktop? If you right click and drag the Rectangles icon to the desktop?

4. Windows Explorer and Shortcuts: Answer the following with respect to the screen in Figure 3.14 on page 139:

a. How do you load the Windows Explorer? What is the difference between clicking the Minimize and Close icons on the title bar?

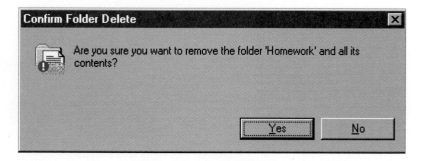

(a) Error Message 1

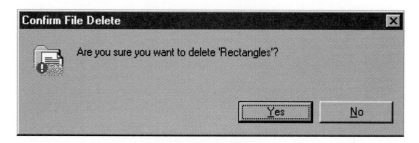

(b) Error Message 2

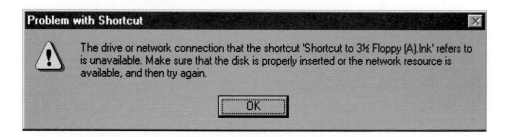

(c) Error Message 3

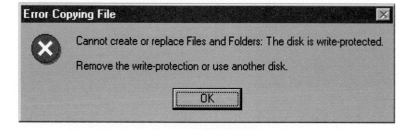

(d) Error Message 4

FIGURE 3.12   Error Messages for Problem 2

b. Which view is displayed in the right pane of the Explorer window? How do you change the view?

c. What would happen if you click the minus icon that is next to the icon for drive C? The plus sign next to the icon for drive A? The icon for drive A rather than the plus sign next to the icon?

d. What would happen if you right click the icon for the Elvis After document? If you double click the icon for the Elvis After document?

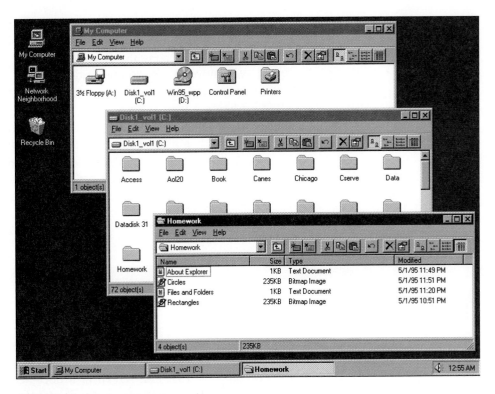

FIGURE 3.13   Screen for Problem 3

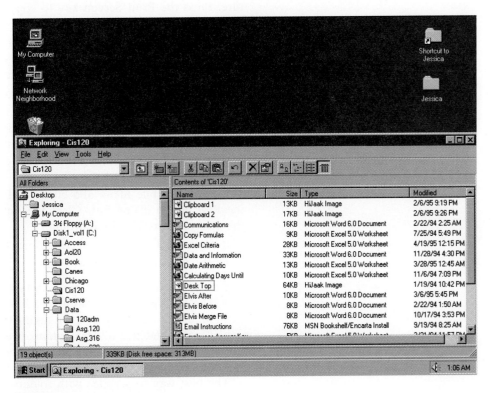

FIGURE 3.14   Screen for Problem 4

e. What is the effect of dragging the icon for the Elvis After document to the icon for drive A? To the icon for the Data folder?

f. How do you copy the Excel Criteria file to the Asg.120 folder? How do you move the file to that folder?

g. How do you find the file called Term Paper, which you know is somewhere on your system?

h. How do you create a shortcut icon for the printer? What would happen if you drag a file icon to the shortcut icon for the printer?

i. What happens if you double click the icon for Jessica on the desktop? If you double click the icon for the Shortcut to Jessica?

j. What would happen if you delete the icon for Jessica? If you delete the icon for Shortcut to Jessica?

PRACTICE WITH WINDOWS 95

1. Screen capture: Prove to your instructor that you have done the hands-on exercises in the chapter by capturing a screen from each exercise and then printing the captured screen in a document to which you add your name. Figure 3.15, for example, occurs in step 6 of exercise 4 (and corresponds to Figure 3.10f) and proves that Jessica Grauer did her homework.

The instructions below show you how to create a document similar to the one in Figure 3.15 using the Paint accessory:

a. Do the hands-on exercise until you come to the screen you want to capture. Press the Print Screen key to copy the screen to the clipboard (an area of memory that is available to every Windows application).

b. Click the Start button, click Programs, click Accessories, then click Paint to open the Paint accessory. If necessary, click the Maximize button so that the Paint window takes the entire desktop.

c. Pull down the Edit menu. Click Paste to copy the screen from the clipboard to the drawing.

d. Click the text tool (the capital A), then click and drag in the drawing area to create a dotted rectangle that will contain the message to your instructor. Type the text indicating that you did your homework. Click outside the rectangle to deselect it.

e. Pull down the File menu and click the Page Setup command to display the Page Setup dialog box. Click the Landscape option button. Change the margins to one inch all around.

f. Pull down the File menu a second time. Click Print. Click OK.

g. Click the Close button to exit Paint.

2. Organize your work: A folder may contain documents, programs, or other folders. The My Classes folder in Figure 3.16, for example, contains five folders, one folder for each class you are taking this semester, and in similar fashion, the Correspondence folder contains two additional folders according to the type of correspondence. We use folders in this fashion to organize our work, and we suggest you do likewise.

The best way to practice with folders is on a floppy disk as was done in Figure 3.16. Accordingly:

a. Format a floppy disk, or alternatively, use the floppy disk you have been using throughout the chapter.

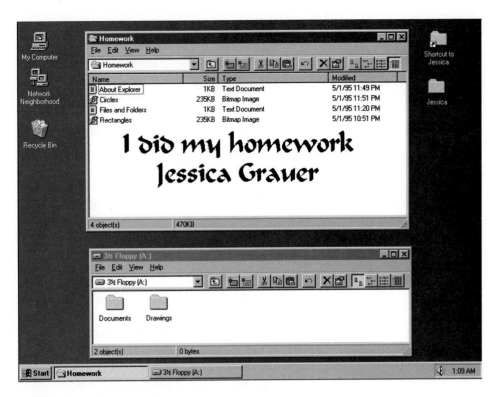

FIGURE 3.15 Practice Exercise 1

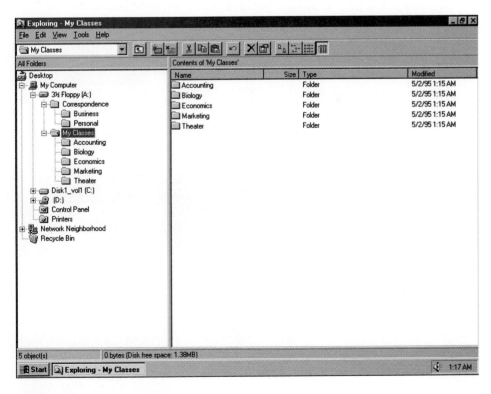

FIGURE 3.16 Practice Exercise 2

b. Create a Correspondence folder. Create a Business and Personal folder within the Correspondence folder as shown in Figure 3.16.

c. Create a My Classes folder. Create a separate folder for each class you are taking within the My Classes folder as shown in Figure 3.16.

d. Use the technique described in problem 1 to capture the screen shown in Figure 3.16. Add your name to the captured screen, then submit it to your instructor as proof that you have done the exercise.

3. Tips and Tricks: Figure 3.17 is similar to Figure 3.7g at the end of Hands-on Exercise 3, but with one very significant difference. Two copies of the Explorer are open in Figure 3.17, as opposed to a single copy as done throughout the chapter. The advantage of opening two copies is that you can see the contents of both the source and destination folders. (Compare Figure 3.17 to Figure 3.7g to appreciate the difference.) Once the contents of both folders are displayed, it is much easier to drag and drop between folders as you have a better appreciation for the file operations that are taking place.

a. Place the formatted disk used throughout the chapter in drive A. Click the Start button, click Programs, and open the Windows Explorer. Open a second copy of the Explorer in similar fashion.

b. Check the Taskbar to be sure that there are no other folders or applications open.

c. Right click a blank area of the Taskbar, then click the command to tile the windows horizontally. Your screen should resemble Figure 3.17.

d. Use the technique described in problem 5 to capture the screen shown in Figure 3.17. Add your name to the captured screen, then submit it to your instructor as proof that you have done the exercise.

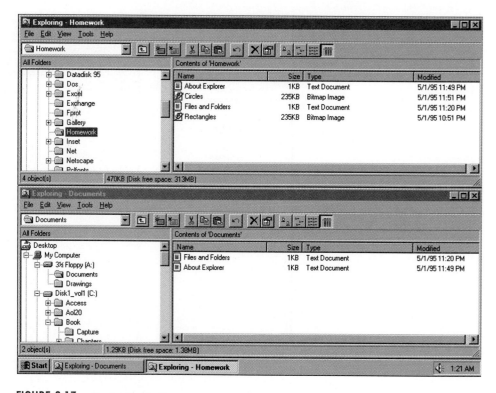

FIGURE 3.17   Practice Exercise 3

4. The Find command can be used to explore your system and locate files of various file types. Windows itself copies many BMP (bitmap) files to various folders during the installation procedure.

   a. Click the Start Button. Click the Find command, then click Files or Folders to display the Find File dialog box in Figure 3.18.

   b. Type *.BMP in the Named text box to search for all files with the BMP extension. If necessary, click the down arrow in the Look in list box to select the hard drive (C:). Check the box to include subfolders.

   c. Check that the settings in your dialog box match those in Figure 3.18. (The names of the BMP files will not yet be visible.) Click the Find Now command button to find all of the BMP files on your system.

   d. You should see many different BMP files since they are installed with a variety of applications. You will not, however, see the identical list of files as in Figure 3.18 since the applications on your system are different from ours. (If you do not see any BMP files at all, verify that your search parameters are the same as ours and try the search again.)

   e. Double click the icon next to any file name that seems interesting to you. (The larger file sizes will return better pictures.) The selected file will open in a Paint window as shown in Figure 3.18.

   f. Pull down the Edit menu and click the Select All command. Pull down the Edit menu a second time and click Copy to copy the bitmap image to the clipboard.

   g. Open WordPad or Microsoft Word. (The Notepad accessory will not work since it saves text files exclusively and thus cannot contain bitmap images.) Pull down the Edit menu and click Paste to paste the drawing into the document. Add your name to the document and include a sentence or two to your instructor describing the picture. Print the document and submit it to your instructor.

FIGURE 3.18   Practice Exercise 4

Planning for Disaster

Do you have a backup strategy? Do you even know what a backup strategy is? You should learn, because sooner or later you will wish you had one. You will erase a file, be unable to read from a floppy disk—or worse yet—suffer a hardware failure in which you are unable to access the hard drive. The problem always seems to occur the night before an assignment is due. The ultimate disaster is the disappearance of your computer, by theft or natural disaster (e.g., Hurricane Andrew). Describe, in 250 words or less, the backup strategy you plan to implement in conjunction with your work in this class.

Your First Consulting Job

Go to a real installation, such as a doctor or an attorney's office, the company where you work, or the computer lab at school. Determine the backup procedures that are in effect. Then write a one-page report indicating whether the policy is adequate and, if necessary, offer suggestions for improvement. Your report should be addressed to the individual in charge of the business, and it should cover all aspects of the backup strategy—that is, which files are backed up and how often, and what software is used for the backup operation. Use appropriate emphasis (for example, bold italics) to identify any potential problems. This is a professional document (it is your first consulting job), and its appearance should be perfect in every way.

The Large File

You've learned your lesson and have come to appreciate the importance of backing up all of your data files. The problem is that you work with large documents that exceed the 1.44MB capacity of a floppy disk. You do *not* have a tape backup device, so you have to find a way to "copy" a large file from your hard drive to a floppy disk. We can think of two different solutions to the problem. Can you?

The Threat of Virus Infection

A computer virus is an actively infectious program that attaches itself to other programs and alters the way a computer works. Some viruses do nothing more than display an annoying message at an inopportune time. Most, however, are more harmful and, in the worst case, erase all files on the disk. When is a computer subject to infection by a virus? What precautions does your school or university take against the threat of virus infection in its computer lab? What precautions, if any, do you take at home? What is the difference between the scan function in an antivirus program versus leaving the antivirus program active in memory? Can you feel confident that your machine will not be infected if you faithfully use a state-of-the-art antivirus program that was purchased in January 1995?

BEYOND THE PC: LOCAL AREA NETWORKS, E-MAIL, INFORMATION SERVICES

OBJECTIVES

After reading this chapter you will be able to:

1. Describe the purpose of a local area network; distinguish between a server and a workstation.
2. Describe the security measures in effect for a local area network.
3. Distinguish between the My Computer and Network Neighborhood icons on the Windows desktop; copy files from a local area network to your computer.
4. Explain the purpose of a modem; use the Hyper Terminal accessory to connect to a remote computer.
5. Use Microsoft Fax to send and receive fax messages.
6. Describe the capabilities of an information service; list three commercial information services.
7. Discuss the basic commands that are present in every e-mail system; send and receive e-mail messages.
8. Define the Internet and explain the structure of an Internet address.

OVERVIEW

The PC that you use at school or purchase for yourself is exactly that, a *personal computer* that functions independently of other computers. It is an incredibly powerful tool that can be made even more powerful by extending its reach beyond the desktop—to local area networks, information services, and the Internet. This chapter explores various ways in which that can be accomplished.

The chapter begins with the definition of a local area network and explains how the network resources are accessed from within Windows. We discuss the Network Neighborhood icon on the desktop and show you how to download files from a network to your PC.

If you are lucky enough to have a PC at home, then you have (or should have) a modem, which is the interface between the PC and the telephone system. We show you how to use the Hyper Terminal accessory to access a remote computer through your modem. We describe the use of the Microsoft Fax accessory to send and receive faxes through your computer. We also explore the use of information services such as the Microsoft Network, CompuServe, America Online, and Prodigy. The chapter describes the capabilities of these services in general terms and suggests ways in which they can enhance your use of the PC.

The last part of the chapter is devoted to e-mail and discusses the basic commands that are present in any e-mail system. It includes an introduction to the Internet (a vast global network of computers) and shows you how to send e-mail to anyone with an Internet address. (Appendix D presents additional information on the Internet and shows you how to browse the World Wide Web.) All told, this is a comprehensive and ambitious chapter, but it is also a chapter that you will enjoy tremendously.

LOCAL AREA NETWORKS

A network is a combination of hardware and software that enables computers to communicate with one another. It may be large enough to encompass computers around the world or it may be limited to the computers on your floor or in your building. The latter is known as a *local area network* or LAN.

The computer that you use at school or work is probably connected to a local area network. The idea behind a LAN is very simple—to enable the connected computers to share resources such as application software, hardware, and data. One printer, for example, can support multiple PCs because not everyone needs to print at the same time.

Networks are common today, but that was not always true. Without a network, you often created a file on one computer, then carried the disk to another machine in order to use the laser printer. Or you might have borrowed a disk containing a specific file to load it on your computer. Or you might have left a message for a friend or colleague in his or her in-box, only to have it get lost under a pile of paper.

All of these situations are examples of network applications, implemented informally in a *sneaker net,* whereby you transferred a file to a floppy disk, put on your sneakers, and ran down the hall to deliver the disk to someone else. A local area network automates the process, and while sneaker net may not sound very impressive, it does illustrate the concept rather effectively.

Figure 4.1 represents a conceptual view of a LAN consisting of multiple workstations, two laser printers, two CD-ROM drives, and two network drives, all connected to a server. A *workstation* (also known as a client or a node) is any PC on which an individual works. There can be different types of workstations (different computers) connected to the network as seen in the figure.

A *server* is a more powerful PC that controls the way the individual workstations share resources. The hard disk(s) attached to the server stores the software and data shared by the individual workstations. The network software handles all requests for network services. Larger networks may have multiple servers, each dedicated to a specific task. A *file server* provides a common place to store data and provides rapid access to that data. A *printer server* manages all printing for the network.

Application programs are stored on a server rather than on individual machines. To use an application, you click the icon to load the program, which issues a request to the network software. The software checks that you are permitted access to the program, then it loads the application into your PC's memory, and the application appears on your screen.

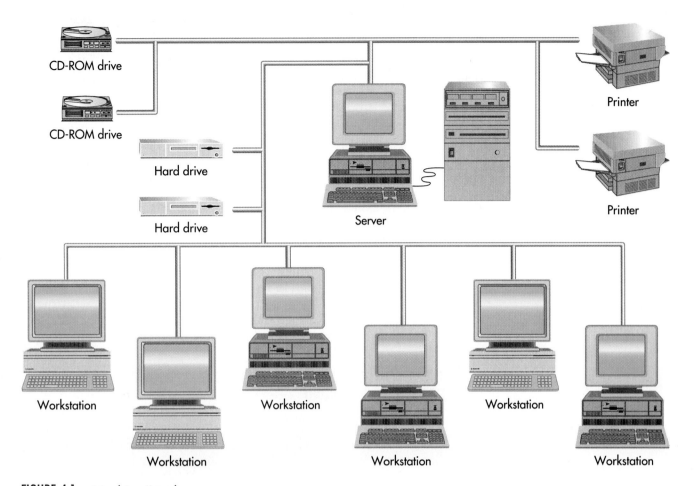

CD-ROM drive

CD-ROM drive

Hard drive

Hard drive

Server

Printer

Printer

Workstation

Workstation

Workstation

Workstation

Workstation

Workstation

FIGURE 4.1   A Local Area Network

The document used with the application may be stored on either a local or a network drive. If the document is stored locally, the network does not come into play. If, however, the document is kept on the network, the server will check that the document is not already in use, then it will open the document for you. It will also prevent other users from gaining access to that document as long as it is open on your machine.

While you're working, other people on the network may load the word processor, but no one else can access your particular document. Anyone attempting to do so gets a message saying the file is in use, because the network locks out everyone else from that file. You finish editing and save the file. Then you execute the print command, and the network prints the document on a network printer(s).

BEYOND THE LAN

A user of a local area network can gain access to other networks and even to mainframe computers through *bridges* or *gateways* installed on the network. The operation of these devices is transparent to the user, but they make it possible for a computer on one network to address a computer on another network as though both machines were on the same network.

Security

The ability to share resources on a network brings with it another requirement, that of protecting the network's resources from unauthorized use. This is typically done by appointing a *network administrator,* and entrusting that person with over-all security for the network.

A *password* is normally required of all users in order to log onto the net-work. Many people choose passwords that are easy to remember, but what is easy for you is also easy for someone trying to break into your account. Thus, you should choose a password consisting of at least six characters, preferably letters *and* numbers or special characters. Keep the password to yourself and change it periodically. You should also avoid proper names and common words, as a hacker will use a program that goes through the dictionary until it is allowed in.

Network security typically extends different privileges to different users for the same file. You would expect, for example, every user to be able to access the word processing or spreadsheet program, but you would not want every user to be able to modify those programs (e.g., to change the program defaults). And you certainly would not want the typical user to be able to delete those programs. Accordingly, all users are empowered to read a program file, but only a few (e.g., system personnel) are allowed to modify or delete these files.

PROTECT YOUR PASSWORD

Almost all computer break-ins occur because of a poorly chosen password consisting of only four characters. A hacker's computer is fast and it doesn't get discouraged if its first several attempts at guessing a password are rejected. A four-letter password has fewer than 500,000 combinations, which can be solved in only 30 seconds of computer time. Opting for eight letters increases the number of combinations to more than 200 billion, which makes the hacker's job much more difficult. And if you include numbers in addi-tion to letters, an eight-character password (letters and numbers) has more than 2 trillion combinations!

Network Neighborhood

The Windows 95 desktop for a computer attached to a local area network con-tains icons for both My Computer and Network Neighborhood. As you already know, My Computer enables you to browse all of the devices that are attached directly to your computer. The *Network Neighborhood* is similar in concept and enables you to browse devices that are on the network (or networks) to which your computer is attached.

You open the Network Neighborhood just as you open My Computer—by double clicking its icon to display a Network Neighborhood window such as Fig-ure 4.2a. The contents of Network Neighborhood will depend on your specific con-figuration, but you can expect to see at least two icons. You will see one icon for the network to which you are attached; for example, Ibis-one in Figure 4.2a. You will also see a second icon for the entire network that shows the other LANs (if any) that exist within the organization.

You can browse the entire network by double clicking the Entire Network icon to display the window in Figure 4.2b. Here you see that the network called Ibis-one is only one of many local area networks within the larger organization. You would be able to log onto any of these networks (in addition to Ibis-one) provided you have the necessary user name and password.

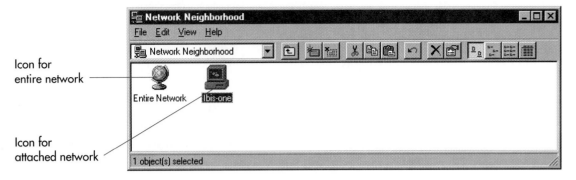

Icon for entire network

Icon for attached network

(a) Network Neighborhood

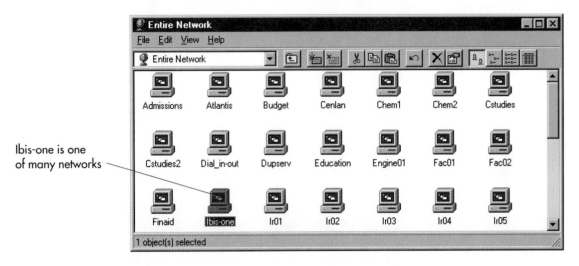

Ibis-one is one of many networks

(b) Entire Network

CD-ROM

Local hard drive

Network drives

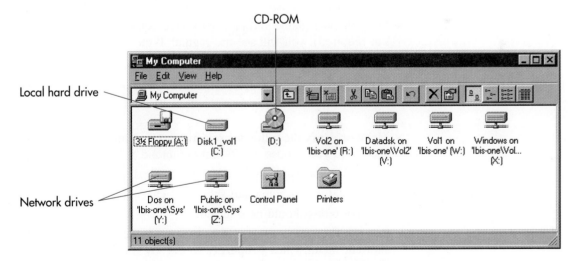

(c) My Computer

FIGURE 4.2   Network Neighborhood

Figure 4.2c shows that logging onto a local area network extends the view within My Computer to include the network drives that are available to you. Look carefully at the My Computer window and note that it contains icons corresponding to six network drives (R:, V:, W:, X:, Y:, and Z:). Note, too, that a different icon is used to distinguish a network connection from a local hard drive.

IT DEPENDS ON YOUR INSTRUCTOR

The exercise that follows has you log onto a local area network, then copy a designated file(s) from a network drive to your computer. The specific file(s) and its (their) location depends on your instructor as he or she must place the file(s) on the network for you. Check with your instructor, before you begin the exercise, to obtain a user name and password, as well as the name and location of the file(s) to copy.

HANDS-ON EXERCISE 1

Local Area Networks

Objective: Log onto a local area network. Open Network Neighborhood and My Computer to view the network resources available to you, then copy a file from the network to your PC. Use Figure 4.3 as a guide in the exercise.

STEP 1: Log on to the Network

➤ Turn on the computer and its peripheral devices. You may (or may not) be required to supply a password to gain access to the network.

- The screen in Figure 4.3a is typical in that it requests a user name, password, and preferred server (the name of the local area network). Enter the required information and click **OK.**

- Do not be concerned if you are not asked for a password as you may log on to the network automatically. Some network administrators enable "guest accounts" with access to the network that do not require a password.

➤ Once the user name and password have been validated (or bypassed if they are not required), you will see the regular Windows desktop.

STEP 2: Network Neighborhood

➤ Double click the **Network Neighborhood icon** to open the window shown in Figure 4.3b. The size and/or position of your window may be different from ours.

➤ Make or verify the following selections. (You have to pull down the View menu each time you choose a different command.)

- The **Toolbar command** should be checked.

- The **Status Bar command** should be checked.

- **Large Icons** should be selected.

➤ Point to the icon for your LAN, then click the **right mouse button** to display a shortcut menu. Click **Properties** to display the Properties dialog box shown in Figure 4.3b. The network in the figure has a maximum of 100 connections, 50 of which are in use.

➤ Close the Properties dialog box.

User name

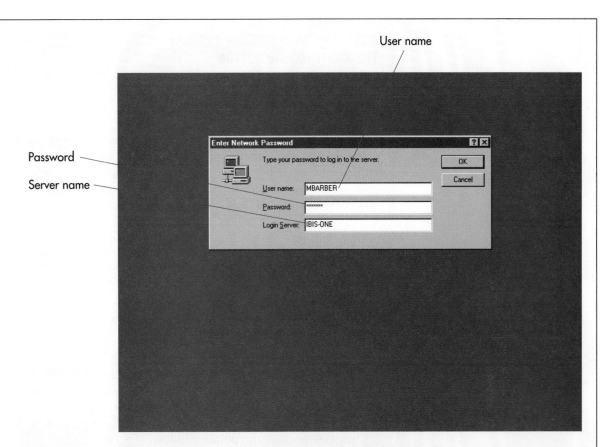

Password

Server name

(a) Log on to the Network (step 1)

Double click to see
Network Neighborhood

Right click icon to
produce shortcut menu

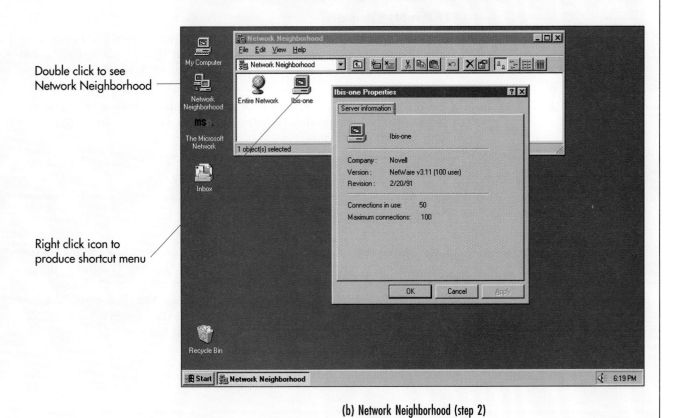

(b) Network Neighborhood (step 2)

FIGURE 4.3   Hands-on Exercise 1 (continued)

THE RIGHT MOUSE BUTTON

Point to the icon for the LAN to which you are attached, then click the right mouse button to display a shortcut menu with commands pertaining to the selected object (the local area network). The Who Am I command identifies the user name (the name under which you logged on to the network). The Log Out disconnects you from the network. The Attach As command (which is unavailable when you are already logged on) enables you to log back on to the network if you log off.

STEP 3: Entire Network

➤ Double click the **Entire Network** icon to open a second window displaying the entire network. The contents of your window will be different from ours, but you should see all the networks within the organization shown in Figure 4.3c.

➤ If necessary, change the view within the Entire Network window to display Large Icons, the Toolbar, and the status bar.

➤ Point to the icon for the network you are attached to (Ibis-one in Figure 4.3), then click the **right mouse button** to display a shortcut menu.

➤ Click the **Who Am I command** to display a popup window similar to the one in Figure 4.3c. The information in the popup window (Mbarber and connection 50) is consistent with the log on of step 1 and the properties displayed in step 2. Click **OK** to close the popup window.

➤ Close the Entire Network window. Close the Network Neighborhood window.

STEP 4: My Computer

➤ Double click **My Computer** to open My Computer as shown in Figure 4.3d. The contents of My Computer will depend on your specific configuration, but you should see the network drives for the local area network to which you are attached.

➤ Point to a network drive, then click the **right mouse button** to display a shortcut menu. Click **Properties.** Note the indication within the Properties dialog box of a network connection.

➤ Close the Properties dialog box. Close My Computer.

CREATE A SHORTCUT TO A NETWORK DRIVE

The fastest way to access a network drive is to create a shortcut for the drive on the desktop. Point to any network drive within My Computer, then use the right mouse button to click and drag the icon to the desktop. Release the mouse to display a shortcut menu, then click the Create Shortcut Here command to create the shortcut. Once the shortcut is created, you can double click the icon to open the drive to which it refers.

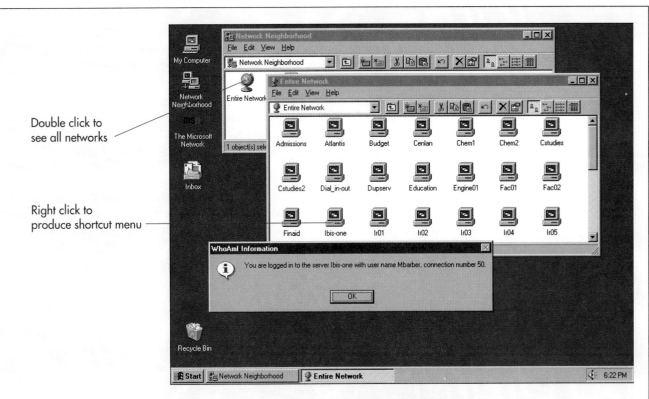

Double click to
see all networks

Right click to
produce shortcut menu

(c) Entire Network (step 3)

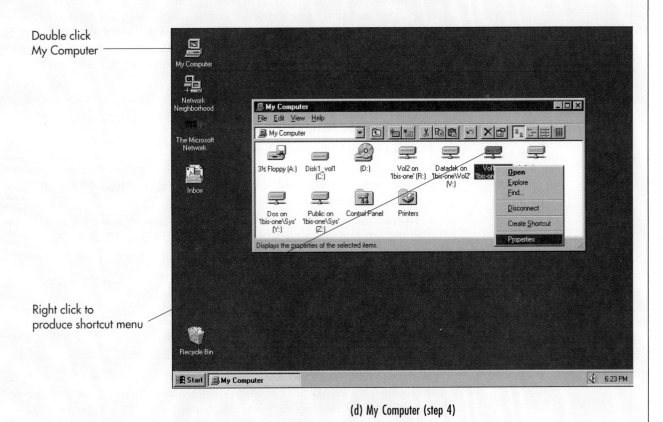

Double click
My Computer

Right click to
produce shortcut menu

(d) My Computer (step 4)

FIGURE 4.3   Hands-on Exercise 1 (continued)

STEP 5: Open the Windows Explorer

➤ Click the **Start button.** Click (or point to) **Programs** to display the Programs menu. Click **Windows Explorer** to open the window in Figure 4.3e. Maximize the Explorer window.

➤ Make or verify the following selections. (You have to pull down the View menu each time you choose a different command.)

• The **Toolbar command** should be checked.

• The **Status Bar command** should be checked.

• **Large Icons** should be selected.

➤ The next several steps depend on your instructor, who will indicate the file(s) you are to copy and the drive(s) on which those files are located. Collapse every drive except the one from which you will copy the file(s). (See boxed tip on the plus and minus signs.)

• There should be a plus sign next to every collapsed device.

• There should be a minus sign next to the expanded network icon.

➤ You are ready to copy files from the network to your floppy disk as described in step 6.

THE PLUS AND MINUS SIGNS

Any drive, be it local or on the network, may be expanded or collapsed to display or hide its contents. A minus sign indicates that the drive has been expanded and that its contents are visible. A plus sign indicates the reverse; that is, the device is collapsed and its contents are not visible. Click either sign to toggle to the other. Clicking the plus sign, for example, expands the drive, then displays a minus sign next to the drive to indicate that the contents are visible.

STEP 6: Copy the Network Files

➤ Place a formatted floppy disk in drive A.

➤ If necessary, expand one or more folders on the network drive until you can see the file or folder you wish to copy. Select (click) the folder—for example, Excldata, in Figure 4.3e.

• To copy the contents of an entire folder, click and drag the folder as it appears in the left pane of the Explorer window to the icon for drive A.

• To copy a file, click and drag the file icon in the right pane of the Explorer window to the icon for drive A.

➤ Copy all files and folders as directed by your instructor.

CREATE A DATA DISK

If you are using other books in the Exploring Windows series, you will need to create a data disk that contains practice files for use with other Microsoft applications. Your instructor will place those files on a network drive and ask you to copy those files to a floppy disk for your personal use.

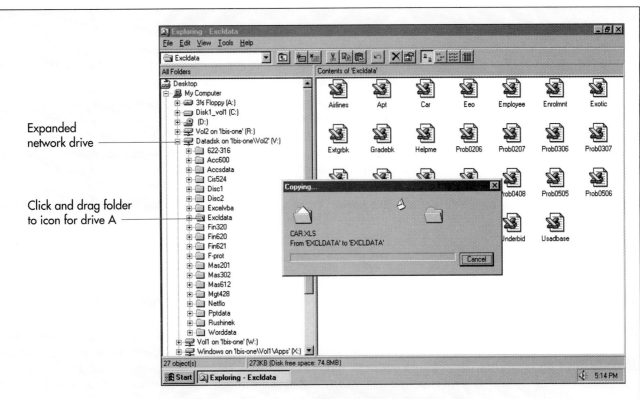

Expanded network drive

Click and drag folder to icon for drive A

(e) Windows Explorer (steps 5 and 6)

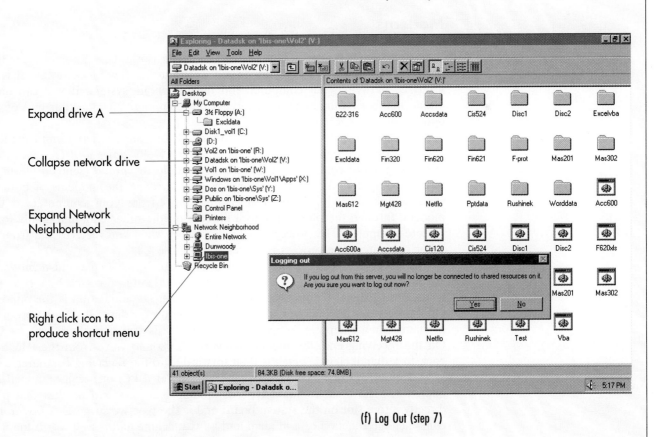

Expand drive A

Collapse network drive

Expand Network Neighborhood

Right click icon to produce shortcut menu

(f) Log Out (step 7)

FIGURE 4.3   Hands-on Exercise 1 (continued)

COMMUNICATING WITH THE OUTSIDE WORLD

The emergence of the local area network in no way eliminates the need for communication with remote computers or information services. Indeed, this type of communication was common well before the advent of the PC and is growing exponentially in the era of the "Information Highway." You need two things to communicate with another computer—a modem and a communications program.

Modems

A *modem* connects your computer to the outside world, be it a remote computer thousands of miles away or your friend's computer a few blocks away. It is the interface between your computer and the telephone system. If you can dial a phone number, your modem can access the computer on the other end of that number.

Once connected, you can enter commands on your computer and have them executed on the remote machine. You can generally *download* (receive) a file from the remote computer, and you may be able to *upload* (send) a file to the remote computer. All data transmission goes through the modems of both the sending and receiving computers. Data passes from your computer to your modem, through the phone line to a modem on the other end, and finally to the remote computer. The process works in reverse when you receive data from the other computer. The process is depicted in Figure 4.4.

The word *modem* is derived from two words, *modulate* and *demodulate*. Modulation is the process of converting the digital data processed by a computer to an analog signal that is used by the telephone. Demodulation is the opposite. On the transmitting end, a modem converts the binary data (1s and 0s) produced by the sending computer to a sound wave, which is sent over the telephone line. On the receiving end, the modem converts the sound wave from the telephone back to a digital signal, which is then forwarded to the receiving computer.

A modem can be purchased when you order a PC, or it can be added at a later time. The most common type of modem is an *internal modem* that plugs directly into a slot on the system board and is the type we suggest. A *fax/modem* combines the function of a modem and a fax machine and is well worth the additional cost (if any). And finally, you need to consider the speed of the modem, which is measured in *bits per second (bps).* A 14,400 bps modem is standard in today's environment. A 28,800 bps modem is more expensive but will return sav-

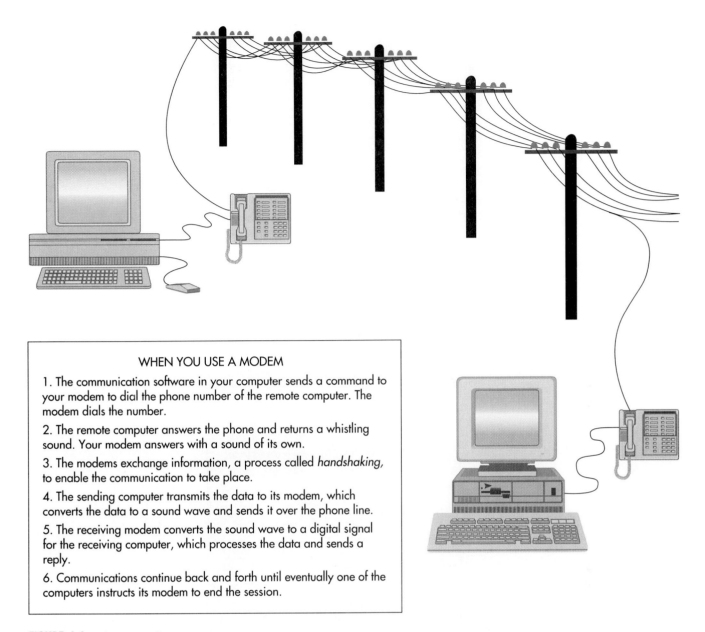

FIGURE 4.4   The Essence of Communication

ings in the form of lower communications costs as you will be transmitting for shorter periods of time.

The Hyper Terminal Accessory

A communications program is required in addition to a modem in order to connect to another computer. The ***communications software*** establishes the protocol (standards) that will be in effect between the two communicating devices. The ***Hyper Terminal accessory*** is the communication program included in Windows 95 and is illustrated in Figure 4.5.

The Connection Description dialog box in Figure 4.5a appears the first time you use Hyper Terminal. You enter a name for the connection (e.g., My School), choose an appropriate icon, then click the OK command button. Next you enter the phone number in the Phone Number Properties sheet of Figure 4.5b, then you dial the number in Figure 4.5c. (The *70 that appears prior to the phone number

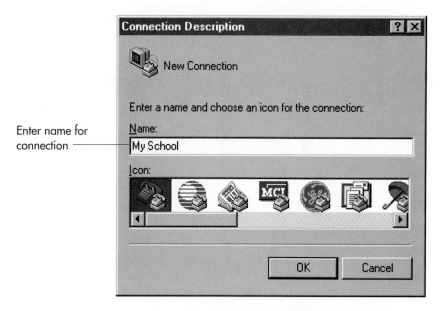

Enter name for connection

(a) Connection Dialog Box

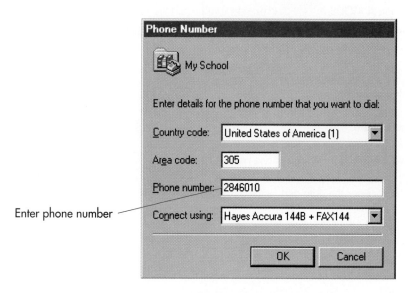

Enter phone number

(b) Phone Number Properties Sheet

FIGURE 4.5   The Hyper Terminal Accessory

is used to block call waiting, as described on page 169.) And finally, you complete the connection and log on to the remote computer as shown in Figure 4.5d. It's easy, and you get a chance to practice in the hands-on exercise that follows shortly.

Figure 4.5d displays the start of a session in which the user has logged on to a remote computer. The user is asked for a username and password, after which she can proceed with the session.

The toolbar in Figure 4.5d has icons for the most common functions in Hyper Terminal. You can create a new connection (e.g., to CompuServe or America Online) or open an existing connection that you previously created. You can click the appropriate icon to connect to the new connection or to disconnect from the present connection. You can upload (send) a file or you can download (receive) a file. You can display the Properties sheet to examine settings for the current connection, and you can use the Help button for additional information.

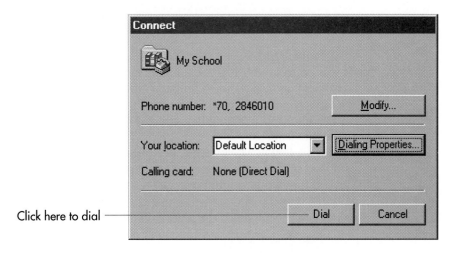

Click here to dial ——————

(c) Dial the Number

Connect   Disconnect   Upload   Download

Toolbar ————

Log onto
remote computer ————

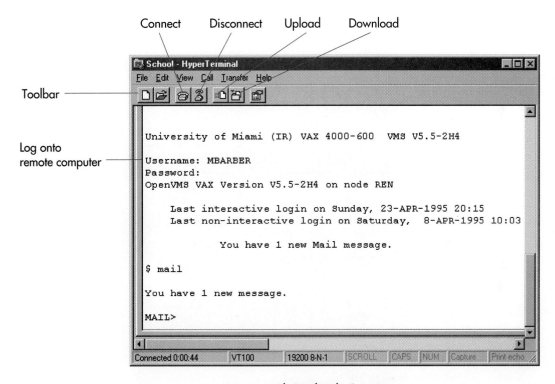

(d) Complete the Connection

FIGURE 4.5   The Hyper Terminal Accessory (continued)

A WORD TO THE WISE

Your computer is at risk to potential infection from a computer virus whenever you download (receive) a file from a remote computer. The chance for infection is virtually nil when you use a major service (e.g., CompuServe or America Online), which implements stringent procedures to safeguard its data. The risk increases dramatically when you are connected to a lesser-known (and less protected) service or bulletin board. Be sure you know as much as possible about the remote computer before you connect.

The Phone Dialer Accessory

The *Phone Dialer accessory* enables the modem to make telephone calls for you. It is used to establish voice communications with another person, not to establish a connection to a remote computer. In essence, you instruct Phone Dialer to dial a number, then you pick up the phone to speak to the person you've called. Use of the Phone Dialer requires a modem and a telephone handset attached to the same line as the modem.

The Phone Dialer is illustrated in Figure 4.6. The accessory looks like an ordinary phone pad and lets you enter phone numbers in different ways. You can click the individual numbers on the number pad or you can type the number directly into the Number to dial text box. The Phone Dialer is smart enough to convert a mnemonic for a phone number (e.g., APAPERS) to the numeric values. You can even use speed dialing just as you can on a telephone.

The Phone Dialer also lets you maintain a log of each completed call that contains the number, date, and time of the call. It enables you to view the log, save it as a text file, or print it to produce a permanent record. You can also copy entries in the log to the clipboard, then paste them into another document.

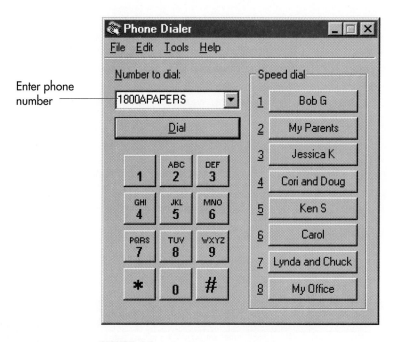

Enter phone number

FIGURE 4.6   The Phone Dialer Accessory

Microsoft Fax

The *Microsoft Fax accessory* enables you to send and receive fax messages provided you have a fax modem on your computer or local area network. The program is accessed through the Accessories submenu and includes a cover page editor with sample pages.

Sending a fax is easy, as you are guided through each step of the process by the Fax Wizard as illustrated in Figure 4.7. Figure 4.7a enables you to enter the recipient's name and phone number explicitly. After entering the recipient(s), click the Next command button to select (omit) a cover page as shown in Figure 4.7b. You can enter information for the cover page as shown in Figure 4.7c, and/or you can browse your computer to attach a file to the fax as shown in Figure 4.7d. It's easy, and you get a chance to practice in the hands-on exercise that follows shortly.

Recipient's name   Recipient's phone number

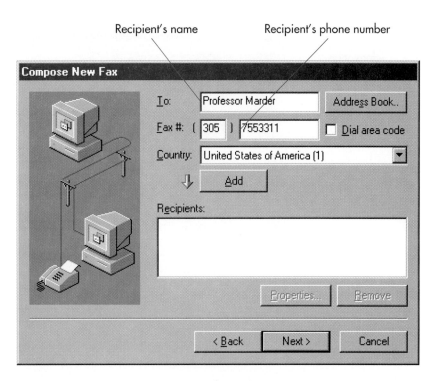

(a) Enter the Recipient

Include a cover page

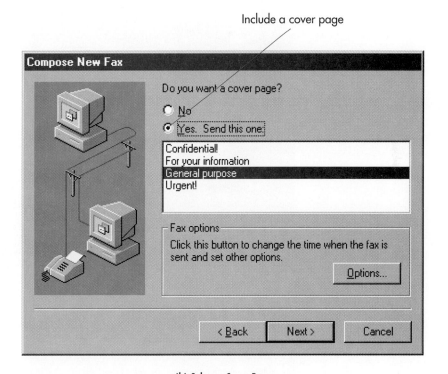

(b) Select a Cover Page

FIGURE 4.7   Microsoft Fax

Information to be included

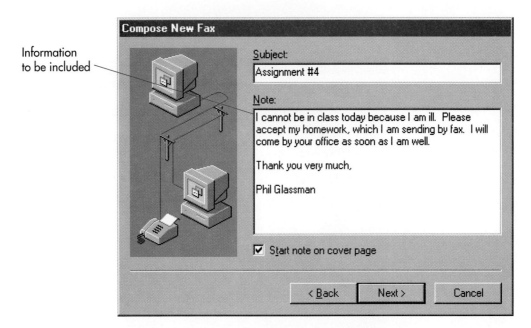

(c) Additional Cover Information

File to be attached

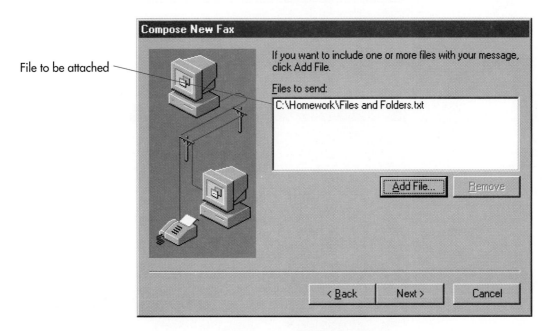

(d) Attach the Files

FIGURE 4.7   Microsoft Fax (continued)

THE ADDRESS BOOK

Use the address book provided by the Fax Wizard to create and maintain a list of fax recipients in a personal address book. Once a recipient's name has been entered into the address book, you no longer have to remember his or her fax number. You just click the address book command button, select the fax recipient, and the Fax Wizard will retrieve the telephone number.

An online ***information service*** provides you with up-to-the-minute information on almost any topic you can think of. Many different services are available, and the most difficult task may well be choosing which service to use.

America Online®, CompuServe®, and ***Prodigy®*** (shown in Figure 4.8a, 4.8b, and 4.8c, respectively) are the largest and best-known services. Each has been in existence for several years and each has a devoted following. Figure 4.8d displays the opening screen in the ***Microsoft Network,*** which made its debut in August 1995. The latter is part of Windows 95, which includes an option to sign up for the service in conjunction with the installation of Windows itself. (This is a point of bitter contention for Microsoft's competitors, who complain about the advantage afforded the Microsoft Network in acquiring new users.)

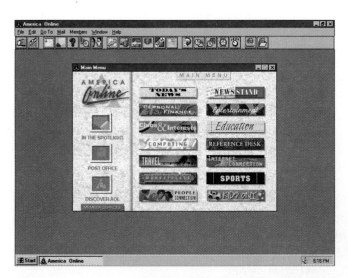

(a) America Online

(b) CompuServe

(c) Prodigy

(d) Microsoft Network

FIGURE 4.8   Online Information Services

Each information service started with a distinct audience in mind. CompuServe, for example, targeted the business user, whereas America Online and Prodigy were geared more toward the home. As the services evolved, however, they grew more alike, making the choice between the services more difficult. Prodigy and America Online now offer the business user much more than they did initially, while CompuServe has strengthened its nonbusiness areas. You can't go wrong with any of the major services, but there are two criteria to keep in mind—content and cost.

The content of a service is why you are online in the first place. All of the services provide information in similar areas, but the depth and timeliness of that information will vary significantly. All services promise the latest news, sports, weather, and financial information, but differ in how complete and how recent the information is. Ask yourself why you want to use an online service, then investigate several services in that specific area. If, for example, you are seeking technical support from a specific vendor, make sure that vendor is online to the service you are considering.

Once you are satisfied with the content, be sure that the cost of the service is in line with your expectations. Information services bill in different ways, usually a combination of a fixed monthly fee and an online charge for every hour that you are connected. Don't automatically select the service with the lowest monthly fee, because it is the total cost that counts. Be aware of additional costs for premium services such as extra charges for faster modems or specialized information.

GO FOR A TEST DRIVE

Look for magazine advertisements offering a free trial period (typically 10 hours) on one of the major information services. You can send in the postage-paid reply card or you can call the 800 number provided. The advertisements appear in a variety of magazines (e.g., *Time* or *US News and World Report*) in addition to computer publications. You're also apt to find the offer for a free trial in the documentation that accompanies your modem.

LEARNING BY DOING

The exercise that follows is typically not done in a school or university environment as it requires a modem and access to an outside telephone line. You can, however, do the exercise on your home computer provided you have a modem. The exercise illustrates the Phone Dialer and Hyper Terminal accessories, which are built into Windows 95. The exercise also has you try the Microsoft Network, but it could have been done just as easily with any other information service. The exercise is intended to show you what you can expect from an information service, and *not* as an endorsement of one service over another.

INSTALLING A MODEM

Windows 95 will automatically detect a modem if it is there at the time Windows is installed. If, however, you subsequently add a modem (or change the modem you do have), then you must run the Add Hardware Wizard to install the modem. Open the Control Panel within My Computer, then double click the Add New Hardware icon to begin the installation process.

Using a Modem

Objective: Use the online registration capability to register Windows 95. Demonstrate the Phone Dialer, Hyper Terminal, and Microsoft Fax accessories. Experiment with the Microsoft Network and/or other information services. Use Figure 4.9 as a guide in the exercise. *The exercise requires a modem and your own copy of Windows 95.*

STEP 1: Check for the Modem

➤ Open **My Computer.** Double click the **Control Panel icon** within My Computer to open the Control Panel. Do not be concerned if the size and/or position of the windows on your desktop is different from ours.

➤ Double click the **Modems icon** to display the Properties for Modems popup window shown in Figure 4.9a. It doesn't matter what type of modem is shown as long as your system recognizes a modem.

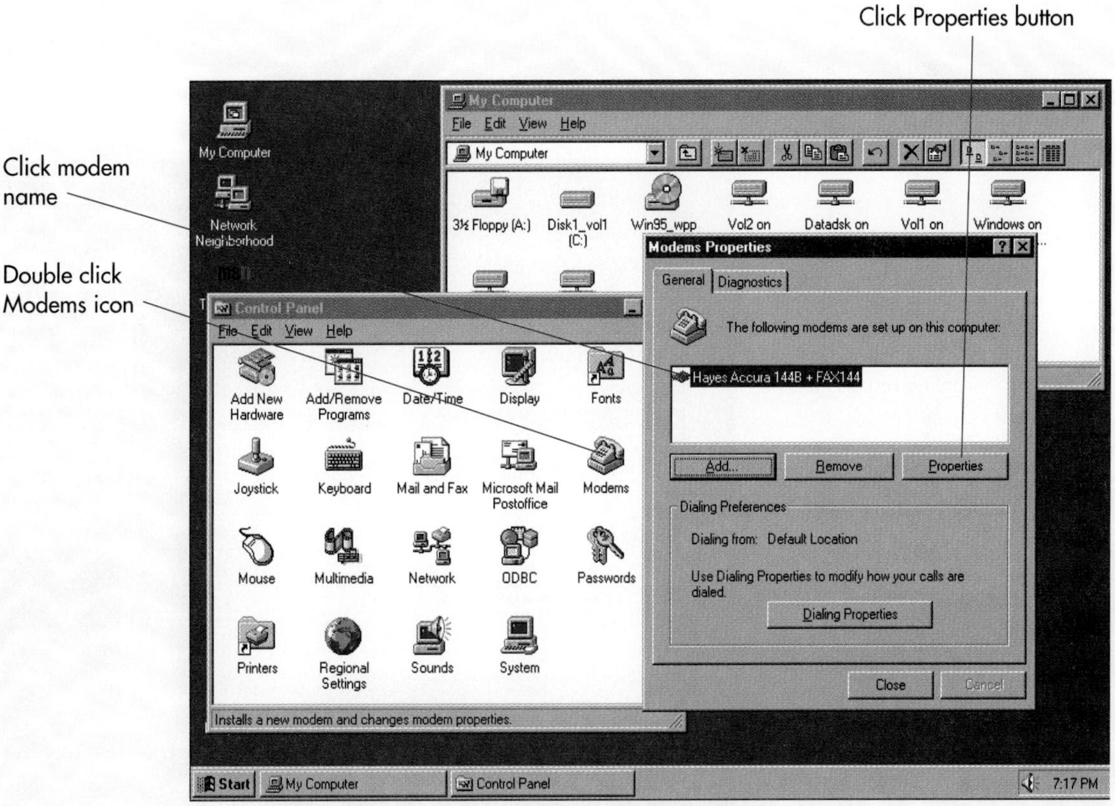

Click Properties button

Click modem name

Double click Modems icon

(a) Check for the Modem (step 1)

FIGURE 4.9 Hands-on Exercise 2

➤ Click the modem name, then click the **Properties command button** to display the properties for your modem (the communications port and the maximum speed). Be sure that the settings are correct.

➤ Now that you know your system has a modem, you are ready to proceed with the rest of the exercise.

➤ Close all open windows.

STEP 2: Register Now

➤ The Welcome to Windows 95 window contains a command button for online registration. To run the Welcome program:

- Click the **Start button** to display the Start menu. Click **Help.** If necessary, click the **Index tab.**
- Type **registration** in the text box to indicate the topic you are searching for. The index entry **registration, online** is selected for you.
- Click the **Display command button** to display the Help window in Figure 4.9b.
- Click the **jump button** in the Help window to display the Welcome to Windows 95 dialog box in Figure 4.9b.
- Click the **Online Registration command button.**

➤ You should see the screen in Figure 4.9b. Read the information, then click the **Next command button** to continue.

(b) Register Now (step 2)

FIGURE 4.9   Hands-on Exercise 2 (continued)

➤ Enter the information requested in the dialog box. Press the **Tab key** to move from one text box to the next. (You can also press **Shift+Tab** to return to the previous text box should you need to correct the information.)

➤ Click the **Next command button** to move to the next screen. Continue to follow the onscreen instructions until you have completed the registration process.

WHEN YOU USE A MODEM

The noise you hear when your modem first dials the number of a remote computer is that of the two modems exchanging information about the communication that is to take place, a process known as *handshaking.* The modems agree on the transmission speed (e.g., 14,400 bits per second), the number of bits used to transmit each character (7 or 8), the number of bits that will signal the end of a character (1 or 2), and parity checking (odd, even, or null).

STEP 3: Phone Dialer

➤ Click the **Start button.** Click (or point to) the **Programs command,** click (or point to) the **Accessories command,** then click the icon for **Phone Dialer.**

➤ The Phone Dialer should appear on your desktop as shown in Figure 4.9c. Click in the **Number to dial** list box, then enter the number you want to dial:

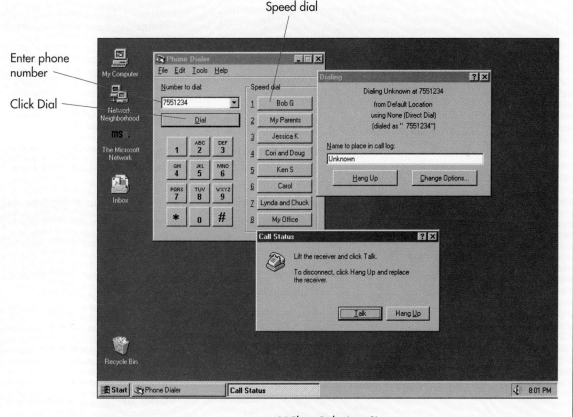

(c) Phone Dialer (step 3)

FIGURE 4.9   Hands-on Exercise 2 (continued)

- Enter just the number if it is a local call—for example, 7551234
- Include the area code for a long distance call—for example, 3057551234

➤ Click the **Dial command button** to dial the number, then pick up the phone. It may take a second or two, but you should hear a regular dial tone, followed by the sound of a dialing number. Pick up the telephone and talk to your friend.

➤ You can use speed dialing to access the numbers you dial frequently:
- Click the **Speed Dial button** on which you want to store the number. The Program Speed Dial dialog box will be displayed.
- Click in the **Name text box** and enter the person's name. Click the **Number to dial text box** and enter the number. (Include the area code if it's a long distance number.)
- Click the **Save command button** to close the Program Speed Dial dialog box. Click the **Speed dial button** to try the number.

➤ Click the **Minimize button** to close the Phone Dialer window, but leave the program active in memory. (You can reopen the Phone Dialer window by clicking its button on the Taskbar.)

TROUBLESHOOTING

If you're having difficulty dialing a long distance number or accessing an outside line, it's probably because the dialing properties are set improperly. Pull down the Tools menu and click Dialing Properties. Enter the appropriate instructions in the check boxes, indicating how you dial from this location; for example, 9 and 1, to access an outside local or long distance line, respectively. Click OK to save the settings and return to Phone Dialer.

STEP 4: Hyper Terminal

➤ To use Hyper Terminal you will need the phone number of a remote computer, plus an account on that computer. (Your instructor may be able to provide you with access to your school's computer.)

➤ Click the **Start button.** Click (or point to) the **Programs command,** click (or point to) the **Accessories command,** then click the icon for **Hyper Terminal.**

➤ Double click the icon for **Hypertrm.exe** to display the Connection Description dialog box.

➤ Type the name of the connection—for example, **School.** Select (click) an icon for the connection. Click **OK.**

➤ Enter the phone number of your school's computer in the Phone Number text box. Click **OK** to produce the Connect window in Figure 4.9d.

➤ Click the **Dialing Properties command button** to display the Dialing Properties dialog box.

➤ Confirm that all settings have been selected properly, especially the disabling of call waiting as described in the boxed tip below. Click **OK** to exit the Dialing Properties dialog box.

➤ Click the **Dial command button** to dial the remote computer.

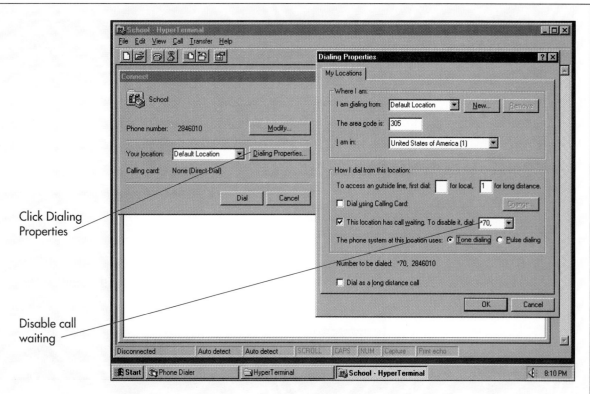

Click Dialing
Properties

Disable call
waiting

(d) Hyper Terminal (step 4)

FIGURE 4.9   Hands-on Exercise 2 (continued)

DISABLE CALL WAITING

If you're dropped suddenly in the middle of a session, it may be due to the call waiting feature on your telephone that signals another call coming in. To prevent this from happening, disable call waiting as a routine procedure prior to initiating calls. Click the Dialing Properties command button within Hyper Terminal, check the box to disable call waiting, and click the down arrow on the associated list box to display the ways to do so. Select the appropriate setting (e.g., *70), then click OK to exit the dialog box.

STEP 5: Hyper Terminal (continued)

➤ Follow the log-on procedure of the host computer, which normally prompts you for your account number (user name) and password. The account number uniquely identifies you to the host computer, and your password protects your account from unauthorized access.

➤ Conduct your business; for example, check and respond to your e-mail messages. (The use of e-mail is covered in detail, beginning on page 173.)

➤ Double click the **modem icon** at the right of the status bar to display the popup window in Figure 4.9e, showing the status of your modem. Click **OK** to close the popup window.

Log on with user
name and password

Double click
Modem icon

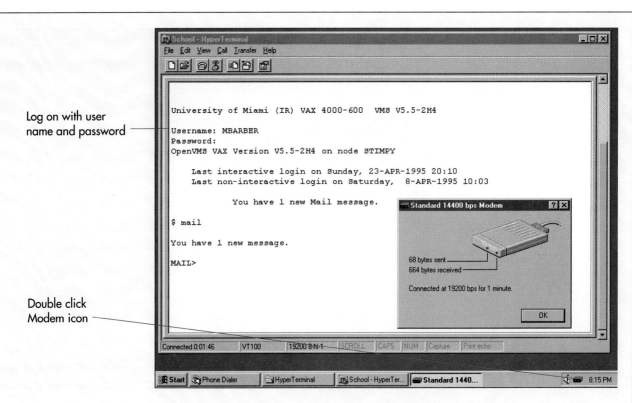

(e) Conduct your Business (step 5)

FIGURE 4.9   Hands-on Exercise 2 (continued)

➤ Be sure to log off properly from the host computer. Failure to do so can make it difficult for you to subsequently log on and/or can result in additional communication charges.

➤ Pull down the **File menu,** click **Exit,** then click **Yes** when asked whether to disconnect.

➤ Click **Yes** when asked whether to save the sessions for School. Close the Hyper Terminal window.

E-MAIL AND YOUR MODEM

There are many different ways to send and receive e-mail as described in the next section. At school, for example, you are on a network and can access the e-mail system directly. If the network has dial-up capability, you can also access e-mail by connecting to the network via a modem from your PC at home.

STEP 6: Microsoft Fax

➤ Click the **Start button.** Click (or point to) the **Programs command,** click (or point to) the **Accessories command,** click (or point to) the icon for **Fax,** then click the command to **Compose New Fax.**

➤ You may (or may not) see a screen asking the location from where you are dialing. If so, choose the default location, then click the **Next command button,** which should display the screen in Figure 4.9f.

TROUBLESHOOTING

If you are unable to load Microsoft Fax, it is most likely because it was not installed properly. Open My Computer, double click Control Panel, then double click the icon to Add/Remove programs. Click the Windows Setup tab, then check that Microsoft Exchange and Microsoft Fax are both installed. If you still have a problem, you may want to call Microsoft for technical support.

STEP 7: Microsoft Fax (continued)

➤ Follow the instructions on the screen to send a fax:

- Enter the recipient's name and fax number. Click the **Next command button.**
- Click the option button to include a **cover page.** Choose the type of page you want. Click **Next.**
- Enter the subject of the fax together with a brief note. Click **Next.**
- Click the **Next command button** if you do not wish to add an existing file to your fax; otherwise, click the **Add file command button,** locate the file, and double click to select it.

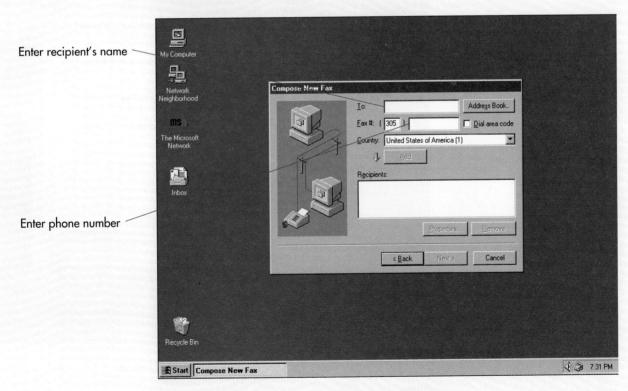

(f) Microsoft Fax (step 6)

FIGURE 4.9   Hands-on Exercise 2 (continued)

➤ You should see a final screen indicating that the Fax Wizard has all of the information it needs. Click the **Finish command button** to send the fax.

THE SEND TO COMMAND

Point to any file in My Computer or the Windows Explorer, then click the right mouse button to display a shortcut menu. Click Fax Recipient, which automatically opens the Fax accessory and takes you directly to the Fax Wizard, which will fax the selected file.

STEP 8: Try an Information Service

➤ Select an information service to try. The software for the Microsoft Network is built into Windows 95, but it is by no means the only service you should consider.

➤ Click the **Start button** to display the Start menu. Click (or point to) **Programs,** then click **The Microsoft Network.**

• If this is your first time connecting to the network, you will see the sign-up screen in Figure 4.9g, asking for your name and other information. Follow the onscreen instructions, which prompt you for your name and address and method of payment.

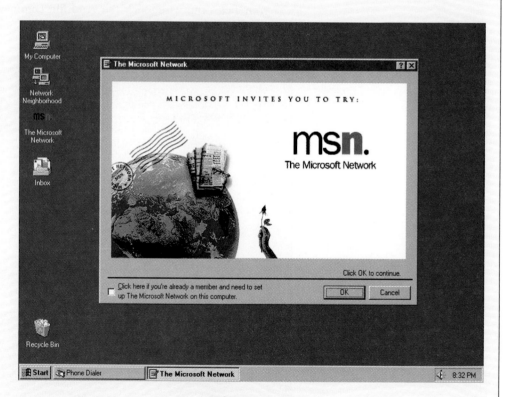

(g) Try an Information Service (step 8)

FIGURE 4.9   Hands-on Exercise 2 (continued)

- If you have previously signed up for the network, you will be asked for your Member ID and password. Enter the information, then click the **Connect command button.**
➤ Once you have logged on to the network, you will have full access to all network services. The possibilities are endless.

COST AND CONTENT

Don't let the ease of signing up for the Microsoft Network lull you into thinking that that is the only service you should consider. Determine the area (or areas) of greatest interest, then select the service that has the richest content in that area at a reasonable price. See boxed tip on page 164 for suggestions on how to obtain a free trial period for many of the major services.

E-MAIL

E-mail (electronic mail) is a means of communicating by computer that has changed the way people communicate. In essence, you use an editor to create a message, then you send the message just as you would mail an ordinary letter. The message is delivered electronically to the recipient, who upon checking his or her mailbox, finds the message and can respond (or not) as he or she sees fit.

You do not have to be at home when the postman delivers a letter to your mailbox. In similar fashion, your computer does not have to be on when an e-mail system delivers a message to your electronic mailbox. You do, however, need access to a local area network, or you must belong to an information service, which provides a host computer and acts as the post office.

All e-mail messages are stored in a central *post office* (an area on disk) that exists on the host computer. Every user has a private mailbox on the host computer, which is analogous to a post office box in a regular post office. You have a key to your post office box and a password for your e-mail mailbox. The post office is controlled by a system administrator who monitors the e-mail system, provides access for individual users, and maintains the disk storage required to hold the electronic mail.

NO MORE TELEPHONE TAG

E-mail has changed the way we communicate and in many ways is superior to the telephone. You send a message when it is convenient for you. The recipient reads the message when it is convenient for him or her. Neither of you has to be online for the other to access his or her e-mail system. Either of you can obtain a printed copy of the message. You can also use a mailing list capability to send the same message to many people. And best of all, e-mail costs a lot less than a long distance phone call.

You can send e-mail in a variety of ways—across a local area network, by logging on to a remote computer at your school or university, or via an information service such as the Microsoft Network. There are many different types of e-mail systems, each with its own unique commands. It would be impossible to cover the details of every system. All systems, however, provide the capability to send and receive mail. Our discussion will focus on the basic commands you can expect to find in any system. We use the *Microsoft Exchange* (an optional component in Windows 95), but the discussion is sufficiently general so that you can apply the concepts to any other system.

The *Microsoft Exchange*

The *Microsoft Exchange* is an integrated messaging and communications system that includes e-mail and fax capabilities. It is designed to be used with many different e-mail systems and includes an editor to compose and read e-mail messages. The *Personal Folders* within Microsoft Exchange include both an inbox and an outbox as well as any other folders the user wishes to create.

Figure 4.10a illustrates Microsoft Exchange as it is implemented on our system. The inbox folder is selected, and it contains previous messages (which you have decided to keep) as well as new messages waiting to be read. The icons displayed next to the various messages indicate their status and/or importance. An exclamation point, for example, indicates a message sent as high priority. A paper clip indicates a file has been attached to (sent with) the message.

All e-mail messages contain certain basic elements as shown in Figure 4.10b. The From and To lines contain the address of the sender and recipient, respectively. The Date line indicates the date and time the letter was received. The Subject line is a one-line summary of the message. The Cc (carbon copy) line indicates the names of other people who are to receive copies of the message. The message itself appears under the header.

E-mail commands are executed by pulling down a menu or by clicking the corresponding icon on the toolbar. The following commands (or their equivalent) are found in every system:

Compose: To create a new message
Send: To send a message that you created
Reply: To respond to a message you received
Forward: To send a message you received to another person

These commands are straightforward and will be illustrated in the hands-on exercise that follows shortly.

RICH TEXT FORMAT

Microsoft Exchange supports the full use of fonts and color and will transmit the rich text format over any e-mail system, including the Internet. If a message is sent to someone who does not use Windows 95, the addressee will receive the plain text equivalent of the message.

New message icon

Attached file is
included with message

Inbox is selected

High-priority message

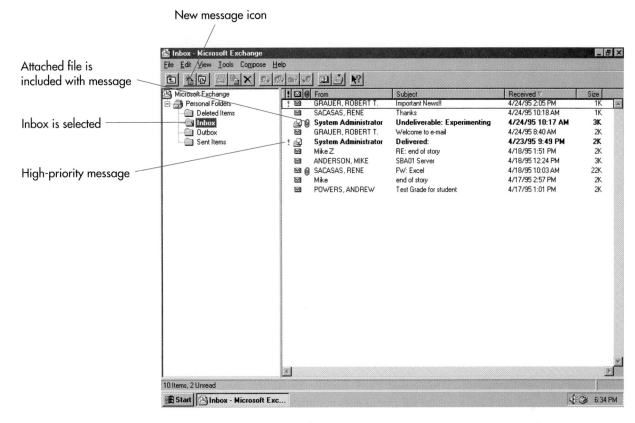

(a) Personal Folders

Sender

Recipient

Message text

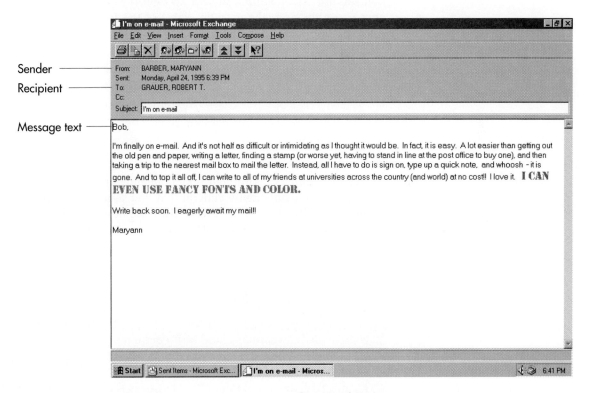

(b) An E-mail Message

FIGURE 4.10   The Microsoft Exchange

The Internet

All e-mail systems enable you to send messages to anyone on your network or information service. You can also send e-mail to individuals outside the network or information service, provided they have an Internet address and your system has access to the Internet.

The *Internet* is a network of networks that connects computers all over the world. It began as an experimental project in 1969 to enable university and governmental laboratories to exchange data with one another. Known originally as the ARPAnet (Advanced Research Projects Agency), the Internet has grown steadily so that it now includes virtually every major university, as well as various government agencies, and an ever increasing number of private corporations.

Each institution that maintains a node on the Internet is responsible for maintaining and administering that node. Organizations that choose to make their computers part of the Internet do so because of the benefits that accrue to their users. A connection to the Internet provides access to an incredible wealth of information (see Appendix D), coupled with the ability to communicate with people all over the world. The latter requires the use of an Internet address to identify the individual and the network to which he or she is attached.

The networks that comprise the Internet are organized into a series of *domains* that enable e-mail (and other files) to be delivered across the network. Universities, for example, belong to the EDU domain. Government agencies are in the GOV domain and commercial organizations (companies) are in the COM domain. Large domains are in turn divided into smaller domains, with each domain responsible for maintaining addresses in the next lower-level domain.

An *Internet address* consists of the username, the host computer, and the domain (or domains) by which the computer is connected to the Internet. The domains are listed in importance from right to left; that is, the highest-level domain appears on the end (the extreme right) of the Internet address. The @ sign separates the username from the host computer. For example:

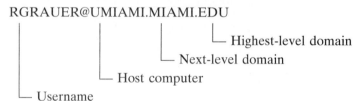

RGRAUER@UMIAMI.MIAMI.EDU
— Highest-level domain
— Next-level domain
— Host computer
— Username

The following exercise demonstrates the basics of e-mail in the context of the Microsoft Exchange. Although the commands in the exercise are specific to that system, they are sufficiently general that you should be able to adapt the exercise to any e-mail system. The exercise also assumes the existence of an e-mail message in your inbox, which (most likely) does not exist on your system.

AN ADDRESS TO REMEMBER

An Internet address is easier to remember when you realize that the address consists of the username, the host computer, and the domain (or domains) by which the computer is connected to the Internet. For example, President Clinton's e-mail address is PRESIDENT@WHITEHOUSE.GOV, where President is the username, Whitehouse is the host computer, and GOV is the domain. Vice President Gore may be reached at VICE-PRESIDENT @WHITEHOUSE.GOV.

E-mail

Objective: Send and receive an e-mail message. The exercise is written for the Microsoft Exchange, but it can be done with any e-mail system. Use Figure 4.11 as a guide in the exercise.

STEP 1: Log On

➤ Sign on to the system you will use for e-mail.

- If you are using a local area network at school, you will need an account (user-name) and a password, which your instructor should provide for you.
- If you are using an information service, you will need to sign up (and pay) for the service in order to obtain an account and username.

➤ It doesn't matter which system you use, since all systems have the same basic capabilities.

TROUBLESHOOTING

Microsoft Exchange is an *optional* component in Windows 95 and is installed only if Custom Setup was selected during installation. You can, however, add the Microsoft Exchange at any time, by opening the Control Panel within My Computer. Double click the Add/Remove Programs icon, click the Windows Setup tab, and check the box for Microsoft Exchange. Click the OK command button, then supply the installation disk(s) as requested.

STEP 2: The Microsoft Exchange

➤ Click the **Start button,** click (or point to) **Programs,** then click the **Microsoft Exchange command.**

➤ You may be asked for your password, after which you should see the Microsoft Exchange window. Maximize the Microsoft Exchange window.

➤ Make or verify the following selections using the **View menu.** (You have to pull down the View menu each time you choose a different command.)

- The **Toolbar command** should be checked.
- The **Status Bar command** should be checked.
- The **Normal view** should be selected under the **Common Views command.**

➤ If necessary, click the **plus sign** to the left of the icon for your personal folders (or Personal Information Store) in order to expand that folder and display its contents.

➤ Click the **Inbox folder** to display the messages currently in your inbox.

➤ Your screen should be similar to Figure 4.11a except that the contents of your inbox will be different from ours, and further, you are not yet reading any mail.

THE RIGHT MOUSE BUTTON

Point to any file (message) in your inbox, then click the right mouse button to display a context-sensitive menu with commands appropriate for that message. You can open (read) the message or you can print the message. You can choose the Reply to Sender command to send a response or you can use the Forward command to send the message to a third party. You can also display the properties of the message, which include the date and time the message was sent and received.

STEP 3: Read Your Mail

➤ Your mail may or may not be delivered automatically when you log on. If necessary, pull down the **Tools menu,** click **Deliver Now Using,** then click **All Services** to receive mail from all services associated with your e-mail system.

➤ To read a message:

- Select the message, pull down the **File menu,** and click the **Open command,** *or*
- Right click the message, then click the **Open command** from the shortcut menu, *or*
- Double click the message

➤ Regardless of which technique you use, a second window will open as shown in Figure 4.11a. (You can click the **Maximize button** to see more of the message.)

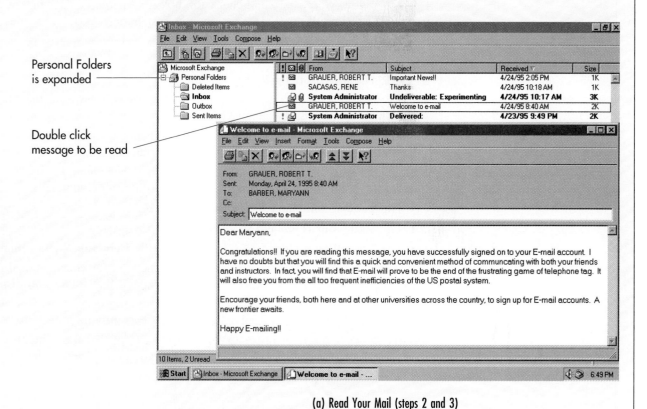

Personal Folders is expanded

Double click message to be read

(a) Read Your Mail (steps 2 and 3)

FIGURE 4.11   Hands-on Exercise 3

FIND A PEN PAL

Everyone likes to get mail, especially when using e-mail for the first time. Find a classmate and exchange e-mail addresses so that you can practice sending and receiving mail. If you have access to the Internet, find another pen pal outside of class so that you can practice sending mail across the Internet.

STEP 4: Reply to a Message

➤ To reply to the message you are reading, pull down the **Compose menu** and click **Reply to Sender** (or click the **Reply button** on the toolbar). The contents of the window will change to enable a reply:

- The address of the person that sent you the message will be entered automatically in the To: box.
- The insertion point will be positioned so that you can start your reply.

➤ Maximize the window so you have more room to work. Enter the text of your reply as shown in Figure 4.11b. Type just as you would using any word processor. Press the enter key only at the end of a paragraph.

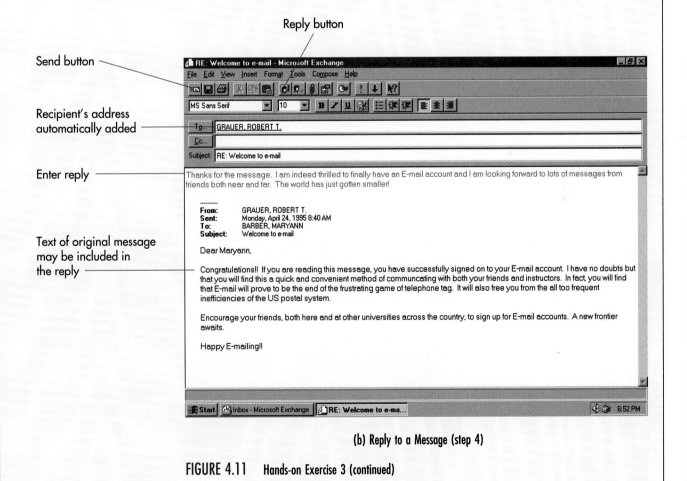

(b) Reply to a Message (step 4)

FIGURE 4.11   Hands-on Exercise 3 (continued)

➤ When you are finished, pull down the **File menu** and click **Send** (or click the **Send button** on the toolbar). The Reply window will close automatically and you will be returned to the Microsoft Exchange window.

RETURN RECEIPT REQUESTED

Would you like confirmation that a message has been delivered, or that it has been read by the recipient after delivery? Pull down the File menu and click the Properties command to display a tabbed dialog box in which you request these options for the current message. The system administrator will send confirmation of these events to your inbox when they occur. To change the options for all messages (rather than just the current message), pull down the Tools menu, click Options for, then click Everything to display a tabbed dialog box, which enables you to set a variety of options. See practice exercise 3 on page 188 for additional information.

STEP 5: Create a Message

➤ Pull down the **Compose menu** and click **New message** (or click the **New Message button** on the toolbar). Maximize the window so you have more room to work.

➤ Enter the name of the recipient.

- If you have an address book, pull down the **Tools menu** and click **Select Address Book** (or click the **Select Names button**). Select the desired address list from the Show Names drop-down list box as shown in Figure 4.11c. Scroll to and double click the recipient's name. (You can type the first few letters of the name to speed up scrolling.) Click **OK.**

- If you do not have an address book: Click in the **To . . .** text box and enter the recipient's address.

➤ The recipient's name should appear in the message, and you are ready to enter its text.

STEP 6: Create a Message (continued)

➤ Click in the **Subject** text box and enter a short description of your message as shown in Figure 4.11d.

➤ Click in the **Message** text box and type your message just as you would using a word processor. The Microsoft Exchange contains a powerful editor that supports rich text format (fonts and color) as well as drag-and-drop editing.

SEND YOURSELF AN E-MAIL MESSAGE

One of the best ways to practice with e-mail is to send yourself a message. Not only does this give you practice with the editor, but it also lets you check that the message is actually delivered to its intended recipient. You open your inbox to view the message, then use the Reply command to send yourself an answer, or use the Forward command to send the same message to someone else.

Select the
address book

Type initial letters to
speed up scrolling process

Double click
recipient's name

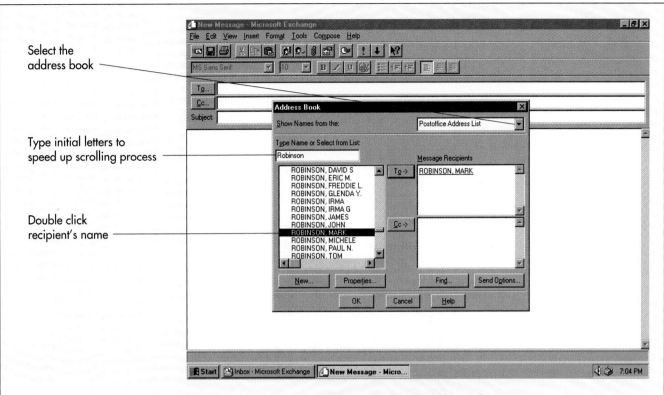

(c) Select a Name from the Address Book (step 5)

Send icon

Enter your
message

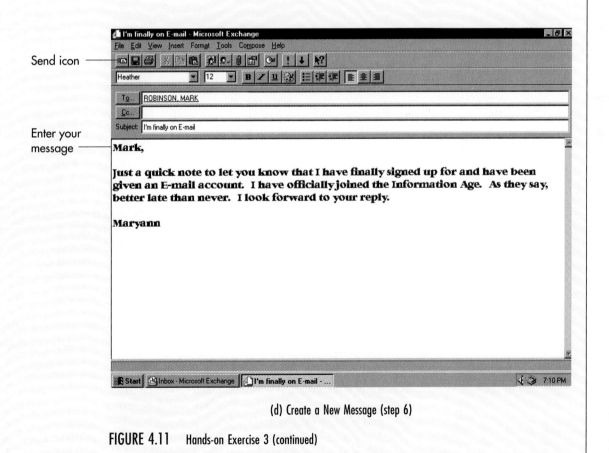

Mark,

**Just a quick note to let you know that I have finally signed up for and have been
given an E-mail account. I have officially joined the Information Age. As they say,
better late than never. I look forward to your reply.**

Maryann

(d) Create a New Message (step 6)

FIGURE 4.11   Hands-on Exercise 3 (continued)

- When you have finished your message, pull down the **File menu** and click **Send** (or click the **Send icon**). The window closes automatically and you will be returned to the Microsoft Exchange window.

STEP 7: Exit Microsoft Exchange

- Keep your mailbox from overflowing (and the disk space from becoming limited) by deleting messages that are no longer necessary.
- To delete a message, select (click) the message, then press the **Del key.** Be sure to delete superfluous messages from all folders within the Personal Information Store, as opposed to just the inbox.
- Click the **Close button** to exit Microsoft Exchange.

ONLINE HELP

Online Help is available for the Microsoft Exchange just as it is for any other Windows application. Pull down the Help menu and select the desired program. (Help for the Microsoft Fax accessory is also available from this menu.) The Contents tab displays an overall table of contents that lets you "drill down" through successive topics by double clicking a closed book icon to display more detailed information. The Index tab enables you to type the first several letters of a specific topic, then displays information on that topic. You can print the contents of any Help screen by right clicking in the screen, then selecting the Print Topic command from the displayed menu.

SUMMARY

A local area network is a combination of hardware and software that lets computers communicate with one another. A workstation is an ordinary PC on which you work. The server is a more powerful PC that controls the way the individual workstations share resources. Larger networks may have multiple servers, each dedicated to a specific task. The network administrator is responsible for administering the security of a network.

A modem is the interface between a PC and the telephone. Data passes from the sending computer to its modem, where it is converted to an analog signal that is transmitted over the phone line. The modem of the receiving computer converts the analog signal back to digital values that are passed to the receiving computer.

A communications program is required in addition to a modem in order to connect to another computer. The Hyper Terminal accessory is the communications program included in Windows 95.

The Phone Dialer accessory enables a modem to make telephone calls for you. It is used to establish voice communications with another person, not to establish a connection to a remote computer.

America Online®, CompuServe®, and Prodigy® are the largest and best-known information services. Each has been in existence for several years and each has a devoted following. The Microsoft Network made its debut in August 1995 and is built into Windows 95.

All e-mail systems have the same basic capabilities. These include the ability to create and send a message, and the ability to receive and reply to a message. The Microsoft Exchange is an integrated messaging and communications system that is built into Windows 95.

The Internet is a network of networks that connects computers all over the world. An Internet address consists of the username, the host computer, and the Internet domain—for example, PRESIDENT@WHITEHOUSE.GOV.

KEY WORDS AND CONCEPTS

America Online®
Bits per second (bps)
Bridge
Communications software
Compose command
CompuServe®
Domain
Download
E-mail
Fax/modem
File server
Forward command

Hyper Terminal accessory
Information service
Internet
Internet address
Local area network (LAN)
Microsoft Exchange
Microsoft Fax accessory
Microsoft Network
Modem
Network administrator
Network Neighborhood

Password
Phone Dialer accessory
Personal Folders
Post office
Printer server
Prodigy®
Reply command
Send command
Server
Upload
Workstation

MULTIPLE CHOICE

1. A local area network is intended to:
   (a) Share data among connected computers
   (b) Share peripheral devices among connected computers
   (c) Share programs among connected computers
   (d) All of the above

2. Which of the following commands is present in every e-mail system?
   (a) Send
   (b) Reply
   (c) Both (a) and (b)
   (d) Neither (a) nor (b)

3. Which of the following folders are found in the Personal Information Source within Microsoft Exchange?
   (a) Inbox and Outbox
   (b) Sent items and Deleted items
   (c) Both (a) and (b)
   (d) Neither (a) nor (b)

4. Which accessory would you use to dial a remote computer in order to access its e-mail capabilities?
   (a) Hyper Terminal
   (b) Phone Dialer

(c) Microsoft Fax

(d) All of the above

5. Which of the following capabilities are built into the Phone Dialer accessory?

(a) Speed dialing

(b) A phone log

(c) Conversion of a mnemonic number to its numerical equivalent

(d) All of the above

6. A virus can be transmitted to your computer when you:

(a) Download files from a remote computer

(b) Upload files to a remote computer

(c) Both (a) and (b)

(d) Neither (a) nor (b)

7. Which of the following is true about the Network Neighborhood and My Computer icons on the Windows desktop?

(a) My Computer is present on every desktop

(b) Network Neighborhood is present on every desktop

(c) Both (a) and (b)

(d) Neither (a) nor (b)

8. Which of the following is found in the heading of an e-mail message?

(a) The addresses of the sender and the recipient

(b) The date and time the message was received

(c) A subject line

(d) All of the above

9. Which of the following is a valid Internet domain?

(a) GOV is the domain for government agencies

(b) COM is the domain for commercial organizations

(c) Both (a) and (b)

(d) Neither (a) nor (b)

10. Given the Internet address, RGRAUER@UMIAMI.MIAMI.EDU

(a) EDU is the highest-level domain

(b) UMIAMI is the host computer

(c) RGRAUER is the username

(d) All of the above

11. Which e-mail command will send a message that you received to another user?

(a) Forward

(b) Reply

(c) Both (a) and (b)

(d) Neither (a) nor (b)

12. Which information service lets you send e-mail over the Internet?

(a) America Online

(b) CompuServe

(c) Prodigy

(d) All of the above

13. The charges for an information service may include:
  (a) A flat monthly fee
  (b) An hourly connect fee
  (c) An additional fee for premium services
  (d) All of the above

14. Which of the following should you consider in the selection of an online service?
  (a) Cost
  (b) Content
  (c) Both (a) and (b)
  (d) Neither (a) nor (b)

15. Which of the following describes network security in a typical network?
  (a) Every user has the same privileges on the network with equal access to all network files
  (b) A password is required to gain access to the network
  (c) Both (a) and (b)
  (d) Neither (a) nor (b)

ANSWERS

1. d	**6.** a	**11.** a
2. c	**7.** a	**12.** d
3. c	**8.** d	**13.** d
4. a	**9.** c	**14.** c
5. d	**10.** d	**15.** b

EXPLORING WINDOWS 95

1. Use Figure 4.12 to match each action with its result; a given action may be used more than once or not at all.

Action

a. Click at 1
b. Click at 2
c. Click at 3
d. Click at 4
e. Click at 5
f. Click at 6
g. Click at 7
h. Double click at 8
i. Right click at 8
j. Click at 9

Result

____ Change the properties for all incoming/outgoing messages
____ Reply to the selected message
____ Create a new message
____ Determine the properties for the selected message
____ Delete the selected message
____ View all deleted messages
____ Forward the selected message
____ Read the selected message
____ Print the selected message
____ Add names to your address book

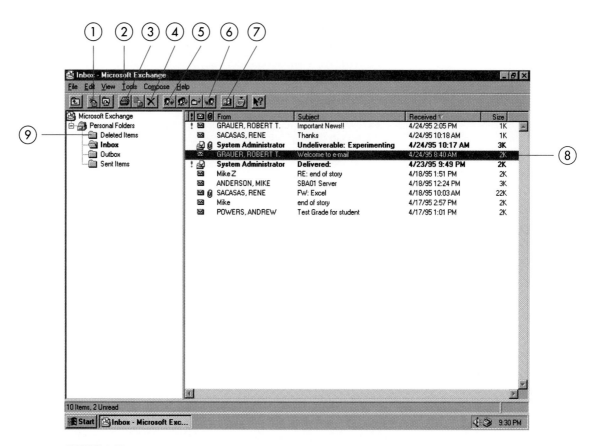

FIGURE 4.12 Screen for Problem 1

2. Local Area Networks: Answer the following with respect to the local area network you used to do the first hands-on exercise.
   a. Who is allowed access to the network?
   b. What type of security is in effect?
   c. What kinds of devices, and how many of each, are on the network?
   d. What application software is available to individuals on the network?
   e. Does the installation's purchase of one copy of a program (e.g., the Microsoft Office) legally entitle every user access to that program? How is the situation handled on the network?
   f. Which data files are available to individuals on the network? Is every user allowed access to every file? What happens if two users attempt to access the same file simultaneously?

3. Communications: Contrary to what the ads of FedEx and its competitors may tell us, there are faster and cheaper ways of transmitting information:
   a. What is the cost of an overnight letter set by FedEx or one of its competitors? How long does it take to deliver the letter?
   b. What is the cost of transmitting the same letter via a fax/modem? What parameters are necessary for you to accurately determine the cost of transmission?

4. Each of the messages in Figure 4.13 appeared (or could have appeared) in conjunction with the hands-on exercises in this chapter. Explain the nature of the message and indicate the necessary corrective action (if any).

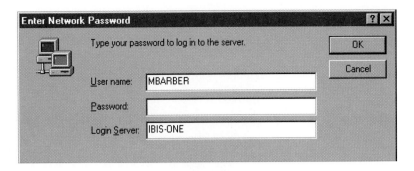

(a) Message 1

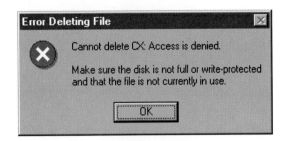

(b) Message 2

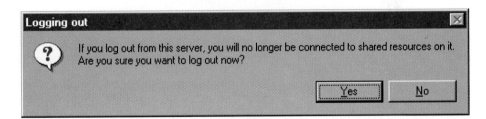

(c) Message 3

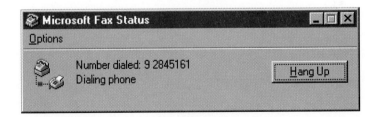

(d) Message 4

FIGURE 4.13   Messages for Problem 4

PRACTICE WITH WINDOWS 95

1. Use the techniques that were described in Chapter 3 to create shortcuts to Hyper Terminal, Phone Dialer, and a network drive (if available) as shown in Figure 4.14. Prove to your instructor that you have done the exercise by

FIGURE 4.14 Practice Exercise 1

capturing the screen and adding your name. (See exercise 7 on pages 40–41 for instructions on screen capture and adding your name.)

2. Information Services: All information services claim to provide similar content, but there is considerable variation from one service to the next. Ask your instructor to divide the class into groups, then assign a different service to each group. Let the class decide on specific information requests, then have each group obtain the information from their assigned service. Some items to consider:

   a. Today's news: Select any relevant news story and see what information is available.

   b. Sports: Obtain the most recent score and related information for the sporting event of your choice.

   c. Entertainment: Choose a specific movie and obtain a review of that movie.

   d. Financial: Obtain the closing price of a specific stock plus all other financial information about that company.

   e. Software support: Determine the online information available in support of Windows 95.

   f. Send an e-mail message to your instructor that summarizes your findings. Keep it brief, but be sure to compare the quantity, quality, and cost of the information, together with your recommendation as to which service to try.

3. Microsoft Exchange: Use Figure 4.15 to answer the following questions regarding settings within the Microsoft Exchange.

   a. Which command in which menu is used to display the Microsoft Exchange dialog box?

   b. How is the user notified of a new message?

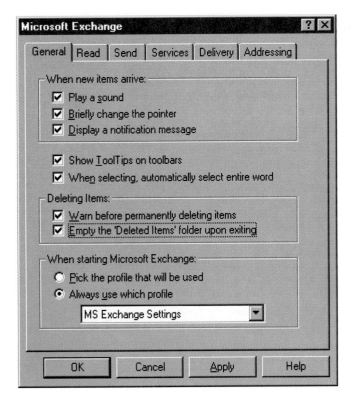

(a) General Settings

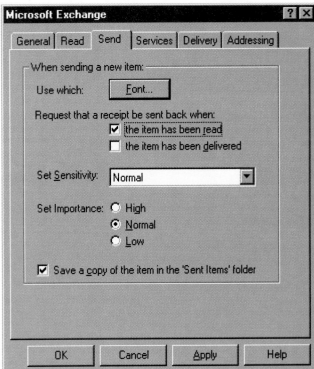

(b) Send Settings

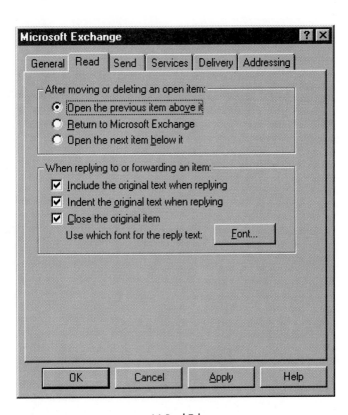

(c) Read Tab

FIGURE 4.15   Practice Exercise 3

c. What is a ToolTip? Will ToolTips be displayed according to the current settings?

d. Which tab is used to modify the Reply and Forward settings?

e. Is the text of an original message included when replying to a message? How would you reverse the setting?

f. What is the What's This button? What is the effect of clicking it?

g. Send the answers to your instructor via an e-mail message.

CASE STUDIES

Adding a Modem

A good friend has asked your advice about installing a modem on a two-year-old machine. Her questions are whether it pays to install a modem (as opposed to buying a new machine), and if so, which modem to get and how much should it cost. Does the installation of a modem require the purchase of any additional software? How difficult is it to install a modem, and would you be able to help install it if she decides to buy? All advice and assistance will be greatly appreciated.

Choosing an Information Service

Now that your friend has acquired a modem, she is very interested in subscribing to an information service. Help your friend decide which service to select by learning about the differences among the major companies. (See the problem on information services on page 188.) Pricing and other information can be obtained by calling the companies directly (each has an 800 number). Investigate three or four different companies, then report back to class with comparative information on the services offered, information content, and pricing policy.

File Compression

Modems are getting faster all the time, but even with a state-of-the-art device, transferring large files over telephone lines can be time consuming (and expensive). Approximately how long does it take to send a 100KB file over a 14,400 bps modem? Over a 28,800 bps modem? Can file compression help, and if so, which program would you use, and where would you get it?

The Internet versus an Information Service

The Internet and World Wide Web (see Appendix D) provide access to a virtually unlimited amount of online information, all of which is free. Is the Internet really free, and if so, why would anyone join an information service when the same information is available at no cost? What special tools, if any, do you need to "surf the net"? To browse the World Wide Web? Does the recent surge of interest in the Internet and World Wide Web mean the end of information services such as CompuServe or America Online?

APPENDIX A: MIGRATING FROM WINDOWS 3.1

A

OVERVIEW

Windows 95, the long-awaited successor to Windows 3.1, is finally here. It took much longer than expected, but we think it was well worth the wait. Windows 3.1 did away with the DOS prompt and put a friendly face on the computer. It gave us the graphical user interface, multitasking, and object linking and embedding. The goal of Windows 95 is to make the PC even easier to use while simultaneously making it more powerful.

Windows 95 was a huge undertaking (the source code is six times larger than the code of Windows 3.1). Not only did Microsoft have to get the new technology right, but they had to ensure compatibility with the more than 120 million existing copies of Windows 3.1. We cannot cover every aspect of Windows 95, nor do we intend to try. Instead, we focus on the new user interface and how it differs from its predecessor.

The most important goal of Windows 95 is to make the PC easier to use. To develop the new interface, Microsoft conducted extensive usability testing of Windows 3.1. It became apparent that program groups were confusing to new users, that double clicking was not intuitive, and that the novice had difficulty finding and launching applications. These findings led to a simpler desktop for Windows 95. The user goes directly to the Start button from which 95 percent of all Windows tasks can be performed.

The study also showed that task switching (via the Alt+Tab shortcut) was not intuitive and that too few users ran (or even knew they could run) multiple applications simultaneously. The result was the Taskbar, which shows all open applications and enables push-button task switching.

Microsoft also discovered that almost half of the general Windows population did not use File Manager because its dual pane and hierarchical view were too intimidating. This led to the introduction of the My Computer browsing model, which lets the user go from the desktop to a disk drive, to a folder (subdirectory), to a file in a more natural (albeit slower) progression.

Ease of use is sometimes accomplished at the expense of efficiency in that it takes an extra mouse click here and there to perform a specific task. While new users are up and running more quickly, there is an adjustment for the experienced Windows user who finds that some treasured shortcuts are no longer necessary or no longer available. Rest assured, however, that there are more powerful features waiting to be discovered, and that once you adjust to the new interface, you will find yourself working much more efficiently than in the past.

This appendix is written for the person knowledgeable in Windows 3.1, as opposed to the computer novice. Unlike the rest of the text, there are no detailed hands-on exercises, but there are boxed tips and associated one- or two-step techniques for you to try. Microsoft has taken long enough to deliver Windows 95 and we don't want to add to the delay. Let's begin.

TRY THIS:

Take the Windows 95 Tour

Windows 95 greets you with a Welcome window (see Figure A.1) that contains a command button to take you on a 10-minute tour of Windows 95. Click the command button and enjoy the show. You might also try the What's New command button for a quick overview of changes from Windows 3.1. If you do not see the Welcome window when you start Windows 95, click the Start button, click Run, type C:\WINDOWS\WELCOME in the Open text box, and press enter.

A SIMPLER DESKTOP

Figure A.1 displays the desktop that appears when Windows 95 is installed on a new computer. The initial desktop has only a few icons, but you can customize the desktop to your personal preference. You can, for example, add additional icons (or shortcuts) that provide immediate access to the applications or documents you use most frequently. It is the simplicity of the desktop, however, that helps the user to focus on what's important.

The *Start button,* as the name suggests, is the place to begin. Click the Start button and you are presented with the menu shown in Figure A.1. There is no need to double click, and the user is presented immediately with a functional menu that provides access to 95 percent of all Windows functions. Consider:

➤ The *Programs menu* provides access to all programs on the system and is the equivalent of Program Manager under Windows 3.1. (All program groups that existed under Windows 3.1 are automatically converted to submenus on the Programs menu. Any program that is subsequently installed under Windows 95 is automatically added to the Programs menu.)

➤ The *Documents menu* lists the last 15 documents that were opened and offers immediate access to those documents. The user simply selects a document name, which automatically loads the associated application and opens the document. The Documents menu promotes the concept of "documentcentricity," where the user is able to think in terms of a document rather than an application.

Start button ——

Taskbar

FIGURE A.1 A Simpler Desktop

> The **Settings menu** takes you to an improved Control Panel that enables you to change the settings of any device on the computer. It also allows you to customize the Taskbar, which in turn lets you add additional menu options to the Start button itself.

> The improved **Find command** goes far beyond the File Search command in Windows 3.1. The File Search command was difficult to find and most users never even knew it existed. And even if they knew of the command, users were limited in that they could search only one drive at a time, and further, they could search only for a file name, rather than text within a file. All of these restrictions have been eliminated.

> The improved **Help facility** is more intuitive than its predecessor and uses a reference book as a metaphor. There is a Contents tab and an Index tab. The Contents tab is organized like the table of contents in a real book. The Index tab functions just like a regular index. The Help topics themselves are short and functionally oriented, with a shortcut button that enables immediate execution of the task at hand.

> The **Run command** is identical to the File Run command in Windows 3.1, but is accessible directly from the Start button.

> The **Shut Down command** is the recommended way to exit Windows 95 as it clears buffers and erases temporary files created during the session.

In addition to the Start button, the desktop in Figure A.1 contains three additional icons. **My Computer** enables the novice to browse the system in intuitive fashion and is covered in Chapter 3. **Network Neighborhood** extends the view of the computer to include the accessible drives on the network to which the machine is attached, if indeed it is part of a network. (You will not see this icon if you are not connected to a network.) The **Recycle Bin** enables you to recover a deleted file.

The **Taskbar** at the bottom of the desktop shows all of the programs (Welcome in Figure A.1) that are currently running (open in memory). It contains a button for each open program and lets you switch back and forth between those programs, by clicking the appropriate button. The Taskbar is discussed further in the section on multitasking on page 196.

TRY THIS:

Slide, Don't Click

How many times do you click the mouse in a Windows session? Microsoft is trying to lower the number and, in the process, possibly reduce the incidence of carpal tunnel syndrome. Click the Start button, then slide (don't click) to the Programs item, slide (don't click) to any item followed by an arrow (e.g., Microsoft Office ▶), then click the desired program (e.g., Word for Windows). In other words, you don't have to click to produce a submenu—just slide to the higher-level menu and the submenu will appear automatically.

Properties Everywhere

Our favorite new feature in Windows 95 is the context-sensitive right mouse button that enables you to **rightclick** any object and display an appropriate shortcut menu. This enables you to display a **properties sheet** through which you can configure the object by changing one or more of its settings.

Each of the property sheets in Figure A.2 was displayed by right clicking the indicated object—the Desktop, Taskbar, My Computer icon, and Drive C icon (within My Computer), respectively. The first thing we saw about the Windows 95 dialog boxes was their improved appearance with beveled three-dimensional surfaces and command buttons, slick-looking icons, and cleaner modern typography. More important, however, is the increased functionality as each property sheet contains one or more **tabbed dialog boxes** that provide access to multiple sets of options.

TRY THIS:

Change the Resolution

It took an adventurous soul to change the resolution in Windows 3.1 because the procedure was both complicated and time consuming. It's much easier in Windows 95 and can be done in a matter of seconds, *without* having to restart Windows. Right click anywhere on the desktop to display the Properties sheet for the Display (Figure A.2a). Click the Settings tab, then drag the Desktop area slider bar to one of the other resolutions supported by your video card. Click OK, then follow the onscreen prompt.

Tabs   What's This button   Close button

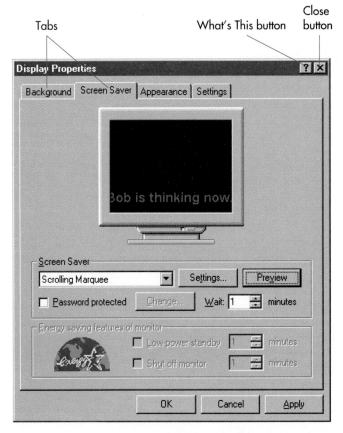

(a) The Desktop

(b) The Taskbar

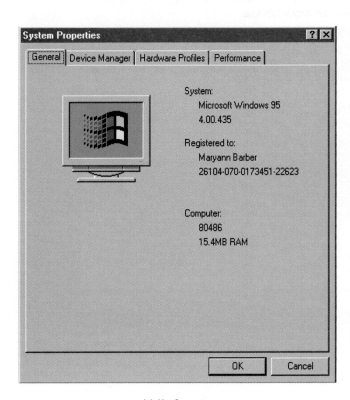

(c) My Computer

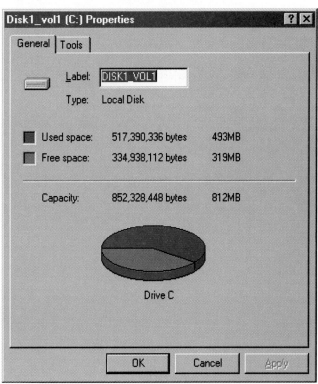

(d) Drive C

FIGURE A.2   Properties Everywhere

Note, too, the new icons on the title bar of each property sheet. The **What's This button** (a question mark) explains any item in the property sheet. Click the button, then click the item in the Property sheet about which you want additional information. (Click outside the resulting popup window to close the informational window and continue working.) The **Close button** (an X) at the right of the title bar is present in every window and closes the window.

The Taskbar

Multitasking, the ability to run multiple applications at the same time, is at the heart of Windows. Most novices, however, did not take advantage of the capability in Windows 3.1 because it was not obvious. Hence the Taskbar, which makes task switching as easy as changing channels on a television set.

Every open window, be it an application or a folder, has a corresponding button on the Taskbar as shown in Figure A.3. To change to a new task, all the user has to do is click the corresponding button on the Taskbar. There is no need to minimize an application and no more concern for disappearing windows. The user always sees all of his or her active tasks simply by looking at the Taskbar.

Each button on the Taskbar appears automatically when its application or folder is opened and disappears upon closing. The buttons are even resized automatically according to the number of open windows. The Taskbar itself can be resized by dragging its inside edge. The Taskbar can also be moved to the left or

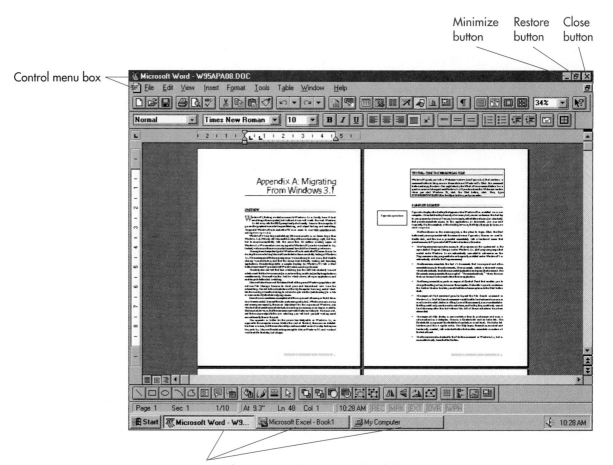

FIGURE A.3   Multitasking and the Taskbar

right edge of the desktop, or to the top of the desktop, by dragging a blank area of the Taskbar to the desired position. You can also right click the Taskbar to display a menu to tile or cascade the open applications.

If you are among the Windows 3.1 users who knew of the Alt+Tab shortcut to switch between applications, you'll be glad to know the shortcut still works, but has been improved to display the icons for all open applications simultaneously. The Ctrl+Esc combination (to display the Windows 3.1 task list) has been changed, however, and now displays the Start menu (it previously displayed the Windows 3.1 task list). Try either shortcut and see the result for yourself.

TRY THIS:

Task Switching

Open My Computer, then open Drive C within My Computer, noting that as each window is opened, a corresponding button appears on the Taskbar. Use the Start button to open at least two applications, and again, note the corresponding buttons on the Taskbar. Maximize the window that you are currently in, then switch to a different window by clicking the corresponding button on the Taskbar.

A New Title Bar

Figure A.3 also illustrates the new look of the Windows 95 title bar. The icon for the control menu box in both the application and document windows has been changed to reflect the icon of the application (Microsoft Word in Figure A.3). The icons for the Minimize, Maximize, and Restore buttons have been changed. A Close button has been added and appears at the extreme right of the title bar.

IMPROVED FILE MANAGEMENT

If you have worked with Windows 3.1 for any length of time, you should have mastered File Manager. You can move or copy a file from one drive or directory to another, you can rename a file, and you can delete a file. (You might even be able to recover a deleted file through the Undelete command that is accessible from the Microsoft Tools group introduced in DOS 6.0.) Although you may take these abilities for granted, they were not easy to learn. Many novices do not understand File Manager and are intimidated by its dual pane view and hierarchical tree structure.

Accordingly, Windows 95 had as a primary objective, the introduction of an easier model for file management. This resulted in the development of My Computer, which is a more intuitive (albeit less efficient) way to browse a system. At the same time, Windows 95 sought to retain the powerful features inherent in File Manager, which led to the even more powerful Windows Explorer.

It doesn't matter whether you use My Computer or the Explorer (we find ourselves switching back and forth between the two) as long as you can accomplish what you need to do. My Computer is intuitive and geared for the novice, as it opens a new window for each successive folder. The Windows Explorer, on the other hand, is more sophisticated and provides a hierarchical view of the entire system in a single window. A beginner will prefer My Computer, whereas a more experienced user will opt for the Explorer.

The contents of My Computer (or any other window) are displayed in one of four different views (Large Icons, Small Icons, Details, and List). Double click the My Computer icon on the desktop to open the My Computer window, then pull down the View menu and click the Toolbar command if the toolbar is not visible. Click each of the four view icons (a ToolTip appears when you point to an icon) to cycle through the different views in order to see the characteristics of each view. Choose the view that is most appropriate for you.

My Computer

My Computer is present on every desktop, but its contents will vary depending on the specific configuration. Our system has one floppy drive, one hard disk, and a CD-ROM as can be seen in Figure A.4. To open My Computer, simply double click the icon on the desktop. Once it's open, you can move or size the My Computer window just as you can any other window.

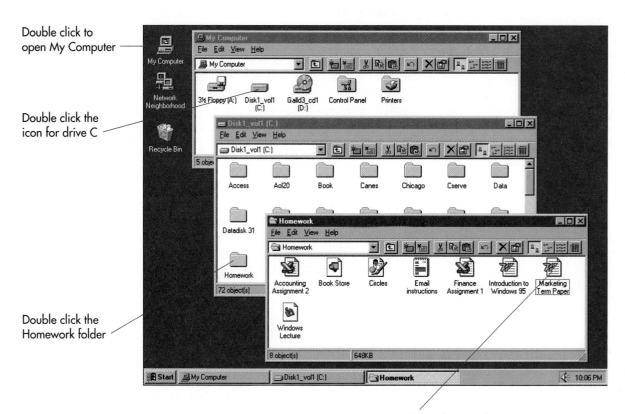

Double click to open My Computer

Double click the icon for drive C

Double click the Homework folder

To copy this file to drive A, drag its icon to drive A icon in My Computer

FIGURE A.4   My Computer

My Computer provides an intuitive way to browse a system in order to find a specific file or subdirectory (known as a folder in Windows 95). Assume, for example, that you wanted to continue working on the term paper you began last night. You would start by double clicking the My Computer icon on the desktop to open the My Computer window. Next you would double click the icon for drive C to open a second window and display all of the folders on drive C. And finally, you would double click the icon for the Homework folder to open that folder, find your document, and start working.

You can also use the open windows within My Computer to move or copy files from one folder to another. To create a backup copy of the term paper, for example, simply drag its icon from the Homework folder to the icon for drive A.

TRY THIS:

Right Click and Drag

Regardless of whether you use My Computer or the Windows Explorer, you need to be able to move and copy with confidence. You can click and drag a file from one folder (directory) to another, just as you did in Windows 3.1, but you have to remember the rules for whether the file will be moved or copied. (Windows 95 is consistent with Windows 3.1.) Better yet, you can click and drag a file with the right mouse button to display a ***shortcut menu,*** which asks which operation you want to perform (move or copy). Try this the next time you need to move or copy a file.

Windows Explorer

My Computer is designed for the novice. It is time consuming to use and it creates desktops cluttered with open windows. The more experienced user will opt for the ***Windows Explorer,*** an improved version of the Windows 3.1 File Manager. The Explorer does not do anything that could not be done through My Computer, but it performs those tasks more quickly.

Like File Manager, the Windows Explorer displays the hierarchy of subdirectories (called folders in Windows 95) as well as the contents of the selected folder. The Explorer window is divided into two panes as seen in Figure A.5. The left pane contains a tree diagram of the entire system, showing all drives and optionally the folders in each drive. One (and only one) object is always selected in the left pane and its contents are displayed automatically in the right pane.

You can change the view in the right pane just as you can in My Computer. You can also move or copy a file(s) by selecting the file(s) in the right pane, then dragging the selected file(s) to the destination folder in the left pane. (Windows 95 is consistent with Windows 3.1 with respect to selecting multiple files through the use of the Shift and Ctrl keys.) And don't forget the right mouse button. You can right click any file or folder to display a shortcut menu with commands appropriate for the selected object.

The Windows 95 Explorer is a significant improvement over File Manager, but there is one capability we miss. We would frequently open two directory windows in File Manager, then tile the open windows so that we could see the contents of both the source and destination directories. This is not possible in the Windows 95 Explorer. You can, however, open two copies of the Explorer at the same time, minimize all other open windows, then right click the Taskbar to tile the two Explorer windows. It's awkward, but it is the only way to see the contents of two folders simultaneously.

Contents of selected folder

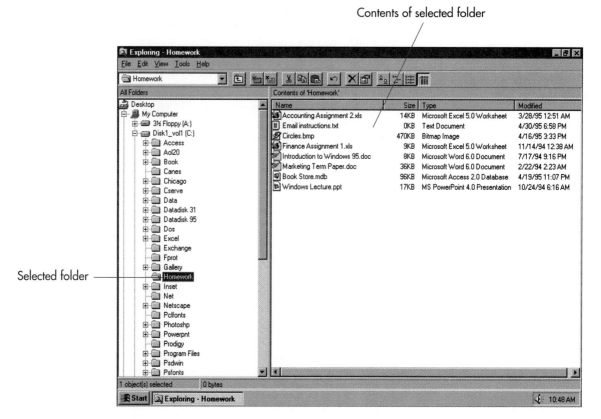

FIGURE A.5 Windows Explorer

TRY THIS:

Think of the Document, Not the Application

Windows 95 lets you create a document without having to load the associated application. Use My Computer or the Explorer to open the folder that is to contain the document, then right click an empty space within that folder. Click the New command in the resulting shortcut menu, then choose the type of document you want to create. (The list of document types reflects the applications installed on your system.) Once a document has been created, you can double click its icon to automatically load the associated application and open the document. In other words, you can think in terms of a document without thinking of the application.

Long File Names

Windows 95 allows file names of up to 255 characters (spaces are permitted but commas are not). Anyone using Windows 95 for the first time will take descriptive names such as *Accounting Assignment 2* for granted, but those familiar with Windows 3.1 will appreciate the improvement over the 8.3 DOS restriction (eight-character file name and optional three-character extension).

The DOS extensions are retained internally, but can be hidden at the user's discretion if a file is associated with an application. The Word for Windows document, *Introduction to Windows 95.doc* for example, can be displayed with or without the DOC extension according to the option specified through the View menu. (The extensions are hidden in Figure A.4 but displayed in Figure A.5.)

Windows 95 maintains compatibility with older applications that are unable to accommodate **long file names** by converting a long name to its DOS equivalent. Only the first eight characters are used, which leads to potential conflicts when shortening similar names; for example, *Term Paper for History* and *Term Paper for Marketing.* To resolve the conflict, Windows 95 adds a tilde (~) and a number to the DOS name, shortening the names to *Term P~1* and *Term P~2,* respectively.

TRY THIS:

Create a Long File Name

Use My Computer or the Windows Explorer to open a folder, then right click any file to display a shortcut menu. Select the Rename command, enter a name longer than eight characters (include the extension if it was shown originally), and press the enter key. Now double click the file icon to load the associated application and open the file. The title bar will show the name of the application and reflect the new file name (which includes a ~ if the application does not support long file names).

The Recycle Bin

The **Recycle Bin** is a special folder that contains all files previously deleted from any hard disk on the system. Think of the Recycle Bin as being similar to a wastebasket. You throw out (delete) a report by tossing it into a wastebasket. The report is gone (deleted) from your desk, but it can be recovered by taking it out of the wastebasket before the basket itself is emptied.

The Recycle Bin works the same way. Files are not deleted from the hard disk per se, but are moved to the Recycle Bin from where they can be recovered. The Recycle Bin should be emptied periodically or else you will run out of space on the disk. Once a file is removed from the Recycle Bin, it can no longer be recovered.

TRY THIS:

Recover a Deleted File

Use My Computer or the Windows Explorer to open a folder. Select (click the icon of) any document (be sure you have a backup copy), press the Del key, then click Yes when asked whether to delete the document. The file disappears from the folder. Double click the icon for the Recycle bin (on the desktop or within the Explorer), right click the icon of the deleted file, then click the Restore command from the shortcut menu. Return to the folder that you opened originally (you can click its button on the Taskbar if the folder was opened using My Computer), and the document is back in place.

Undo Command

How many times have you accidentally deleted, renamed, moved, or copied a file? Windows 95 enables you to recover from your mistake with a multilevel **Undo command** that reverses the effect of the last several commands. The Undo command is accessible from the Edit menu or by right clicking within the folder containing the affected file(s).

TRY THIS:

Multiple Level Undo

Use My Computer or the Windows Explorer to open a folder, then select any file in that folder. Click and drag the file icon to the desktop to copy the file. Right click the copied file in order to rename the file. Right click the file a second time and delete the renamed file. Now, right click anywhere on the desktop and undo the Delete command. Right click the desktop a second time and undo the Rename command. Right click the desktop a third and final time and undo the Copy command.

SHORTCUTS

Shortcuts are powerful tools that let you open a folder, drive, document, or application through a desktop icon, as opposed to going through a series of menus. Consider, for example, the desktop in Figure A.6, which contains a variety of different shortcuts. Two of the shortcuts are for applications (Excel and Word for Windows). Two are for documents associated with those applications (Modems.doc and 1040.xls). There is also a shortcut to drive A, a shortcut to the Homework folder, and a shortcut to the printer. All shortcuts are distinguished from other icons on the desktop by the **jump arrow** that is part of every shortcut icon.

All of the shortcuts provide a quick way to get to the indicated object. Double click the shortcut to Excel, for example, and you load Excel into memory without having to click the Start button and go through the associated menu(s). Double clicking a document shortcut is even quicker. Double click the shortcut to Modems.doc, for example, and it loads Word for Windows (the associated application), then opens the Modems document.

Double clicking a shortcut for a folder or drive opens the object and displays its contents. Double clicking the shortcut to the printer displays the printer queue (the jobs that are printing or awaiting printing) and lets you see the progress of a document as it is printed. You can then use the printer queue to change the priority of a pending job and/or cancel a job if you change your mind about printing. You can also drag a document icon to the shortcut for a printer to print the document without having to open it.

A Windows 95 shortcut corresponds to program icons in Windows 3.1. Thus, deleting a shortcut deletes just the shortcut and not the object to which the shortcut refers. Be sure, however, that the icon you are deleting is a shortcut icon and that it contains the jump arrow. Deleting an icon without the jump arrow deletes the actual file, which is *not* what you intend to do. This is a significant change from Windows 3.1, where deleting an icon in Program Manager deleted just the icon, and not the underlying file.

Jump arrows indicate shortcuts

Double click to load
Excel and open 1040.xls

Double click to open
Homework folder

FIGURE A.6   A More Powerful Desktop

TRY THIS:

Create a Shortcut

Creating a shortcut is a two-step process. First you use My Computer or the Windows Explorer to locate the object (a program, document, folder, disk drive, or printer) for which you want a shortcut. Then you click and drag the object with the right mouse button to the desktop, release the mouse, and click the Create Shortcut command. A shortcut icon will appear on the desktop with the phrase "shortcut to" as part of the name. To create a shortcut to the Control Panel, for example, just right click and drag the Control Panel icon from within My Computer to the desktop.

IMPROVED CONTROL PANEL

The ***Control Panel*** in Windows 95 has been expanded in order to group all configuration functions in a single location. The Control Panel can be accessed in several ways, most easily from within My Computer.

Figure A.7 displays the Control Panel as it is implemented on our system. The precise number of icons (tools) within Control Panel depend on the installed devices. You will not, for example, see the Mail and Fax icon unless you have installed the Microsoft Exchange.

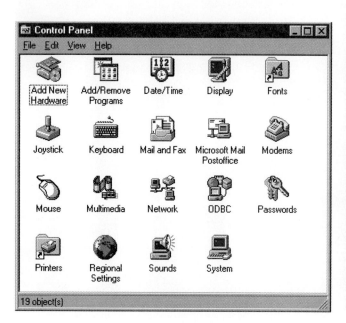

(a) The Control Panel

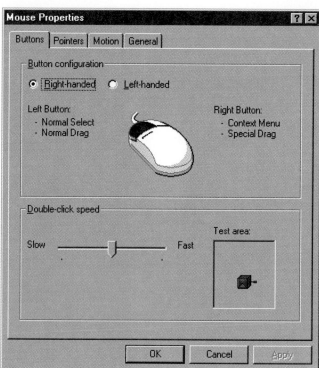

(b) Mouse Settings

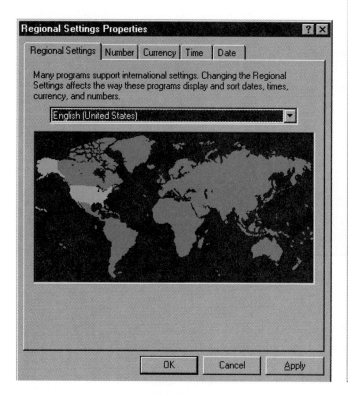

(c) Regional Settings

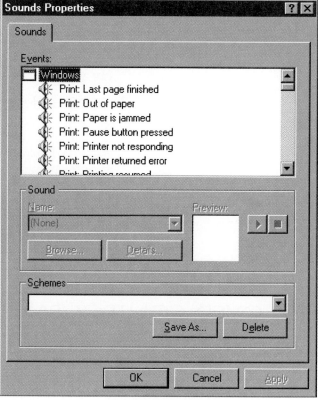

(d) Sound Settings

FIGURE A.7   An Improved Control Panel

Each of the icons within the control panel enables you to change the settings of the associated item. Figures A.7b, A.7c, and A.7d display the property sheets for the Mouse, Regional Settings, and Sounds, respectively. Each property sheet contains multiple tabs with settings as indicated. To change a setting, click the appropriate tab, enter the new setting, then click OK to accept the new setting(s) and exit the dialog box.

The Add New Hardware and Add/Remove Program icons are especially useful. Clicking either icon will take you to a wizard, which prompts you for the necessary information, then performs the indicated task automatically.

TRY THIS:

Create a Font Sampler

Open the Control Panel and double click the Fonts folder to display the fonts available on your system. Right click the icon for any font, click the Print command in the resulting shortcut menu, then click OK to print the selected font. You will get a one-page printed sample of the font, which shows every character in the font together with printed samples of varying point sizes. Select and print additional fonts, then keep the printed samples as a guide for your next desktop publishing project.

SUMMARY

This appendix described the Windows 95 interface from the viewpoint of an individual knowledgeable in Windows 3.1. The most important design criterion for Windows 95 was to make the PC easier to use. The need for a simpler interface became evident during extensive usability testing of Windows 3.1. Microsoft learned that the computer novice was confused by Program Manager, had difficulty finding and launching applications, and typically did not take advantage of multitasking. The result was a simplified desktop with the Start button and Taskbar.

Another finding of the usability study was that much of the Windows 3.1 population did not use File Manager because its dual pane and hierarchical view were too intimidating. This led to the introduction of the My Computer browsing model, which opens a new window for each successive folder. Windows 95 also provides the Windows Explorer, an improved version of the Windows 3.1 File Manager. A beginner will prefer My Computer, whereas a more sophisticated user will opt for the Explorer.

The Windows 95 interface is not only easier than its predecessor, but it is significantly more powerful. The context-sensitive right mouse button enables you to right click any object and display a shortcut menu or property sheet. The Recycle bin lets you recover a deleted file. The multilevel Undo command enables you to recover from unintended move, copy, or rename operations. Long file names (up to 255 characters) are a significant improvement over the DOS 8.3 naming convention.

Shortcuts are analogous to Windows 3.1 program icons and provide immediate access to a program, document, or device. The expanded Control Panel provides access to all configuration settings in a single location. The Add New Hardware and Add/Remove Program icons simplify the installation of new hardware and software.

Close button	Network Neighborhood	Shortcut menu
Control Panel	Programs menu	Shut Down command
Documents menu	Properties sheet	Start button
Find command	Recycle Bin	Tabbed dialog box
Help facility	Right click	Taskbar
Jump arrow	Run command	Undo command
Long file names	Settings menu	What's This button
My Computer	Shortcut	Windows Explorer

APPENDIX B:
A PC BUYING GUIDE

OVERVIEW

Are you confused about all the ads for personal computers? You can buy from hundreds of companies, retail or through the mail, with no such thing as a standard configuration. The microprocessor can be one of many 486 or Pentium chips, each of which can be configured with any amount of memory. You can select a desktop, tower, or notebook configuration. You can choose a variety of monitors in different sizes, and can input data from one of many keyboards, a mouse, a trackball, or even a touch screen. Hard disks run up to 1GB or more. There are fax/modem cards, sound cards, tape backup units, and CD-ROM devices.

The personal computer has, in effect, become a commodity where the consumer is able to select the individual elements in the configuration. And, as with the purchase of any other big-ticket item, you must understand what you are buying, so that the decision you make is right for you. This appendix will familiarize you with the components in a computer system so that you can select the machine best suited to your needs and budget.

DON'T FORGET THE SOFTWARE

Any machine you buy will come with Windows 95, but that is only the beginning since you must also purchase the application software you intend to run. Many first-time buyers are surprised that they have to pay extra for software, but you had better allow for software in your budget. A software suite, purchased at an educational discount through the university bookstore, is generally your best bet. The software is at least as important as the hardware, because it is the software that drives the hardware and determines how successful a system will be in meeting your objectives.

THE PERSONAL COMPUTER

The personal computer is a marvel of miniaturization and technology. We take it for granted, but the IBM PC, which jump-started the industry, is just a teenager. IBM announced the PC in 1981 (three years after the Apple II) and broke a long-standing corporate tradition by going to external sources for supporting hardware and software. The *microprocessor* inside the PC was produced by *Intel Corporation.* The operating system was developed by *Microsoft Corporation.*

In terms of today's capabilities, IBM's initial offering was hardly spectacular. A fully loaded system with two floppy disk drives (a hard disk was not available), monochrome monitor, and 80 cps (character per second) dot matrix printer sold for $4425. Software was practically nonexistent. Lotus 1-2-3 had not yet been released, and WordPerfect was a little-known program not yet modified to run on the PC. Yet the PC, with little software and limited hardware, was an instant success for two reasons. The IBM name, and its reputation for quality and service, meant that corporate America could order the machine and be assured that it would perform as promised.

Of equal, or even greater, significance, was the PC's open design, which meant that independent vendors could offer supporting products to enhance performance. This was accomplished through *expansion slots* that held additional circuit boards that added functionality to the basic PC. IBM made public the technical information to create *expansion cards* (also knows as adapters) so that other companies could build peripherals for the PC, thus enhancing its capabilities. Today you can purchase expansion cards that add sound, increase the number of colors, resolution, and speed of the monitor, or add peripheral devices such as CD-ROMs and tape-backup units that did not exist when the PC was introduced.

PC-compatibles, computers based on the same microprocessor and able to run the same software, began to appear as early as 1982 and offered superior performance for less money. Companies and individuals who were once willing to pay a premium for the IBM name began ordering the "same" machine from other vendors. PC has become a generic term for any computer based on Intel-compatible microprocessors and capable of running Microsoft Windows.

Figure B.1 illustrates a typical Windows workstation. We view the system from the front (Figure B.1a), the rear (Figure B.1b), and from inside the system unit (Figure B.1c). Your system will be different from ours, but you should be able to recognize the various components as they are discussed in this appendix. Whether you choose a desktop or tower for your system unit, or whether you purchase a laptop or notebook computer, you will have to decide on each component of your system.

LET YOUR FINGERS DO THE WALKING

A single issue of a computer magazine contains advertisements from many vendors, making it possible to comparison shop from multiple mail-order vendors from the convenience of home. Computer magazines are also the source of the latest technical information, and thus a subscription to a magazine is a must for the serious user. Our three favorites (*PC Computing, PC Magazine,* and *Windows Magazine*) are found on most newsstands.

THE MICROPROCESSOR

The capability of a PC depends in large part on the microprocessor on which it is based. Intel microprocessors are currently in their fifth generation, with each

(a) Front View

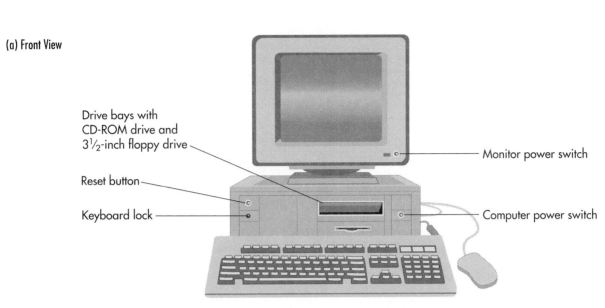

Drive bays with
CD-ROM drive and
3½-inch floppy drive

Reset button

Keyboard lock

Monitor power switch

Computer power switch

(b) Rear View

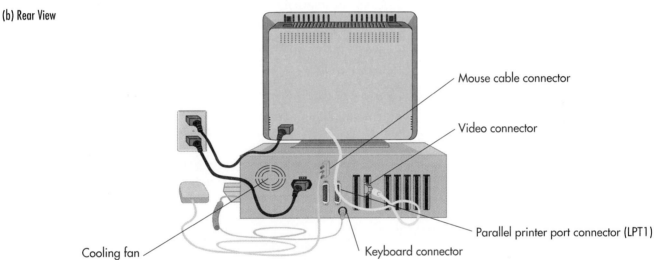

Mouse cable connector

Video connector

Parallel printer port connector (LPT1)

Cooling fan

Keyboard connector

Rear of computer

(c) Inside the Computer

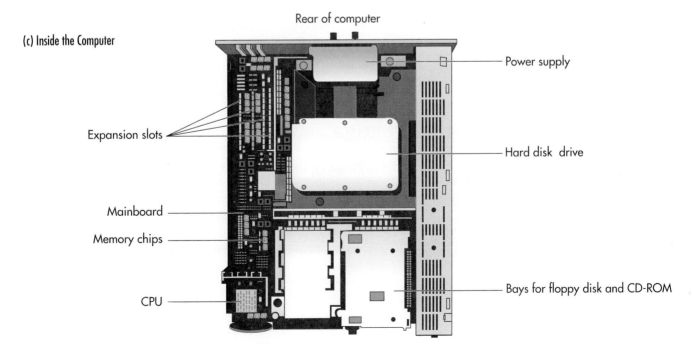

Power supply

Expansion slots

Hard disk drive

Mainboard

Memory chips

Bays for floppy disk and CD-ROM

CPU

FIGURE B.1   The Windows Workstation

generation giving rise to increasingly powerful personal computers. All generations are upward compatible; that is, software written for one generation will automatically run on the next. This upward compatibility is crucial because it protects your investment in software when you upgrade to a faster computer.

Today's purchase decision comes down to a fourth or fifth generation microprocessor, either a 486 or a 586 (e.g., a Pentium), as the earlier generations are obsolete. The 486 is manufactured by several companies beside Intel (e.g., AMD or Cyrix). A Pentium, however, is available only from Intel, because Intel has trademarked the Pentium name to differentiate its product from the competition. 586 chips, without the Pentium name, are available from other vendors.

Each generation has multiple microprocessors, which are differentiated by *clock speed,* an indication of how fast instructions are executed. Clock speed is measured in ***megahertz (MHz).*** The higher the clock speed, the faster the machine. There can also be different versions of a microprocessor at the same clock speed; for example, the SX microprocessor is a less powerful chip than the corresponding DX version.

Intel has also created the DX2 series of chips that double the clock speed of the microprocessor for internal calculations. The DX2/66, for example, is really a 33MHz chip that runs at 66MHz internally, but communicates with other components (e.g., memory) at 33MHz. And finally, Intel has trademarked the DX4 designation to indicate a clock tripling of its 486 chips; for example the DX4/75 is a 25MHz chip that runs internally at 75MHz but communicates with the other components at 25MHz.

Fortunately, however, the technical specifications of the individual microprocessors are not important here. What is important is their relative performance to one another as measured by the ***Intel CPU performance index.*** The index consists of a single number to indicate the relative performance of a microprocessor: the higher the number, the faster the processor. Figure B.2 displays the index values for selected Intel microprocessors (the index does not include Intel-compatible microprocessors manufactured by other vendors). This is the table to use when you are selecting a computer because you want to purchase the fastest machine that you can afford.

Any comparison of one machine to another—for example, an IBM PC to one made by Zeos or Gateway—must be based on the identical microprocessor, or else the comparison will not be valid. Realize, too, that machines based on different microprocessors should reflect a price differential. You would, for example, expect to pay more for a Pentium running at 90 MHz than you would for the same chip running at 66MHz.

CPU	Index Rating
Pentium (166 MHz)	1,308
Pentium (150 MHz)	1,176
Pentium (133 MHz)	1,110
Pentium (120 MHz)	1,000
Pentium (100 MHz)	815
Pentium (90 MHz)	735
Pentium (75 MHz)	610
Pentium (66 MHz)	567
Pentium (60 MHz)	510
486 DX4 (100 MHz)	435
486 DX4 (75 MHz)	319
486 DX2 (66 MHz)	297
486 DX2 (50 MHz)	231
486 DX (33 MHz)	166
486 SX (33 MHz)	136
486 DX (25 MHz)	122
486 SX (25 MHz)	100
386 DX (33 MHz)	68
386 SX (25 MHz)	49

FIGURE B.2   CPU Performance Index

THE MICROPROCESSOR—PAST, PRESENT, AND FUTURE

The IBM PC was based on the 8088 microprocessor, which had the equivalent of 29,000 transistors and was capable of 333,000 instructions per second. Today's Pentium has the equivalent of 3 million transistors and is capable of more than 100,000,000 instructions per second. If the increase in capability continues to hold, and there is every reason to believe that it will, then a 100,000,000 transistor chip, capable of two billion instructions per second, is possible by the year 2000.

The microprocessor is the brain of the PC, but it needs instructions that tell it what to do, data on which to work, and a place to store the results of its calculations. All of this takes place in *memory,* a temporary storage area that holds data, instructions, and results, and passes everything back and forth to the CPU. The amount of memory a system has is important because the larger the memory, the more sophisticated the programs are that the computer is capable of executing, and the more data it can work with.

The *memory* of a computer (also known as *random access memory* or *RAM*) is made up of individual storage locations, each of which holds the same amount of data, one *byte* or one character. In the early days of the PC, memory was measured in *kilobytes (KB).* Today memory is measured in *megabytes (MB).* One KB and one MB are equal to approximately one thousand and one million characters, respectively. (In actuality, 1KB equals 1024 bytes, or 2^{10} bytes, whereas 1MB is 1,048,576 bytes, or 2^{20} bytes.)

A computer's memory is volatile (temporary), and its contents are erased when the power is off. Hence a computer also needs a permanent means of storage that can retain data without power.

DON'T SKIMP ON MEMORY

The more memory a system has, the better its overall performance. Windows and its associated applications are powerful indeed, but they require adequate resources to run efficiently. 8MB of RAM is the minimum you should consider in today's environment, but you should anticipate a future upgrade. Be sure the system you buy can accommodate additional memory easily and inexpensively.

AUXILIARY STORAGE

Unlike memory, magnetic disks are permanent storage devices that retain their contents when the power is off. Disks fall into two categories—*floppy disks* and *hard disks.* A hard disk is also known as a fixed disk because it remains permanently inside the system unit. The floppy disk gets its name because it is made of a flexible Mylar plastic. The hard disk uses rigid metal platters.

A hard disk holds significantly more data than a floppy disk, and it accesses that data much faster. Hard disks are rated by capacity and access time. Capacity is measured in megabytes, and in today's environment you should not purchase any system with less than 750MB of disk space. The *access time* is the time in milliseconds that a disk needs to locate and begin retrieving data. The smaller the access time, the faster the disk, and the more expensive.

The hard disk connects to the motherboard with one of three interfaces: IDE (Integrated Drive Electronics), ESDI (Enhanced Small Device Interface), or SCSI

(Small Computer System Interface). We mention this only because you are likely to see these initials in any advertisement that you read. The IDE technology is the cheapest and most common and more than adequate for the typical Windows user.

A floppy disk (and the corresponding drive) comes in two sizes, 3½ and 5¼ inches. The latter is nearly obsolete and no longer a consideration. The capacity of a 3½ floppy disk is either 720KB or 1.44MB, depending on whether the disk is double density or high density. A **high-density drive** (the only kind you can buy today) can read either a **double-density disk** or a high-density disk. We suggest, however, that you use high-density disks exclusively.

MASS STORAGE: BUY MORE THAN YOU NEED

Windows 95 takes approximately 15 MB of disk space and requires another 20 to 30MB for a swap file. The typical Windows application takes approximately 10 to 15MB of disk space. Multimedia applications require even more. The best advice, therefore, is to buy a bigger disk than you think you need. *A 750MB disk is a minimum.* You should also check that the system unit has room for a second hard disk that can be added in the future.

VIDEO

The video system consists of the monitor and display adapter (video card). The first consideration is the **resolution** of the monitor, which is defined in terms of **pixels** (the tiny dots or *pic*ture *ele*ments that make up a picture). Resolution is stated as the number of pixels across by the number down; for example, **VGA** is 640 across by 480 down. **Super VGA,** another common resolution, is 800 pixels across by 600 pixels down. The higher the resolution, the more of the document (or spreadsheet) you can see at one time.

Any image at a given resolution always contains the same number of pixels; for example, a Windows screen in Super VGA (800 × 600) contains 480,000 pixels regardless of the size of the monitor on which it is displayed. The advantage to the larger monitor is that the individual pixels are bigger and thus the image on the screen is easier to read. The advantage of the higher resolution is that more pixels are displayed and hence you see more on the screen at one time—for example, more columns in a spreadsheet or more pages in a word processing document. Figure B.3 lists the available resolutions with the recommended size of the monitor.

The desired resolution and monitor size are selected in conjunction with one another, so that the image displayed on a screen can be easily read. It would be foolish, for example, to display a 1024 × 768 image on a 14-inch screen because the individual pixels would be too small and the display unreadable. Higher resolutions demand bigger monitors, which are significantly more expensive.

The **video (display) adapter** is a separate card that is placed in an expansion slot within the system unit. The video card accepts information from the CPU (central processing unit) and sends it to the monitor, which displays the image. For best performance, the video card should have its own processing capability in the form of an accelerator chip. This enables the CPU to perform other tasks while the image is displayed, thus improving the overall performance of the system. The video card should also have its own memory. A minimum of 1MB is suggested but 2MB is preferable.

Resolution	Number of Pixels	Minimum Screen Size
640 × 480 (VGA)	307,200	14 inches
800 × 600 (Super VGA)	480,000	15 inches
1024 × 768 (Extended VGA)	782,462	17 inches
1280 × 1024	1,310,720	19 inches

FIGURE B.3   Resolution and Monitor Size

THE FINER POINTS OF CHOOSING A MONITOR

Do some monitors produce a sharper, crisper picture than others, even at the same resolution? Does the image on one monitor appear to flicker while the image on another remains constant? The differences are due to information that is often buried in the fine print of an advertisement

The *dot pitch* is the distance between adjacent pixels. The smaller the dot pitch, the crisper the image; or conversely, the larger the dot pitch, the more grainy the picture. Choose a monitor with a dot pitch of .28 or less.

The *vertical refresh rate* determines how frequently the screen is repainted from top to bottom. A rate that is too slow causes the screen to flicker because it is not being redrawn fast enough to fool the eye into seeing a constant pattern. A rate of 70Hz (70 cycles per second) is the minimum you should accept.

A *noninterlaced monitor* repaints every line whenever the electron gun moves down the screen. An interlaced monitor scans every other line; all even lines are drawn on the first pass and all odd lines on the next pass. An interlaced monitor is *unacceptable* in today's environment because the pixels have more time to fade and thus flicker is more common.

THE LOCAL BUS

The *bus* is the circuitry on the motherboard that provides the path by which data travels from one component to another. (The motherboard, or system board, is the main board within the system unit that holds the microprocessor, memory, and adapter cards.) All peripheral devices—including the hard disk, video display adapter, and printer—transmit data along the same bus. As you might expect, the more data that is traveling within the system, the more crowded the bus, and like any highway, bottlenecks will occur if traffic moves too slowly.

Older PCs used the *ISA (Industry Standard Architecture)* bus, which was 16 bits wide and ran at 8MHz. The ISA bus was sufficient in the early days of the PC with low-speed devices and low data requirements, but it proved inadequate in the Windows environment with its high graphic requirements. The constant need to refresh the screen, especially with displays that rendered 256 colors (or more), overwhelmed the ISA bus and slowed the overall system. The problem with the ISA bus is twofold—it runs at 8MHz (regardless of the speed of the microprocessor), and it fails to take advantage of the 32-bit path available with 80386 (and higher) microprocessors.

To solve the problem, the industry created a second bus called the *video local bus (VLB),* which is 32 bits wide and runs at the speed of the microprocessor. Equally important, the VLB bus connects the microprocessor directly to the video display adapter, which no longer has to share the ISA bus with other devices.

Think of the new bus as a super highway where traffic goes directly from one place to another, with a higher speed limit (the speed of the microprocessor versus 8MHz), and has twice as many lanes (32 bits versus 16) as previously.

Intel has recently designed the PCI bus in conjunction with the Pentium processor. Either a VLB or PCI bus is standard on today's machines, and you should not consider a system without one or the other. Both designs also support other high-speed devices (e.g., a fixed disk). Look for a system that offers multiple local bus slots on the motherboard.

PRINTERS

Printers vary greatly in terms of design, price, and capability, with dot matrix, ink jet, and laser printers the most common in today's environment. The type of printer you choose depends on your budget and the quality of output you require.

A ***dot matrix printer*** represents the oldest technology and is the least expensive. These printers produce an image on paper by driving a series of small pins against a ribbon. They create letters, numbers, symbols, and/or graphics out of a series of dots, and can print any shape at all depending on the accompanying software. The disadvantage to a dot matrix printer is the less than perfect print quality since its characters are formed as a pattern of dots. The introduction of the 24-pin print head (in place of the 9-pin version used in earlier models) has improved the quality of output but has done nothing to reduce the noise level.

The ***inkjet printer*** offers improved speed and print quality over a dot matrix printer. It is also quiet since the ink is squirted onto the page rather than hammered onto it as with the dot matrix. The purchase price is slightly higher than a dot matrix printer, but it is well worth the investment.

Laser printers are the top-of-the-line devices, and have created new expectations in terms of print quality, speed, and quietness of operation. They produce consistently dense characters and graphics, suitable for both reports and presentations. The resolution of a laser printer is measured in dots per inch (dpi). Laser printer speed is measured in pages per minute (ppm). Entry-level laser printers at 600 dpi and 4 ppm are available for approximately $600 in today's environment.

FAX/MODEM

A ***modem*** connects your computer to the outside world, be it an information service such as Prodigy or CompuServe, or your friend two blocks away. All means of data communications process data in its most elementary form, as a series of electronic pulses represented numerically as ***bits*** (***bi***nary digi***ts***). Every message transmitted by a computer, be it words, numbers, or pictures, is broken down into a series of 1s and 0s, which are sent over the transmission medium. The telephone uses an analog signal, whereas a computer uses a digital signal and thus some type of conversion is necessary.

Modulation is the process of converting a digital signal to an analog one; demodulation is the reverse process. A modem (derived from the combination of modulate and demodulate) performs both functions. On the transmitting end, a modem converts binary signals (1s and 0s) produced by the computer to analog signals, which can be sent over the telephone system. On the receiving end, the modem converts the analog signal from the telephone back to a digital signal, which is forwarded to the computer or peripheral device.

The speed of a modem—that is, the maximum rate at which it can transmit or receive data—is measured in ***bits per second (bps).*** A 14,400 bps modem is standard in today's environment. A 28,800 bps modem is more expensive but will return savings in the form of lower communications costs as you will be transmitting for shorter periods of time. A *fax/modem* combines the functions of a modem and a fax machine into a single card and is our recommendation for you.

CD-ROM

The data on a compact disk can be read, but it cannot be erased, hence the name *CD-ROM,* for Compact Disk/Read Only Memory. A single CD-ROM holds approximately 650MB of data, making it an ideal medium for the mass distribution of data and absolutely essential for multimedia applications.

The performance of a CD-ROM is measured by two parameters, access time and transfer rate. *Access time* is the average time to find a specific item (the smaller, the better). *Transfer rate* is the amount of data that is read every second (the higher, the better).

The first CD-ROM drives for the PC had access times of approximately 600 milliseconds (ms) and transfer rates of approximately 150KB per second. As with all technology, both parameters have improved significantly. A double-speed drive (300 ms access time and 300KB/sec transfer rate) is already obsolete, as quadruple-speed devices (150 ms access time and 600 KB/second transfer rate) are today's standard. Six-speed CD-ROMs are becoming increasingly common.

AUDIO

The standard PC comes with a simple speaker that is capable of little more than a beep, which you hear when you press the wrong key. True sound requires the installation of a sound card and the availability of speakers. A microphone is necessary if you want to record your own sound.

A *sound card* has two basic functions—to play a previously recorded sound and to record a new sound. Thus every sound card contains (a minimum of) two chips. One chip converts the sound from a microphone to a digital form the PC can store on disk. The second chip works in reverse and translates a digital file into sound. More sophisticated (and more expensive) *audio cards* include additional capabilities, such as voice recognition, that enable you to talk to your computer and have it respond to your commands.

If you intend to run multimedia applications, look for a sound card that supports wave table synthesis (as opposed to older cards that used a technique known as FM synthesis). A wave table produces higher-quality musical notes because it stores samples of actual instruments, then uses those samples to reproduce the music. And don't forget the speakers. No matter how good your sound card, you will be disappointed if you don't have a correspondingly good pair of speakers.

RESOLUTION AND SAMPLING RATE

The specifications of a sound card include its resolution and maximum sampling rate. The resolution is the number of bits (binary digits) used to store each sample. The more bits, the better. Eight-bit cards are obsolete, making 16-bit sound today's standard. The sampling rate is the number of samples per second and is measured in KHz (thousands of samples a second). The higher the sampling rate, the better. CD-quality recording and playback requires a sampling rate of 44KHz.

The purchase of a computer should be approached in much the same way as any other big-ticket item and requires similar research and planning. First and foremost, do not walk into a computer store without some idea of your hardware requirements, or you will spend too much or buy the wrong system. Know the technical specifications in advance, in order to ask intelligent questions about the various brands and systems. Stick to your requirements and don't be swayed to a different item if the vendor is out of stock. You've waited this long to buy a computer and another week or two won't matter.

The best place to start is often the university's computer center, which may allow a local vendor or manufacturer(s) to maintain a store on the premises. The university will use its buying power to secure a favorable price or educational discount, and the promise of additional business guarantees continuing service and support. In addition, people you know will purchase similar equipment, which means additional sources of help later on. Alternatively, you may consider the retail store (be it local or part of a national chain) or mail order. Either or both may be appropriate, and you may avail yourself of both sources, at different times and for different equipment.

CHECK OUT A NOTEBOOK BEFORE YOU BUY

The purchase of a notebook computer has additional considerations beyond those of a desktop configuration—weight, size, battery life, keyboard, and screen. Is the computer light enough so that you won't leave it behind when you travel? Is the life of the battery sufficient to accomplish what you need to do? Can you type comfortably on the keyboard over long periods of time? Is the screen readable in different levels of light? Is the hard disk large enough to accommodate all of your applications? Does it have a modem so that you can communicate when you take the machine on the road? Be sure to see the machine and test it before you buy so that you won't be disappointed later.

Mail order will almost always offer better prices than a retail establishment, but price should not be the sole consideration. Local service and support are also important, especially if you are a nontechnical new user. A little research, however, and you can purchase through the mail with confidence, and save yourself money in the process. A good way to choose a vendor, mail-order or retail, is to ask your friends where they purchased their systems, because a satisfied customer is always the best recommendation.

If you buy by mail, confirm all orders in writing, stating exactly what you are expecting to receive and when. Include the specific brands and/or model numbers and the agreed-upon price, including shipping and handling, to have documentation in the event of a dispute. State that the seller is not to deviate from the terms in your letter without prior written agreement.

Look for a steady advertising history by the mail-order firm, searching back issues of the magazine to see if the company has been in business over time. Avoid companies that appear to be in financial difficulty; for example, a company that previously ran four-page full-color ads and now runs a half-page, black-and-white advertisement. Check out service in advance, by calling the toll-free technical support number to determine the level of service you can expect. You might also inquire about the cost of on-site service. If you buy locally, try to choose a vendor with an on-site facility.

Pay with a credit card that offers a buyer protection plan to double the manufacturer's warranty (up to an additional year). The use of a credit card also gives you additional leverage if you are dissatisfied with an item. If you are purchasing by mail, make sure the charge is not entered until you receive the merchandise. Do not buy from anyone, retail store or mail order, that insists all sales are final, that offers a store credit in lieu of a refund, or that charges a restocking fee on returned items. Settle for nothing less than a no-strings-attached, 30-day, money-back guarantee, and be sure the vendor guarantees in writing a rebate if the price goes down within 30 days.

Make bundling (unbundling) work for you by obtaining credit for substituted items—for example, a name-brand monitor in place of the vendor's off-brand monitor, which often sacrifices quality for price. Software bundling may or may not be a good deal; for example, Windows should be included, but you may not need the application software; ask for credit if you don't take it. Conversely, bundled software may be a good deal if you don't already have the application.

Our experience has been that the vast majority of dealers, both retail and mail order, are reputable; but as with any purchase, *caveat emptor*. Good luck and good shopping.

BE KIND TO YOURSELF

Are you the type of person who will spend thousands on a new computer, only to set it up on your regular desk and sit on a $10 bridge chair? Don't. A conventional desk (or the dining room table) is 30 inches high, but the recommended typing height is 27 inches. The difference accounts for the stiff neck, tight shoulders, and aching backs reported by many people who sit at a computer over an extended period of time. Be kind to yourself and include a computer table with lots of room as well as a comfortable chair in your budget. Proper lighting is essential.

CAN YOU READ A COMPUTER AD?

This is not a regular chapter and as such does not have the exercises you have seen throughout the text. Nevertheless, we think it worthwhile to leave you with an examination of sorts, that of Figure B.4, which displays a typical computer advertisement to see whether you can read between the lines.

The prices in the ad are not important per se; after all, they will only go down and may well be obsolete by the time our book is in print. In similar fashion, the capabilities in the ad will only increase, and may be dwarfed by what is available in the future. The format of the ad, however, is fairly typical and indicative of what you are likely to see. Accordingly, see if you can answer the following questions, based only on this appendix and the information in the ad:

1. What is the minimum configuration (as recommended by the authors) for running Windows? How much does it cost?
2. What are the major differences between packages 2 and 3? between packages 3 and 4?

	Package 1 8MB RAM, 500MB hard drive, 14-inch NI monitor	Package 2 8MB RAM, 750MB hard drive, 15-inch NI monitor 4X CD-ROM	Package 3 16MB RAM, 1GB hard drive, 15-inch NI monitor 4X CD-ROM	Package 4 24MB RAM, 2GB hard drive, 17-inch NI monitor 6X CD-ROM
Pentium-75	$1595	$1995	$2395	$2895
Pentium-100	$1795	$2195	$2595	$3095
Pentium-120	$1995	$2395	$2795	$3295
Pentium-133	$2195	$2595	$2995	$3495
Pentium-166	$2495	$2895	$3295	$3795

Standard on all systems: 3.5" 1.44MB floppy drive, two PCI and five ISA expansion slots, a video accelerator card with 2MB of video memory, mouse, 101 keyboard, Windows 95, one-year warranty. All systems are expandable to 192MB RAM. All CD-ROMs are shipped with a sound card and speakers.

Standard on packages 3 and 4: Microsoft Office Professional

FIGURE B.4   Can You Read a Computer Ad?

3. What premium is the vendor charging for a Pentium-100 microprocessor? For a Pentium-120 processor? For a Pentium 166 processor?
4. How much memory is offered in the most powerful configuration? Can the memory be expanded beyond the current offering?
5. Which configurations will support multimedia applications?
6. Will the user be comfortable running at 1024 by 768 with packages 2 or 3?
7. Can a second hard drive and/or tape backup unit be added to all configurations?
8. Is Windows bundled with all configurations? Which application programs, if any, are bundled in the various offerings?
9. What additional component (if any) do you need to add in order to use e-mail?
10. What warranty does the vendor offer? How can you extend the warranty at no additional cost?
11. What additional costs can you expect to incur that are not mentioned in the ad?
12. What is the vendor's return policy?

DON'T BE FRUSTRATED WHEN PRICES DROP

The system you buy today will invariably cost less tomorrow. To add insult to injury, tomorrow's machine will run circles around today's most powerful system. The IBM/XT, with an 8088 microprocessor, a 10MB hard disk, 128KB of RAM, and monochrome monitor, sold for $5,000 in 1983; today you can buy a Pentium processor with 16 MB of memory, a 1GB hard drive, a 15-inch Super VGA monitor, a quad-speed CD-ROM, and a sound card, all for less than $2500. The point of this example is that you should enjoy the machine you buy today without concern for what it will cost tomorrow.

The open design of the PC enabled companies other than IBM to build a functionally equivalent PC-compatible; IBM today has only ten percent of the market it was so instrumental in creating. Intel and Microsoft, IBM's original partners, continue to dominate their respective areas.

The capability of a PC is determined by the microprocessor on which it is based. The relative performances of the various Intel microprocessors are provided in Figure B.2.

The more memory in a system, the better its overall performance; we recommend a minimum of 8MB. The best advice regarding a hard disk is to buy one larger than you think you need; a 750MB hard disk is our suggested minimum, but larger disks are well worth the investment.

The resolution of a system is the number of pixels displayed on the monitor; the higher the resolution, the greater the detail and the larger the supporting monitor should be. The performance of the video adapter can be improved significantly with an accelerator card.

The ISA (Industry Standard Architecture) bus is 16 bits wide, runs at 8MHz, and is shared by all peripheral devices. The video local bus (VLB) is 32 bits wide, runs at the speed of the microprocessor, and is dedicated to the video display adapter.

The purchase of a computer should be approached in much the same way as any other "big-ticket" item. Mail order will almost always offer better prices than a retail establishment, but local service and support may outweigh price considerations for first-time buyers.

The price of software must be included in the budget for a computer system. A software suite, purchased at an educational discount through the university bookstore, is generally your best bet.

The purchase of a laptop computer has additional considerations beyond those of a desktop configuration: weight, size, battery life, keyboard, and screen.

OUR RECOMMENDATION

As technology continues to advance, yesterday's top-of-the-line system has become today's entry-level computer. We recommend, therefore, that you settle for nothing less than a Pentium 75MHz processor with 8MB of RAM, a 750MB hard disk, quad-speed CD-ROM with 16-bit sound card, a 15-inch monitor with .28 dot pitch, and a 14,400 bps modem. If your budget can stand it, go beyond this configuration to buy a faster CPU, more memory, a larger disk drive, and a faster modem.

KEY WORDS AND CONCEPTS

Access time	Byte	Double-density disk
Audio card	CD-ROM	Expansion card
Bit	Clock speed	Expansion slot
Bits per second (bps)	Dot matrix printer	Fax/modem card
Bus	Dot pitch	Floppy disk

Hard disk
High-density drive
Inkjet printer
Intel Corporation
Intel CPU performance
    index
ISA (Industry Standard
    Architecture)
Kilobyte (KB)
Laser printer

Local bus
Megabyte (MB)
Megahertz (MHz)
Memory
Microprocessor
Microsoft Corporation
Modem
Noninterlaced monitor
PC-compatible
Pixel

Random access
    memory (RAM)
RAM
Resolution
Sound card
Super VGA
Transfer rate
Vertical refresh rate
VGA
Video adapter

APPENDIX C: INTRODUCTION TO MULTIMEDIA

C

OVERVIEW

Multimedia combines the text and graphic capability of the PC with high-quality sound and video. The combination of different media, under the control of the PC, has opened up a new world of education and entertainment. The uses of multimedia are limited only by the imagination. Hundreds of applications already exist, with new ones added on a daily basis.

Multimedia is possible only because of recent advances in technology that include faster microprocessors, the CD-ROM, and sophisticated sound and video boards. But how fast a microprocessor do you really need? What type of CD-ROM and sound card should you consider? Questions abound and we begin, therefore, with a discussion of hardware requirements as stated by the Multimedia PC Marketing Council, which publishes a recognized multimedia standard.

This appendix also explains the basic concepts underlying a multimedia application. We describe the file types associated with multimedia applications and the necessity for file compression. We focus on the multimedia capabilities within Windows 95 and end with a hands-on exercise that enables you to experiment with these capabilities.

THE MULTIMEDIA COMPUTER

A few years ago multimedia was an extra. Today it is a virtual standard, and you are well advised to buy a system with multimedia built in. But what exactly constitutes a multimedia computer? The answer is critical to both the consumer and the developer.

The consumer wants a system that is capable of running "typical" multimedia applications. The developer, on the other hand, wants to appeal to the widest possible audience and must write an application so that it runs on the "typical" configuration. To guide developers, and to let the public know the specific hardware required, the Multimedia PC Marketing Council (MPC) established a minimum specification for a multimedia computer as shown in Table C.1.

The first standard *(MPC-1)* was published in 1991 and had as its objective, a system retailing for less than $2,000. A second standard *(MPC-2)* was published in 1993 and was also based on a retail price of $2,000. The MPC-3 standard was published in 1995 and again fell within the $2,000 guideline.

If your budget can afford it, you may want to go beyond the minimum configuration to a faster microprocessor, more memory, and a larger hard drive. Don't forget to include speakers to amplify the sound, a microphone if you want to record your own sounds, and a joystick for games. (See Appendix B: A PC Buying Guide for additional information on CD-ROMs and sound cards.) And finally, be sure to buy a modem so that you will be able to download sound and movie clips.

THE MULTIMEDIA UPGRADE

Computer magazines are filled with advertisements for multimedia upgrades, kits that contain a sound card and CD-ROM, but are they worth the investment? If you already have Windows 95 and a modem, and if your existing system meets our other minimum requirements, a 486/66 processor, 8MB of RAM, and a 750 MB disk, by all means upgrade. If, on the other hand, you're lacking one or more of these components, you are better off waiting until you are ready to replace the entire system. And one final piece of advice if you do decide to upgrade: Installing a CD-ROM and sound card on an existing system is not easy! Purchase the upgrade at a local store and have a professional do it for you.

TABLE C.1   The Multimedia PC

	MPC-1 (1991)	MPC-2 (1993)	MPC-3 (1995)
CPU	80386 16MHz	80486SX 25MHz	75MHz Pentium
RAM	2MB	4MB	8MB
Disk Capacity	30MB	160MB	540MB
Sound Card	8-bit	8-bit	16-bit with multivoice internal synthesizer
CD-ROM	Single-speed	Double-speed	Quadruple-speed
Video System	VGA (640 × 480)	SVGA (800 × 600)	30 frames/second at 320 × 240 pixels

THE BASICS OF MULTIMEDIA

Everyone has their favorite multimedia application. But did you ever stop to think of how the application was created? Or of the large number of individual files that are needed for the sound and visual effects that are at the heart of the application? We said at the beginning of this appendix that multimedia combines the text and graphics capability of the PC with high-quality sound and video. In this section we look at the individual components, the sound and video files, that comprise a multimedia application.

Sound

The sound you hear from your PC is the result of a sound file (stored on disk or a CD-ROM) being played through the sound card in your system. There are, however, two very different types of sound files, a WAV file, and a MIDI file. Each is discussed in turn.

A **WAV file** is a digitized recording of an actual sound (a voice, music, or special effects). It is created by a chip in the sound card, which converts a recorded sound (e.g., your voice by way of a microphone) into a file on disk. The sound card divides the sound wave into tiny segments (known as samples) and stores each sample as a binary number. The quality of the sound is determined by two factors—the sampling rate and the resolution of each sample. The higher each of these values, the better the quality, and the larger the corresponding file.

The **sampling rate** (or frequency) is the number of samples per second and is expressed in KHz (thousands of samples per second). The higher the sampling rate, the more accurately the sound will be represented in the wave file. Common sampling rates are 11KHz, 22KHz, and 44KHz.

The **resolution** is the number of bits (binary digits) used to store each sample. The more bits, the better. The first sound cards provided for only eight bits. Sixteen bits are standard in today's environment.

WAV files, even those that last only a few seconds, grow large very quickly. Eight-bit sound, for example, at a sampling rate of 11KHz (11,000 samples a second) requires approximately 11KB of disk space per second. Thirty seconds of sound at this sampling rate will take some 330KB. If you improve the quality by using a 16-bit sound card, and by doubling the sampling rate to 22KHz, the same 30 seconds of sound will consume 1.3MB or almost an entire high-density floppy disk!

A **MIDI file** (Musical Instrument Digital Interface) is very different from a WAV file and is used only to create music. It does not store an actual sound, but rather the instructions to create that sound. Thus, a MIDI file is the electronic equivalent of sheet music. The advantage of a MIDI file is that it is much more compact than a WAV file because it stores instructions to create the sound rather than the actual sound. A WAV file, however, can represent any type of sound (a voice, music, or special effects) because it is a recorded sound. A MIDI file can store only music.

Video

An **AVI** (Audi-Video Interleaved) **file** is the Microsoft standard for a digital video (i.e., a multimedia) file. It takes approximately 4.5MB to store one second of *uncompressed* color video in the AVI format. That may sound unbelievable, but you can verify the number with a little arithmetic.

A single VGA screen contains approximately 300,000 (640 × 480) pixels, each of which requires at least one byte of storage. Allocating one byte (or 8 bits) per pixel yields only 256 (or 2^8) different colors. It is more common, therefore, to define color palettes based on two or even three bytes per pixel, which yield 65,536 (2^{16}) and 16,777,216 (2^{24}) colors, respectively. Realize, however, the more colors you have, the larger the associated file.

To fool the eye, and create the effect of motion, the screen must display at least 15 screens (frames) a second. If we multiply 300,000 bytes per frame, times 15 frames per second, we arrive at the earlier number of 4.5MB of data for each second of video. Storage requirements of this magnitude are clearly prohibitive in that an entire 640MB CD would hold less than three minutes of video. And even if storage capacity were not a problem, it's simply not possible for a CD-ROM to deliver almost 5MB of data per second of data to the PC. Clearly, something has to be done.

Full-motion video is made possible in two ways, by reducing the size of the window in which the video clip is displayed, and through *file compression.* Think, for a moment, of the video clips you have seen (or consider the Skiing.avi file in Figure C.1) and realize that they are displayed in a window that is 320 × 240, or one quarter of a VGA screen. The smaller window immediately reduces the storage requirement by a factor of four.

Even more significant than a reduced window is the availability of sophisticated compression-decompression algorithms (known as *codecs*), which dramatically reduce storage requirements. In essence, these algorithms do not store every pixel in every frame, but only information about how pixels change from frame to frame. The details of file compression are not important at this time. What is important is that you appreciate the enormous amount of data that is required for multimedia applications.

Realize, too, that even with the smaller window and file compression, AVI files are still inordinately large. The 10-second Skiing.avi file in Figure C.1, for example, requires 1.4MB, or the equivalent of an entire high-density floppy disk. Nevertheless, compare these storage requirements to our earlier calculations, which showed that an uncompressed video running 10 seconds in a VGA screen would take 45MB.

DANCING POSTAGE STAMPS AND CREDIT CARDS

The AVI format was introduced in 1992 at a time when the standard size for a video clip was 160 × 120, or one sixteenth of a VGA screen. The "dancing postage stamp" was derided by the public, but cheered by technicians who realized how difficult it was to accomplish. The introduction of the local bus, double-speed CD-ROM, better compression algorithms, and faster microprocessors have created today's standard clip of 320 × 240, or one quarter of a VGA screen. Critics still refer to "dancing credit cards," but video of this size has proved compelling enough to result in the avalanche of multimedia titles that are found in the retail market.

WINDOWS 95 AND MULTIMEDIA

Windows 95 provides software tools in the form of accessories in order to play various types of multimedia files. The tools can be accessed from the Start button or through shortcuts in the Multimedia folder shown in Figure C.2a. The appropriate accessory is also opened automatically when you open the corresponding media.

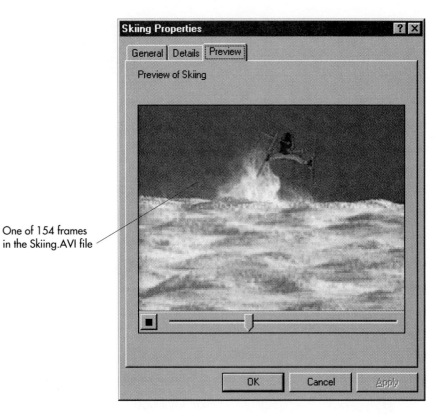

One of 154 frames
in the Skiing.AVI file

(a) Preview

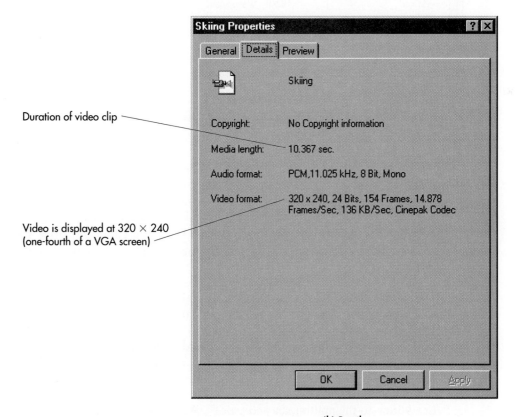

Duration of video clip

Video is displayed at 320 × 240
(one-fourth of a VGA screen)

(b) Details

FIGURE C.1   SKIING.AVI (1.4MB)

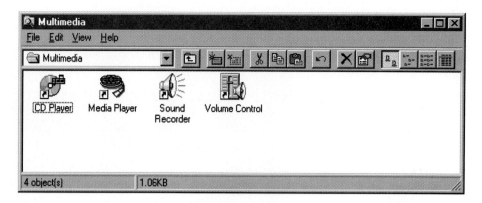

(a) Multimedia Tools

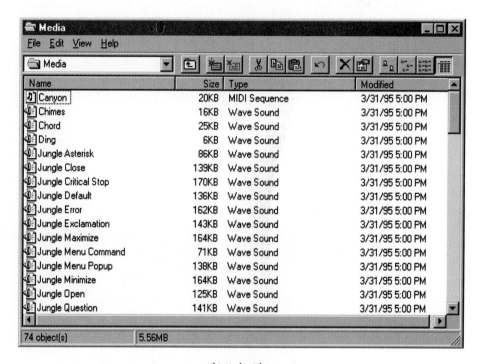

(b) Media Files

FIGURE C.2   Multimedia Support

The **CD Player** enables you to play audio CDs in a CD-ROM drive while you work on your PC. The controls on the Windows CD player look just like those on a regular CD player. It also has many of the same features, such as random play and a programmable playback order.

The **Media Player** lets you play audio, video, or animation files. **Volume Control** enables you to control the volume or balance of your sound card.

The **Sound Recorder** is used to record and play back a WAV file. Options within the Sound Recorder enable you to record at different sampling rates for different quality sound (e.g., CD or radio). You can also add special effects to a recorded sound, such as an echo, or you can speed up or slow down the recording. You can even play it backwards.

In addition to the multimedia accessories, Windows also provides sample files on which you can experiment. The files are stored in the Media folder as shown in Figure C.2b. The exercise that follows has you locate the Media folder on your system, then use the Windows accessories to play various files in the folder. The exercise requires a sound board and microphone (if you want to record your own sounds). It does not require a CD-ROM drive.

HANDS-ON EXERCISE 1

Introduction to Multimedia

Objective: Use the Media folder in Windows 95 to demonstrate WAV, MIDI, and AVI files. Use the Sound Recorder to create a sound file, then assign that file to an event via the Control Panel. Use Figure C.3 below as a guide in doing the exercise.

STEP 1: The Find Command

➤ Click the **Start Button.** Click (or point to) the **Find command,** then click **Files or Folders** to display the dialog box in Figure C.3a. (No files will be listed since the search has not yet taken place and the Media folder will not be displayed.) The size and/or position of the dialog box may be different from the one in the figure.

➤ Type **media** (the folder you are searching for) in the Named text box. Click the **down arrow** in the Look in list box. Click **My Computer** to search all of the drives on your system. Be sure the **Include subfolders** box is checked as shown in Figure C.3a.

Enter media

Look through My Computer (all drives)

Include subfolders

Double click Media folder to open it

Search results

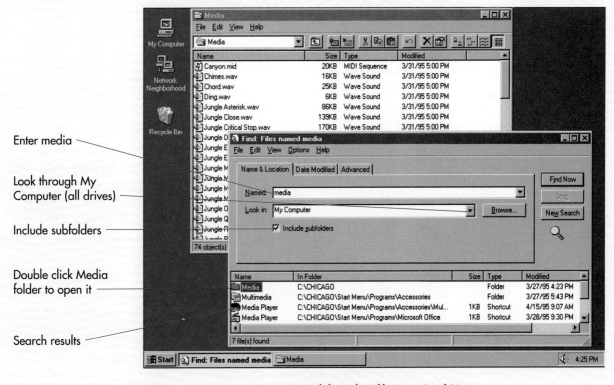

(a) Find the Media Folder (steps 1 and 2)

FIGURE C.3 Hands-on Exercise 1

➤ Click the **Find Now button** to begin the search, then watch the status bar as Windows searches for the specified files and folders.

➤ The results of the search are displayed within the Find Files dialog box and should contain a Media folder as shown in Figure C.3a. (Your view may be different from ours.) If you do not see the folder, check the search parameters:

• Be sure that you spelled **Media** correctly and that you are looking in **My Computer.**

• Click the **Date Modified tab.** Click the **All Files option button.**

• Click the **Advanced tab.** Be sure that **All Files and Folders** is specified in the Of Type list box and that the Containing text box is clear.

• Pull down the **Options menu** and verify that the Case-sensitive option is off (i.e., that the option does not have a check).

• Click the **Find Now button** to repeat the search with these parameters.

➤ If you still do not see a Media folder, ask your instructor about reinstalling the multimedia component in Windows 95.

ORDINARY FILES

A multimedia file is just like any other file with respect to ordinary file operations. Point to the file, then click the right mouse button to display a menu, which enables you to cut or copy the file, rename or delete the file, or display its properties. You can also use the right mouse button to click and drag the file to a different drive or different folder or create a shortcut on the desktop.

STEP 2: The Media Folder

➤ Double click the **Media folder** to open a window for this folder as shown in Figure C.3a. The size and position of your window may be different from ours.

➤ To display the Details view and the file extensions within that view:

• Pull down the **View menu.** Click **Details.**

• Pull down the **View menu** a second time. Click **Options,** then click the **View tab** in the Options dialog box. Clear the box (if necessary) to **Hide MS-DOS file extensions.** Click **OK.**

FILE EXTENSIONS

Long-time DOS users will recognize the three-character extension at the end of a file name, which indicates the file type. The extensions are displayed or hidden according to an option set in the View menu. Windows 95 maintains the file extension for compatibility, and in addition, displays an icon next to the file name to indicate the file type. The icons are more easily recognized in the Large Icons view, as opposed to the Details view. WAV and MID denote a waveform and MIDI file, respectively. An AVI (Audio-Video Interleaved) file is the Microsoft standard for a multimedia file with video and sound.

➤ The view in your Media window should match Figure C.3a. You may, however, see a different number of files.

➤ Click anywhere in the **Find window** (or click its button on the Taskbar). Click the **Close button** in this window so that only the Media folder remains open on the desktop.

STEP 3: WAV Files

➤ Point to the **Chord.wav** file, then click the **right mouse button** to display a menu with commands pertaining to the selected file.

➤ Click **Properties** to display the property sheet for the file. Click the **Details tab** as shown in Figure C.3b. Note that the duration of the sound (the media length) is just a little over one second, yet the file requires 25KB of storage.

➤ Close the Properties dialog box.

➤ Play the sound:

   • Double click the icon next to the file name *or*

   • Right click the file, then click the **Play command.**

➤ The Sound Recorder will appear briefly on the screen as the sound is played, then disappear after the sound has played.

➤ Double click the other WAV files to play the other sound files. The sounds should be familiar; the Critical Stop, for example, plays by default when you make a mistake.

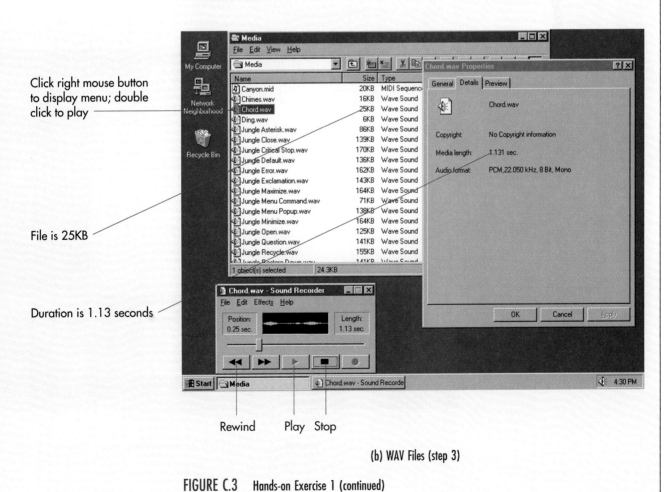

Click right mouse button to display menu; double click to play

File is 25KB

Duration is 1.13 seconds

Rewind   Play Stop

(b) WAV Files (step 3)

FIGURE C.3   Hands-on Exercise 1 (continued)

THE DOCUMENT, NOT THE APPLICATION

Windows 95 is document oriented, meaning that you can create or modify a document (file) without having to explicitly start the associated application. To create a new sound (wav) file, right click in the folder that is to contain the file, click New, then click Wave Sound to specify the type of object you want to create. Change the default file name, then double click the file to open the Sound Recorder. Click the Record button to start recording and the Stop button when you have finished. Click the Play button to hear the recorded sound. To modify an existing sound file, right click the file and click the Open command. To play an existing sound file from within Explorer, double click the file.

STEP 4: MIDI Files

➤ Play either the **Canyon.mid** or the **Passport.mid** file:
 • Double click the icon next to the file name *or*
 • Right click the file to select the file and display a menu. Click **Play.**

➤ The Media Player will appear on the screen as shown in Figure C.3c. Unlike the Wav files, which last but a second, the MIDI files are musical compositions that last two minutes each.

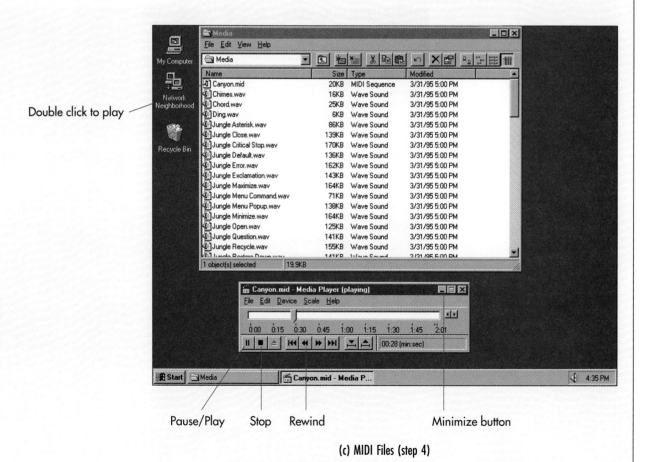

Double click to play

Pause/Play   Stop   Rewind   Minimize button

(c) MIDI Files (step 4)

FIGURE C.3   Hands-on Exercise 1 (continued)

➤ Experiment with the controls on the Media Player:
  • Click the **Pause button** to suspend playing.
  • Click the **Play button** (which appears after you click the Pause button) to resume playing.
  • Click the **Stop button** to stop playing.
  • Click the **Rewind button** to return to the beginning of the recording.
➤ End this step with the Media Player still open and positioned at the beginning of the recording.

WAV FILES VERSUS MIDI FILES

A WAV file stores an actual sound, whereas a MIDI file stores the instructions to create the sound. Because a WAV file stores a recorded sound, it can represent any type of sound—a voice, music, or special effects. A MIDI file can store only music. WAV files, even those that last only a few seconds, are very large because the sound is sampled thousands of times a second to create the file. MIDI files, however, are much more compact because they store the instructions to create the sound rather than the actual sound.

STEP 5: Online Help

➤ Click the **Play button** to play the MIDI file selected in the previous step. Click the **Minimize button** on the title bar of Media Player, which closes the window. The Media Player remains in memory, however, and the file continues to play.
➤ Click the **Start button** to display the Start menu. Click **Help** to open the Help window in Figure C.3d. Click the **Index tab** (if necessary) to enable you to search the index. Notice that the music continues to play because of the multitasking capability inherent in Windows.
➤ Type **mul** (the first letters in "multimedia," which is the topic you are searching for). The Help system automatically displays the topics beginning with the letters you enter.
➤ To display instructions for a specific topic (e.g., assigning sound for program events), select the topic, then click the **Display button** to open a popup window with the help you requested. Do not do anything further with the information at this time. Close the Help window.

MULTITASKING

Multitasking, the ability to run several programs at the same time, is one of the major benefits of Windows. You can run a word processor in one window and a spreadsheet in another. You can even use the CD player to play music from an audio CD as you work. Pull down the Start menu, click Programs, click Accessories, click Multimedia, then click the CD Player to open the program. Place the CD in the CD-ROM drive, then click the appropriate button on the CD Player.

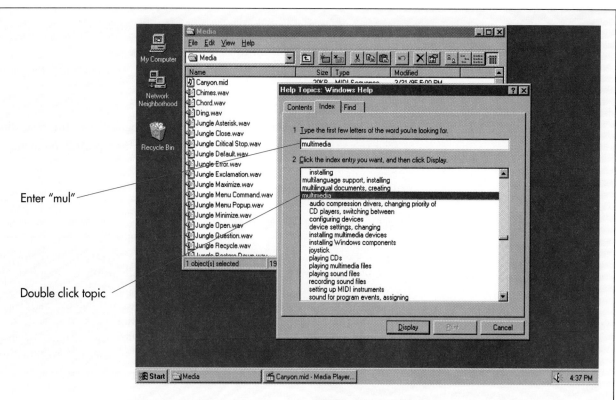

Enter "mul"

Double click topic

(d) Online Help (step 5)

FIGURE C.3 Hands-on Exercise 1 (continued)

➤ The music should still be playing (unless you've taken more than two minutes to complete this step). Click the **Media Player button** on the Taskbar, then close the Media Player.

STEP 6: The Sound Recorder

➤ This step requires a microphone as you will create your own sound file.

➤ Click the **right mouse button** anywhere within the Media window. Click (or point to) the **New command** to display a menu of different file types. Click **Wave Sound** as the type of file to create.

➤ The icon for a new sound file will appear with the file name (New Wave Sound.wav) highlighted. Press **enter** to accept the name of the file.

➤ Double click the **icon** to open the Sound Recorder as shown in Figure C.3e. The Sound Recorder looks just like a tape recorder with buttons to rewind, fast forward, play, stop, and record.

➤ Let's create a sound file that will bid you goodbye on exiting Windows:

  • Pick up the microphone. Click the **Record button** to begin recording.

  • Speak clearly into the microphone to record the message—for example, "Goodbye for now, see you soon." Click the **Stop button** to cease recording.

  • Click the **Play button** to hear the recording.

➤ The easiest way to change a recording is to rerecord. Press the **rewind button** to return to the beginning of the tape, then record the new message. Pull down the **Edit menu** and click **Delete After Current Position** to erase any portion of the previous recording.

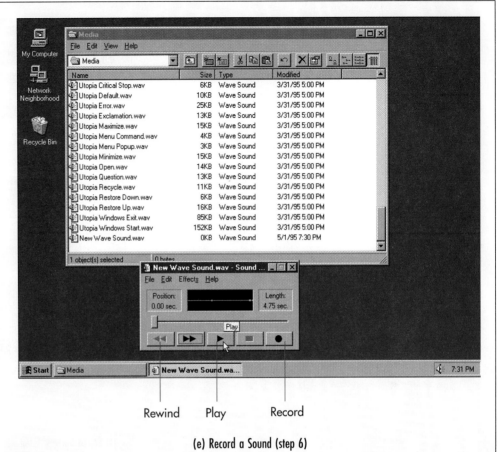

Rewind   Play   Record

(e) Record a Sound (step 6)

FIGURE C.3   Hands-on Exercise 1 (continued)

➤ Pull down the **File menu.** Click **Save** when you are satisfied with the recording. Click the **Close button** to exit the Sound Recorder.
➤ Click anywhere in the Media window and press the **F5 key** to refresh the window. The sound file you just created is several thousand bytes in length even though it lasts only a few seconds. Close the media window.

SOUND EFFECTS

The Effects menu in the Sound Recorder enables you to add special effects to a recorded sound. Record the sound as you usually do, then pull down the Effects menu and click Increase (Decrease) Speed to double (halve) the speed of the recording. Other commands let you add an echo or play the sound in reverse. It's easy, and it's fun. Try it!

STEP 7: Sound Settings

➤ Double click the **My Computer icon** to open My Computer. Double click the **Control Panel icon** to open a second window as shown in Figure C.3f. Double

Exit Windows
event

Sound file
created in step 6

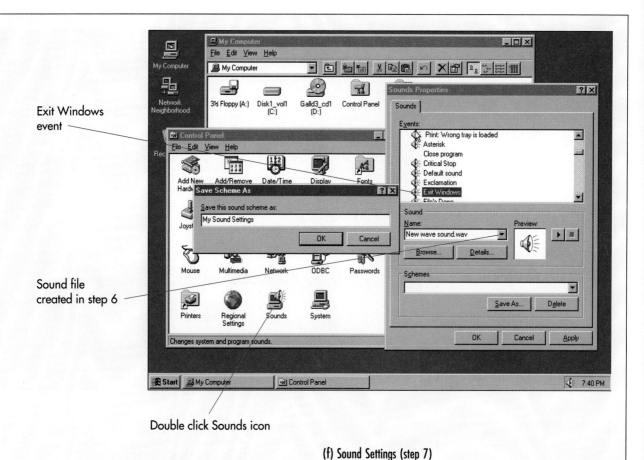

Double click Sounds icon

(f) Sound Settings (step 7)

FIGURE C.3   Hands-on Exercise 1 (continued)

click the Sounds icon within the Control Panel. The size and/or position of your windows will be different from ours.

➤ Click the **down arrow** on the scroll bar in the Events list box until you can select (click) the Exit Windows event.

➤ Click the **down arrow** in the Name box until you can select (click) the New Wave Sound created in the previous step. Click the Play button in the Preview box to hear the sound you selected.

➤ Click the **Save As command button** to open the Save As dialog box shown in Figure C.3f. Enter My Sound Settings as the name for the new settings. Click **OK** to exit the Save As dialog box. Click **OK** a second time to accept the settings and exit the Properties for Sounds dialog box.

STEP 8: Exit Windows

➤ Close the Control Panel. Close My Computer.

➤ Click the **Start Button,** then click the **Shut Down command.** Click **Yes** when you see the dialog box asking whether you are sure you want to exit Windows.

➤ You should hear your recording from step 7, after which you will see the screen indicating that it is safe to turn off the computer.

➤ Turn off the power if you truly want to exit or press **Ctrl, Alt,** and **Del** to restart the computer and continue working. Welcome to multimedia!

The Multimedia PC Marketing Council has established a minimum specification for a multimedia computer intended to guide both the consumer and the developer. Two standards, MPC-1 and MPC-2, have been published to date.

There are two different types of sound files, WAV files and MIDI files. A WAV file records an actual sound and requires large amounts of disk space because the sound is sampled several times a second to create the file. A MIDI file is much more compact than a WAV file because it stores the instructions to create the sound rather than the actual sound. A WAV file can represent any type of sound (a voice, music, or special effects) because it is a recorded sound. A MIDI file is the electronic equivalent of sheet music and can store only music.

An AVI (Audi-Video Interleaved) file is the Microsoft standard for a digital video (multimedia) file. AVI files are optimized to play at a resolution of 320 × 240 (one quarter of a VGA screen) to reduce the storage requirements. File compression of digital video is essential and is accomplished through various codecs (compression/decompression algorithms) supplied with Windows.

Windows 95 provides the software tools necessary to play the different types of multimedia files. The accessories can be accessed through the Start button or through shortcuts in the Multimedia folder.

KEY WORDS AND CONCEPTS

AVI file	MIDI file	Sound Recorder
CD Player	MPC-1	Volume Control
Codec	MPC-2	WAV file
File compression	Resolution	
Media Player	Sampling rate	

APPENDIX D: THE INTERNET AND WORLD WIDE WEB

OVERVIEW

The Internet. You read about it in magazines such as *Time* or *Newsweek*. Television programs provide their Internet addresses so they can be contacted by viewers. You use e-mail to communicate with your friends at other universities. The media make continual references to the Information Highway. But what exactly is the Internet and how does a message or file get from one computer to another?

This appendix provides basic information about the Internet, what it is, and how it works. It describes the World Wide Web and the under-lying concept of hypertext and hypermedia. The appendix also includes an introduction to Mosaic and Netscape, the powerful Windows-based tools that brought ease-of-use to the Internet and, more than any other piece of software, are responsible for the explosion of interest in the Internet and World Wide Web.

E-MAIL AND THE INTERNET

E-mail is indeed a powerful means of communication, but it is only one of many services provided through the Internet. If you have never used e-mail, then read the discussion in Chapter 4 beginning on page 173. If you are already familiar with e-mail, but do not use the Internet in any other way, you are in for a treat as you move through this appendix.

THE INTERNET

The *Internet* is a network of networks that connects computers across the country and around the world. It grew out of a government project that began in 1969 to test the feasibility of a network where scientists and military personnel could share messages and data no matter where they were. The government imposed the additional requirement that the experimental network be able to function with partial outages in times of national emergency, when one or more computers were down.

The proposed solution was to create a network with no central authority. Each node would be equal to all other nodes, with the ability to originate, pass, and receive messages. The path that a particular message took in getting to its destination would be insignificant. Only the final result was important as the message would be passed from node to node until it arrived at its destination.

The experiment was (to say the least) successful. Known originally as the **ARPAnet** (Advanced Research Projects Agency), the original network of four computers grew exponentially to include thousands of computers at virtually every major university and government agency, and an ever-increasing number of private corporations. To say that the Internet is large is a gross understatement, but by its very nature, it's impossible to say just how large the Internet really is. (One commonly accepted estimate is 25 million users.) The Internet is not a single network, but a collection of networks. How many networks there are, and how many users are connected to those networks, is of no importance as long as you yourself have access.

Unlike an ordinary network, such as the LAN you may be connected to at school, there is no single computer (or server) that controls the Internet. There is, however, a requirement that any computer connected to the Internet follow a uniform **protocol** (set of rules) that specifies how data is to be sent. That agreement, and the adoption of the Transmission Control Protocol/Internet Protocol (or TCP/IP), has led to the global network of interconnected computers we know as the Internet.

Each institution that maintains a node on the Internet is responsible for supporting and administering that node. The National Science Foundation, however, maintains the backbone of the Internet, which consists of a series of super computers that provide long distance communications links across the country.

THE INTERNET IS NOT FREE

The fact that there is no "Internet Incorporated" to collect a usage fee has given many people the mistaken idea that the Internet is free. The Internet is not free, although you may be lucky enough to have free access through your school or university, which has elected not to pass the cost on to you. The computers that make up the Internet cost money, and each node (e.g., your university) must pay its own way by funding its own network connection. The US taxpayer also funds the backbone of the Internet through the NSFNet (National Science Foundation Network) that provides the long distance communication links.

How It Works

The postal system provides a good analogy of how (but certainly not how fast) information travels across the Internet.[1] (E-mail is infinitely faster than "snail-mail.") When you mail a letter, you drop it in a mailbox, where it is picked up with a lot of other letters and delivered to the local post office. The letters are sorted and sent on their way to a larger post office or substation, where the letters are sorted again, until eventually each letter reaches the post office closest to its destination. The local mail carrier at the receiving post office then delivers each letter to its final destination.

[1]Krol, Ed, *The Whole Internet,* O'Reilly and Associates, Inc., Sebastopol, CA, 1992, pages 24, 26.

There is no direct connection between the origin and destination because it is impossible to connect every pair of cities within the United States. If you were to send a letter from Coral Springs, Florida, to Englewood Cliffs, New Jersey, the post office would not charter a plane from Coral Springs to Englewood Cliffs. Instead it would route the letter from one substation to the next, making a new decision at each substation—for example, from Coral Springs, to Miami, to Newark, to Englewood Cliffs.

Each postal substation considers all of the routes it has available to the next substation and makes the best possible decision according to the prevailing conditions. This means that the next time you mail a letter from Coral Springs, Florida, to Englewood Cliffs, New Jersey, the letter may travel a completely different path. If the mail truck from Coral Springs to Miami had already left or was full to capacity, the letter could be routed through Fort Lauderdale to New York City and then to Englewood Cliffs. It really doesn't matter because your only concern is that the letter arrive at its final destination.

The Internet works the same way, as data travels across the Internet through several levels of networks until it gets to its destination. E-mail messages arrive at the local post office (the host computer) from a remote PC (connected by modem), or from a node on a local area network. The messages then leave the local post office and pass through a more powerful computer (known as a router) that connects the networks on the Internet to one another.

A message may pass through several networks to get to its destination. Each network has its own router that determines how best to move the message closer to its destination, taking into account the traffic on the network. A message passes from one network to the next, until it arrives at the local area network on the other end, from where it can be sent to its final destination. The process is depicted graphically in Figure D.1.

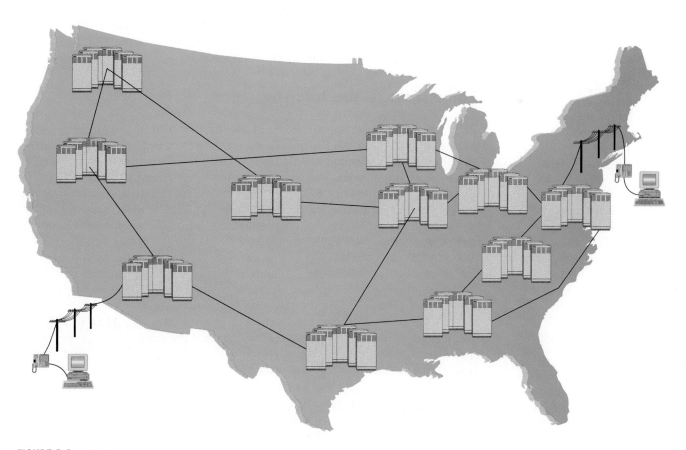

FIGURE D.1   The Internet

The TCP/IP Protocol

Let's pretend for a moment that the Post Office no longer accepted packages and that you wanted to send a book to your friend across the country. Your only alternative would be to rip the pages out of the book, put each page in its own envelope, mail the individual envelopes, then trust in your friend to open the envelopes and put the book back together. That may sound awkward, but that is a truer picture of how the Internet works.

Information is sent across the Internet in *packets,* with each packet limited in size. The rules for creating and sending the packets are specified by the *TCP/IP protocol* (Transmission Control Protocol/Internet Protocol) that governs the flow of data across the Internet. The TCP portion divides the file that you want to send into pieces, then numbers each piece so that the message can be reconstructed at the other end. The IP portion addresses each packet by specifying the address of the sending and receiving computer so that the routers will be able to do their job.

Why, you might ask, are files divided into packets rather than being sent in their entirety? The answer has to do with ensuring that data is transmitted correctly. Static or noise on a telephone line is merely annoying to people having a conversation, but devastating when a file (especially a computer program) is transmitted and a byte or two is garbled. The larger the file being sent, the greater the chance that noise will be introduced and that the file will be corrupted. Sending the data in smaller pieces (packets), and verifying that the packets were received correctly, helps ensure the integrity of the data.

The Internet is built in layers that revolve around the TCP/IP protocol. At the sending computer, the application layer creates the message and passes it to the TCP layer, where the message is divided into packets. The packets are addressed at the IP layer, then sent across the Internet over the hardware layer (the various levels of networks through which the data must travel to get to its destination). The process is reversed at the receiving computer. The IP layer receives the individual packets, then passes the packets up to the TCP layer, where they are reassembled and sent to the application layer to display the message.

Connecting to the Internet

The way in which you are connected to the Internet is of little concern as long as you can do what you want to do. There are, however, different ways to connect, and the distinction becomes important when you are connecting for the first time—for example, when you are setting up a home computer.

A full (dedicated) *TCP/IP connection* connects directly to the Internet over a high-speed transmission line 24 hours a day. This is the most powerful (and by far the most expensive) type of connection and is suitable only for universities and large corporations. A TCP/IP connection makes the site a node on the Internet and provides each workstation at that site with full Internet access. Anything that can happen between networked computers can occur at any workstation. You can run client/server software such as Mosaic or Netscape (see discussion on page 242), and you can download files directly onto your workstation.

The best way to access the Internet at home is through a *SLIP* or *PPP connection,* which is obtained through a local service provider. This type of connection provides direct access to all Internet services over a high-speed modem (14,400 bps or higher), but is significantly slower than a full TCP/IP connection. It does, however, enable you to download files directly onto your computer, and to run graphic client/server software such as Mosaic or Netscape.

A simple dial-up account is less expensive than a SLIP or PPP connection. It is also a more limited type of connection in that your PC functions as a "dumb terminal" of the host computer, which prevents you from running client/server software. Nor can you download a file directly to your computer since your computer is not known to the Internet. Instead, the file is saved first on the host computer. Then you must go through the extra step of downloading from the host to your computer. Nevertheless, you have access to basic Internet services (e.g., e-mail), and hence it might be all you need.

CONNECTING TO THE INTERNET

Your school or university probably has an Internet connection, in which case all you have to do is ask your instructor for information on how to access the connection. You can also obtain Internet access through the Microsoft Network (see page 163) or through other services such as America Online, Prodigy, or CompuServe.

THE DOMAIN NAME SYSTEM

Most people are introduced to the Internet through e-mail. You can send e-mail to anyone, anywhere in the world, as long as you have access to the Internet and you know the recipient's Internet address. The latter is developed through the *Domain Name System (DNS)*, which ensures that every Internet address is unique.

The Internet divides its component networks into a series of domains that enable e-mail (and other files) to be sent across the network. Universities, for example, belong to the EDU domain. Government agencies are in the GOV domain. Commercial organizations (companies) are in the COM domain. Large domains are in turn divided into smaller domains, with each domain responsible for maintaining unique addresses in the next lower-level domain.

An *Internet address* consists of the username, the host computer, and the domain (or domains) by which the computer is connected to the Internet. President Clinton's e-mail address is PRESIDENT@WHITEHOUSE.GOV, where President is the username, Whitehouse is the host computer, and GOV is the domain. Vice President Gore may be reached at VICE-PRESIDENT@WHITE-HOUSE.GOV. The President's domain and host computer are the same as the Vice President's. The only difference between the two addresses is the username, President and Vice-President, respectively.

THE WORLD WIDE WEB

The original language of the Internet was uninviting, to say the least. You needed a variety of esoteric programs (e.g., Telnet, FTP, Archie, and Gopher), which were derived from the UNIX operating system. You had to know the precise syntax of those programs. And even if you were able to get what you wanted, everything was communicated in plain text (graphics and sound were not available).

The *World Wide Web* was created in 1991 and introduced a new way to connect the resources on the Internet to one another. The Web is based on the technology of *hypertext* and *hypermedia,* which link computer-based documents in nonlinear fashion. Unlike a traditional document, that is read sequentially from top to bottom, a hypertext document includes links to other documents, which can be viewed (or not) at the reader's discretion. Hypermedia is similar in concept except that it provides links to graphic and video files in addition to text files.

Assume, for example, that you're reading a hypertext or hypermedia document about the American Revolution. You come to a reference to the Declaration of Independence, and rather than finishing the descriptive text, you can click a hypertext reference and be linked to the actual document. That in turn may contain a link to Thomas Jefferson or Benjamin Franklin, and those links may contain other links to other topics. You can choose to explore the link about Jefferson or you can go back to reading about the Revolution.

To explore the Web, you need a program called a ***browser,*** which requests files from various nodes on the Internet, then displays the hypertext (or hypermedia) documents on your computer. The first browsers were restricted to text, but were able to follow links from one document to another, even if the documents were on different computers. As users began to create other document types (images, sound, and video), the text browsers evolved naturally into a more powerful GUI tool.

Mosaic was the first Windows-based browser and it introduced point-and-click navigation to the Web. Today there are many different browsers from which to choose, but all browsers offer the same basic capabilities. We have chosen to focus on ***Netscape,*** a newer and more powerful browser than Mosaic. The discussion is sufficiently general to apply to other programs.

Netscape

A Windows browser, such as Netscape, is easy to use because it shares the common user interface and consistent command structure present in every Windows application. You already know several things about Netscape because of your basic understanding of Windows.

Consider, for example, Figure D.2, which displays the Netscape home page. (The ***home page*** is the first document you see at a web site.) You should recognize several familiar elements, such as the control menu box, the title bar, and the Minimize, Maximize (or Restore), and Close buttons. As with any other Windows application, commands are executed from pull-down menus or from command buttons that appear under the menu bar. A vertical and/or horizontal scroll bar appears if the entire document is not visible at one time.

The title bar displays the name of the document (Welcome to Netscape in Figure D.2.). The document itself contains ***hyperlinks*** (graphic icons or underlined items) that point to other documents. The Netscape home page, for example, contains several hyperlinks (Escapes, Company & Products, and so on). Click any link and you are automatically presented with another document that displays the requested information. That document may contain links to other documents, which may take you to still other documents, at other sites anywhere on the Internet.

The location (or address) of a document appears in the location text box and is known as a ***Uniform Resource Locator (URL).*** The URL is the primary means of navigating the Web and indicates the ***Web site*** (computer) on which you are working. Change the URL (we describe how in the next section) and you change the document.

A URL address consists of several parts: the method of access, the computer (web site) where the document is located, the path (if any) to that document, and the file name. For example:

http://home.mcom.com/home/welcome.html

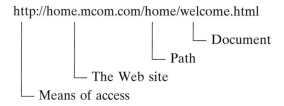

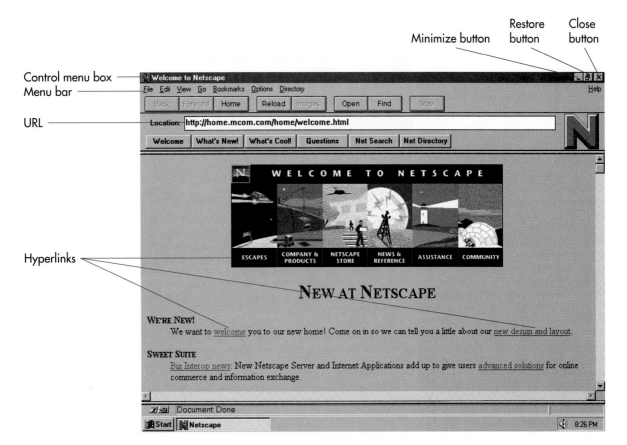

Control menu box
Menu bar
URL
Hyperlinks

Minimize button
Restore button
Close button

FIGURE D.2 The Netscape Home Page

Every URL address begins with the letters **http** to indicate the HyperText Transfer Protocol that specifies the way web documents are requested and retrieved. Two slashes separate the means of access from the Web site (the address of the computer) on which the document is located. The information following the web site indicates the path on the computer to get to the document (e.g., home), and finally the document name (e.g., welcome.html).

To go to a particular site, enter its URL address through the Open URL command in the File menu. (You can also type the address directly in the Location text box.) Just enter the address and off you go.

WHAT IS HTML?

All Web documents are written in **HTML** (HyperText Markup Language). An HTML document consists of tags that describe how to display the text, hyperlinks, and multimedia elements within a document. The letters HTML appear at the end of many URL addresses to indicate this type of document.

Hypertext and Hypermedia

A web document contains hyperlinks to other documents that appear as underlined items or as graphic icons. Consider, for example, the hypermedia document in Figure D.3. We began by choosing a Web site and entering its URL address (http://underground.net/oscarnet) in Figure D.3a. (Yes, it helps to know various sites on the Web, and we suggest several sites in Table D.1 on page 246.) Most of

URL

Click here

(a) Oscar Home Page

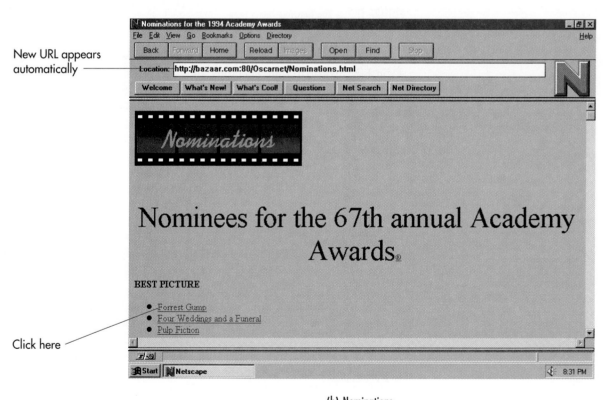

New URL appears automatically

Click here

(b) Nominations

FIGURE D.3   A Hypermedia Document

New URL ——

Click here ——

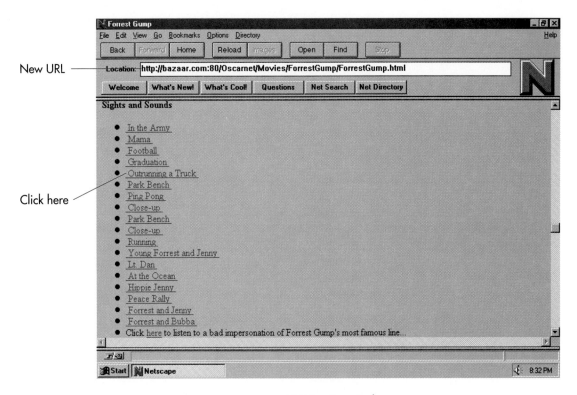

(c) Outrunning a Truck

New URL ——

Graphic can be downloaded
through Save command
in file menu

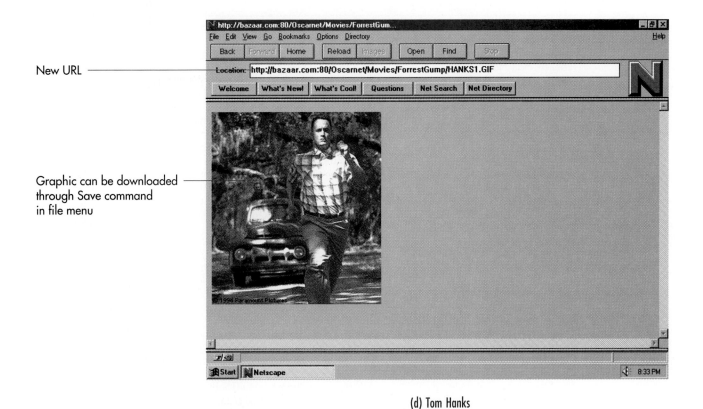

(d) Tom Hanks

FIGURE D.3   A Hypermedia Document (continued)

the time, however, you don't even have to enter the URL address, because Netscape is constantly suggesting sites to explore. And those sites may suggest other sites. The Oscarnet was in fact a "cool site" of the day (see the "What's Cool" boxed tip on page 247) in March 1995, just prior to the Academy Awards.

The first document at a web site is known as a home page. Once you arrive at a home page (e.g., Figure D.3a), click any link that interests you. We clicked on Nominations in Figure D.3a, which took us to the document in Figure D.3b. (The URL address in the location text box changes automatically to reflect the new document.) From there we clicked on Forrest Gump, which took us to the document in Figure D.3c, which led to the picture in Figure D.3d. There is no beginning (other than the starting point or home page) and no end. You simply read a hypermedia document in any way that makes sense to you, stopping to explore whatever topic you want to see next.

The World Wide Web is a "living document" that is constantly changing. The information at many sites is updated daily, and you never know just what you will find. We doubt, for example, that you will be able to retrieve the exact screens in Figure D.3 because a new set of movies will be nominated for next year's Academy Awards. It doesn't matter, because you will always find something of interest.

Your exploration of the World Wide Web is limited only by your imagination. The What's Cool button suggests several interesting sites and is an excellent place to begin your exploration. Alternatively, you may begin with any of the sites listed in Table D.1. Be sure to look at Bob Grauer's home page to download data disks for the *Exploring Windows* series.

TABLE D.1 Exploring the World Wide Web

Site	URL
Bob Grauer's Home Page	http://www.bus.miami.edu/~rgrauer
US Bureau of Census	http://www.census.gov
Web Crawler Home Page	http://webcrawler.cs.washington.edu/WebCrawler/WebQuery.html
Prentice Hall Home Page	http://www.prenhall.com
Microsoft Home Page	http://www.microsoft.com
Star Trek Home Page	http://voyager.paramount.com
Australian National University Art	http://rubens/anu.edu.au/
Map Viewer Home Page	http://pubweb.parc.xerox.com/map
Buena Vista Movie Plex	http://bvp.wdp.com/BVPM/MooVPlex.html
The Whole Internet Home Page	http://nearnet.gnn.com/gnn/wic/newrescat.toc.html
Movies and Television	http://alpha.acast.nova.edu/movies.html
Economy Markets and Investments	http://www.yahoo.com/Economy/Markets_and_Investments
Dow Jones Quote Server	http://www.secapl.com/cgi-bin/qs
JobWeb	http://www.risetime.com/risetime/preview.html
Planet Earth Home Page	http://white.nosc.mil/info_modern.html
Yahoo (Guide to the Web)	http://www.yahoo.com
White House	http://www.whitehouse.gov
Library of Congress	http://lcweb.loc.gov/homepage/lchp.html
Galaxy	http://www.einet.net/galaxy.html
Sports Schedules	http://www.cs.rochester.edu/u/ferguson/schedules/
Internet Movie Database	http://www.cm.cf.au.uk/Movies/Oscars.html
Elvis Shrine	http://www/mit/edu:8001/activities/41 West/Elvis.html
Underground Music Archive	http://sunsittee.unc.edu/IUMA
Travel and Tourist Information	http://www.digimark.net/rec-travel
Best of the Web Awards	http://wings.buffalo.edu/contest
GNN Best of the Net	http://nearnet.gnn.com/gnn/wic/best.toc.html
Cool Site of the Day	http://www.infi.net/cool.html
The Simpsons	http://www.digimark.net/TheSimpsons
Wide Web of Sports	http://tnswww.lcs.mit.edu/cgibin/sports
Ultimate TV List	http://cinenet.net.UTVL/utvl.html
Chocolate Lover's Page	http://www.ios.com/~mb/chocolate
Music	http://www.informatik.tu-muenchen.de/isar/archive/music/
Natural History	coast.http://ucmp1.berkeley.edu/welcome.html
Internet Business Center	http://www.tig.com/IBC/index.html

Searching the Web

The Web is growing on a daily basis and you can spend endless time searching for a document. There are, however, a series of search tools that help you find material more quickly. Netscape, for example, includes an Internet Search command that takes you to several Web sites, from where you can enter search criteria.

The exercise that follows is written for Netscape, but it can be applied to Mosaic or any other Windows-based browser. It is the document (and associated web site) that is important, *not* the particular browser. We suggest a specific starting point (the White House home page) and a progression through that document. You can, however, start with any other home page, and choose any links you want. Going from one document or link to the next is what "Surfing the Net" is all about. Bon voyage!

IT'S ALWAYS CHANGING

The World Wide Web is always changing, so don't be surprised if you cannot duplicate the hands-on exercise exactly. The information at the White House site changes from day to day and the pictures we display may no longer be there. In addition, the Web is quite busy during the middle of the day and hence you may be unable to connect because there are too many other visitors already at the site. Be patient and try again, or try another site. It's worth the wait!

HANDS-ON EXERCISE 1

Surfing the Net

Objective: Load Netscape or another browser. Enter the URL address of a specific Web site and browse the site. Use the Netscape Print and Save commands. Use Figure D.4 as a guide in the exercise.

STEP 1: Load Netscape

➤ Load Netscape to display the opening screen in Figure D.4a. (If you are using a different browser, you will see a different home page, but you can still do the exercise by adapting our instructions to that program.)

➤ Pull down the **File menu.** Click **Open Location** to display the dialog box in Figure D.4a. Type the name of the web site you want to explore—for example, **http://www.whitehouse.gov** in Figure D.4a. Press **enter.**

WHAT'S COOL

The What's Cool button is an excellent place to begin. The list of suggested sites changes every day and you never know what you will find, but the results are always interesting. Click the button and see for yourself.

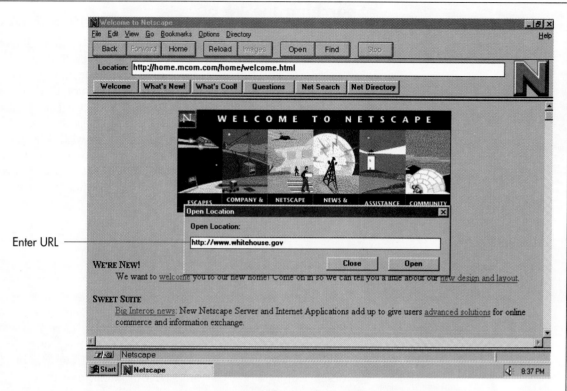

Enter URL

(a) Open Location Command (step 1)

FIGURE D.4   Hands-on Exercise 1

STEP 2: The White House

➤ You should see the home page in Figure D.4b. (The web is always changing and the home page you see may be different from our figure.) If you are unable to get to this site:

- Pull down the **File Menu,** click **Open URL,** and re-enter the address in Figure D.4a. You must type the address exactly as it appears in the figure. Press **enter.**

- If you are still unable to get to the site, it may be because the site is no longer active or because there are too many visitors already at the site. (There have been more than two million visitors since the site opened in October 1994.) Click the **What's Cool button** and select a different site to explore if you can't get to the White House.

➤ Click the hyperlink to the **Executive Branch** on the White House home page.

THE FLASHING LOGO

The Netscape logo (the capital N) in the upper right-hand corner of the Netscape window indicates the status of a Netscape search. The icon will be flashing when Netscape is connecting to a URL, searching for a document, or otherwise involved in data transfer. It will be still otherwise. Click the Stop button to terminate the data transfer if the icon continues to flash for (what seems to be) an unreasonable amount of time.

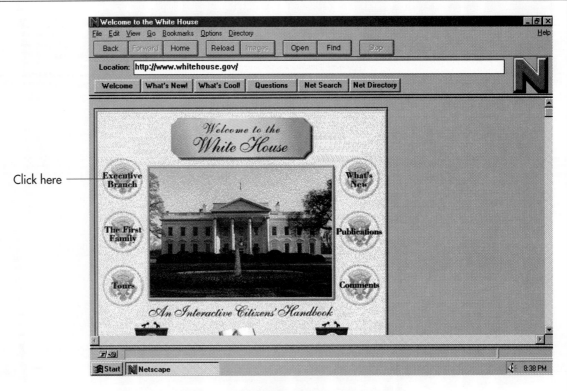

Click here ——

(b) The White House Home Page (step 2)

FIGURE D.4   Hands-on Exercise 1 (continued)

STEP 3: Hyperlinks

➤ You should see the screen in Figure D.4c. Click the hyperlink to the **President's Cabinet** to explore that page.

➤ Click the **Back button** when you have finished looking at the President's Cabinet to return to the Executive Branch. Click the **Back button** a second time to return to the White House home page.

➤ Continue to browse the White House to get a feeling for the information contained at this site.

THE STATUS BAR

The status bar at the bottom of the Netscape window provides continual information as files are downloaded. It signals all attempts at connecting to a web site, then indicates when the connection is completed. It also displays the total number of bytes in a file that is to be downloaded, then displays a running count as the bytes are transferred.

STEP 4: The Print Command

➤ Click the **Back button** several times until you are back at the White House home page. Click the **First Family** hyperlink to display the document in Figure D.4d.

Back button ——

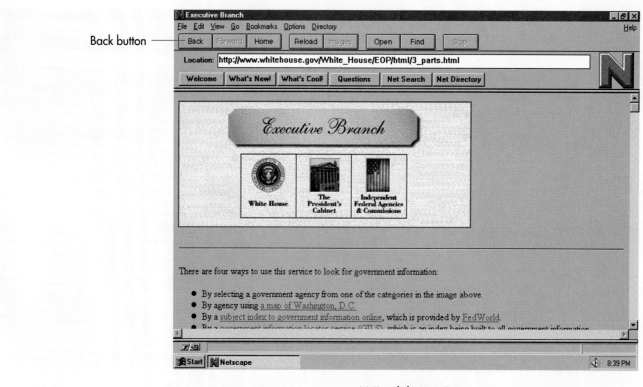

(c) Hyperlinks (step 3)

Preview document ——

Scroll through document ——

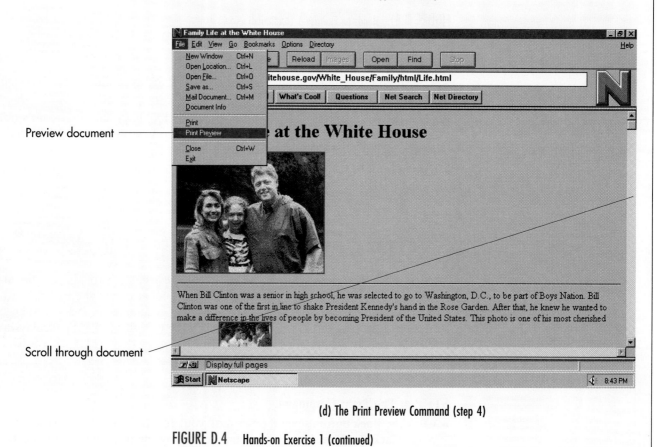

(d) The Print Preview Command (step 4)

FIGURE D.4   Hands-on Exercise 1 (continued)

(You may see a different picture because the contents of the site are always changing.)

➤ Pull down the **File menu.** Click **Print Preview** to preview the document. Click the **Print button** if you want to print the document, or click the **Close button** to exit the preview mode without printing.

THE VIEW HISTORY COMMAND

The View History command lists the places you have visited during the current session. Pull down the Go menu, then click the View History command to display a window with the list of sites. Double click any site (then close the View History window) to return to that site. You can also pull down the Bookmarks menu to add the current site to a list of favorite places for access in a future session.

STEP 5: The Save Command

➤ Figure D.4e shows another document from the White House. We got to this document by scrolling through the First Family page (step 4), then clicking on the small icon of President Clinton on the saxophone. (Note the different URL address.)

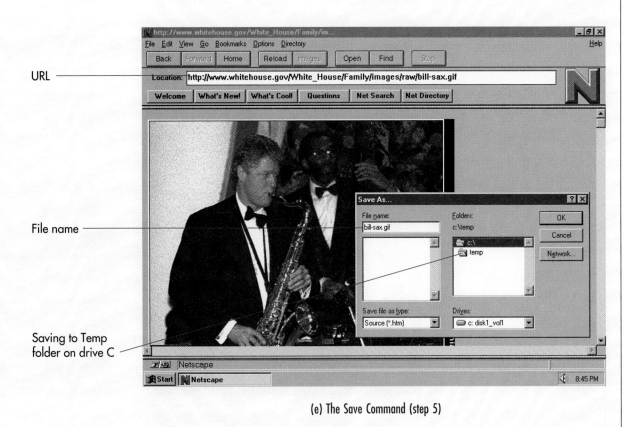

(e) The Save Command (step 5)

FIGURE D.4   Hands-on Exercise 1 (continued)

➤ Pull down the **File menu.** Click **Save** to display the dialog box in Figure D.4e. Choose the drive and directory on which you want to save the file (e.g., the Temp directory on drive C). Click **OK.**

➤ The picture of President Clinton will be downloaded to your hard drive and saved as bill-sax.gif in the indicated directory.

THE INSERT PICTURE COMMAND

The Insert Picture command in Word 6.0 enables you to include a GIF file in a Word document. Pull down the Insert menu, click Picture, select the appropriate drive and directory, then choose the name of the picture (e.g., bill-sax.gif) to insert. Click OK and the picture is inserted into the Word document. Right click the picture and click the Insert Frame command to facilitate moving and sizing the frame within a Word document.

STEP 6: Internet Search

➤ Pull down the **Directory menu.** Click **Internet Search** to display a list of search sites.

➤ Click the **down arrow** on the vertical scroll bar to scroll through the list of search sites until you can see **Web Crawler Searching** as shown in Figure D.4f.

➤ Click the hyperlink for the **Web Crawler.**

Click here to select
Web Crawler search tool —

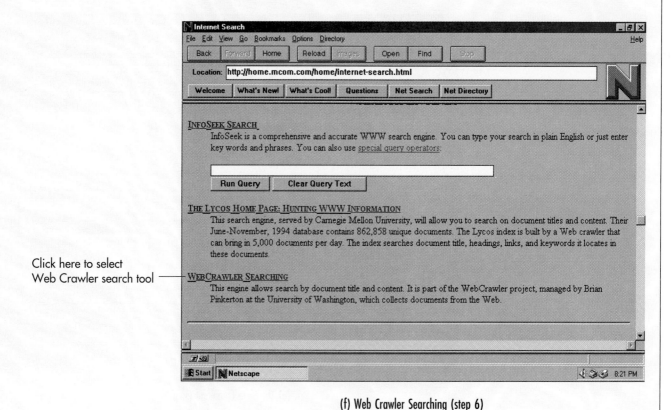

(f) Web Crawler Searching (step 6)

FIGURE D.4   Hands-on Exercise 1 (continued)

STEP 7: The Web Crawler

➤ The Web Crawler home page should be displayed on your screen as shown in Figure D.4g. (The URL address is identical to the address shown in Table D.1. The appearance of the page may have changed since we last accessed this site.)

➤ Click in the **text box.** Type **Congress** as the key word in your search, then click the **Search button** to begin the search.

➤ You will see a message indicating that the information you have submitted is insecure and could be observed by a third party. Click the **Continue** button.

➤ The Web Crawler returns a list of sites with documents that satisfy the search criteria.

BOOKMARKS

The ability to add (and return to) a specific site is one of the best features of Netscape. Pull down the Bookmark menu and click Add Bookmark to save the URL address of the current document. (The Web Crawler is a good bookmark, as it enables you to quickly initiate a search.) The next time you want to return to the site for which you set the bookmark, pull down the Bookmark menu and click the View Bookmark command. Select (click) the desired bookmark, then click the Go To button.

Bookmark menu enables you to return to a previous site

URL address is identical to entry in Table D.1

Click here to enter search criteria

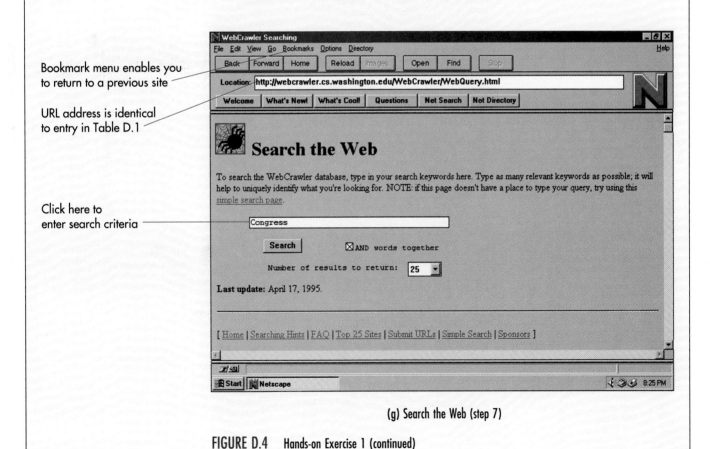

(g) Search the Web (step 7)

FIGURE D.4   Hands-on Exercise 1 (continued)

STEP 8: The Search Results

➤ Click **US Government Resources - Legislature Branch.** You are now at the seat of our Federal government as shown in Figure D.4h.

➤ Click the hyperlinks that interest you, which in turn will take you to other documents at that site (or even at a different site). Save or print the documents that you find as you see fit.

➤ Exit Netscape when you are finished exploring.

SET A TIME LIMIT

We warn you that it's addictive, and that once you start "surfing the Net," it is difficult to stop. We suggest, therefore, that you set a time limit before you begin, and that you stick to it when the time has expired. Tomorrow is another day with new places to explore.

Hyperlink to a previous page

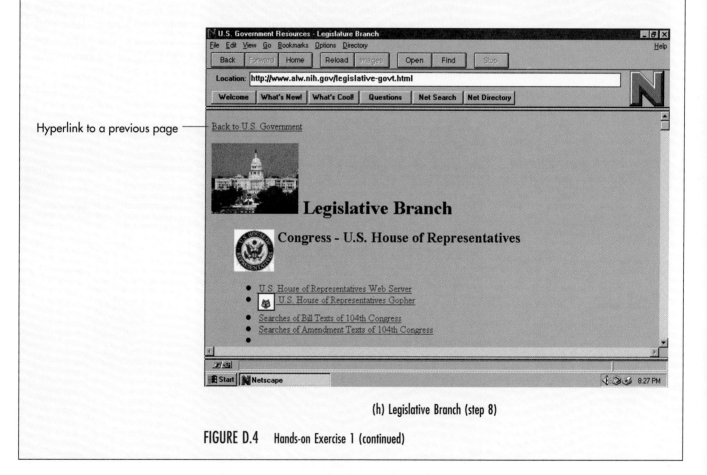

(h) Legislative Branch (step 8)

FIGURE D.4   Hands-on Exercise 1 (continued)

SUMMARY

The Internet is a network of networks that connects computers across the country and around the world. It began as an experimental project in 1969 to test the possibility of creating a network where scientists and military personnel could share messages and data no matter where they were. Today the Internet includes virtually every major university, various government agencies, and an ever-increasing number of private corporations.

Each institution that maintains a node on the Internet is responsible for supporting and administering that node. Thus, each individual user pays its own way, although the National Science Foundation maintains the backbone of the Internet—a series of super computers that provide long distance communications links across the country.

A full (dedicated) TCP/IP node connects directly to the Internet over a high-speed transmission line 24 hours a day. This is the most powerful (and by far the most expensive) type of connection and is suitable only for universities and large corporations. The best way to access the Internet at home is through a SLIP or PPP connection, which is obtained through a local service provider. This type of connection provides direct access to all Internet services over a high-speed modem (14,400 bps or higher), but is significantly slower than a full TCP/IP connection. A simple dial-up account is less expensive than a SLIP or PPP connection. It is also a more limited type of connection in that your PC functions as a "dumb terminal" of the host computer, which prevents you from running client/server software.

The World Wide Web is a way of connecting resources on the Internet to one another so that the user is unaware of where (on which computer) each resource is located. Web documents are created using hyperlinks that enable a user to move through a document in nonlinear fashion. Many Web sites contain search tools (e.g., the Web Crawler) that help search for specific documents.

To explore the Web (or surf the Net), you need a Windows-based browser such as Mosaic or Netscape. The URL (Uniform Resource Locator) is the heart of Web navigation and contains the address of the document you are viewing. Table D.1 suggests specific sites for exploration.

KEY WORDS AND CONCEPTS

ARPAnet	Internet	TCP/IP protocol
Browser	Internet address	Uniform Resource
Domain Name System	Mosaic	Locator
Home page	Netscape	URL
HTML	Packet	Username
HTTP	Protocol	Web site
Hyperlinks	PPP connection	World Wide Web
Hypermedia	SLIP connection	
Hypertext	TCP/IP connection	

INDEX

Access time, 212
    for CD-ROM, 215
Active window, 24
Add New Hardware, 205
Add/Remove Programs, 205
Address book, 162
America Online®, 163
Application software, 2
ARPAnet, 238
Attach As command, 150
Audio card. *See* Sound card
Auto Arrange command, 18
Auxiliary storage, 211–212
AVI file, 223

Background color (in Paint), 62
Backup strategy, 104, 109
Bit, 214
Boldface, 58
Bookmark (in Netscape), 253
Bridge, 147
Browser, 242. *See also* Netscape
Bus, 213
Buying Guide, 207–220
Byte, 211

Call waiting, disabling of, 169
Cascade command, 24–26, 28
CD Player, 226
CD-ROM, 215
Check box, 15
Click, 4
Clipboard, 50
Clock speed, 210
Close button, 13
Codec (compression/decompression), 224
Color box (in Paint), 61–62
Common user interface, 46–48
Communications software, 157
Compose command (in e-mail), 174
Compound document, 70–71
CompuServe®, 163
Contents tab (in Windows Help), 5–6, 8–9
Control Panel, 23–24
Copy command, 50, 58–60, 68
CPU Performance Index, 210
Cut command, 50, 58–60

Data file, 92
Delete command, 104
Desktop, 2–3
    customization of, 31
Details view, 20

Dialog box, 15
Dimmed command, 14
Disk properties, 22
Display, properties of, 195
Document (versus application) orientation,
    95, 200
Documents menu, 192
Domain, 176
Domain Name System, 241
Dot matrix printer, 214
Dot pitch, 213
Double click, 4
Double-density disk, 17, 212
Download, 156
Drag, 5
Drawing color (in Paint), 62
Drop-down list box, 15

Edit menu, 50
Ellipsis, 14
E-mail, 173–182
Expansion card, 208
Expansion slot, 208
Extended VGA, 213
Extension. *See* File extension

Fax/modem, 156, 214. *See also* Microsoft Fax
File
    copying of, 109
    moving of, 119
    selection of, 122
File compression, 224
File extension, 55, 92
    hiding of, 106
    for sound files, 228
File menu, 48–50
File name, 50, 92, 200–201
File server, 146
File type, 66, 92
Find command, 123–125, 127–128, 227
Fixed disk, 211–212
Floppy disk, formatting of, 17, 20–21
Folder, 92
    collapsed, 114, 115, 154
    copying of, 118
    creation of, 118
    expanded, 114, 115, 154
Font, 50–51
Font sampler, 205
Formatting
    floppy disk, 17, 20–21
    in WordPad, 50–52
Forward command (in e-mail), 174

Gateway, 147

Handshaking, 167
Hard disk. *See* Fixed disk
Help command, 5–6
High-density disk, 17
Home page, 242
    list of, 246
Horizontal scroll bar, 13
HTML, 243
HTTP, 242–243
Hyperlink, 242, 249
Hypermedia, 241, 243–246
HyperTerminal accessory, 157–158, 168–170
Hypertext, 241, 243–246

IBM PC, announcement of, 208
Index tab, in Windows Help, 5–6, 10
Information service, 163–164
Inkjet printer, 214
Insertion point, 48
Intel Corporation, 208
Internet, 176, 237–255
Internet address, 176, 241–242
ISA (Industry Standard Architecture), 214
Italics, 58

Jump arrow. *See* Shortcuts

Keyboard shortcuts:
    boldface, italics, and underline, 58
    cut, copy, and paste, 73
    moving in a document, 58
Kilobyte (KB), 211

Laser printer, 214
Local Area Network (LAN), 146–156
Local bus, 213–214
Long filenames, 200–201

Maximize button, 13, 19
Media folder, 226, 228–229
    finding of, 227
Media player, 226
Megabyte (MB), 211
Megahertz (MHz), 210
Memory, 211
Menu bar, 13
Microprocessor, 208, 210–211

Microsoft Exchange, 174–175, 177–182
    options in, 188–189
Microsoft Fax, 160–162, 170–172
Microsoft Network, 163, 172–173
MIDI file. *See* Sound file
Minimize button, 13, 19
Minimize versus closing, 77
Modem, 156
    installation of, 165
    practice with, 165–172
Monitor, purchase of, 213
Mosaic, 242
Mouse
    customization of, 28, 204
    operations with, 3–5
    problems with, 8
    tips for, 64
Mouse pointer, 5
Move a window, 12–13, 18–19
Move command. *See* Cut and paste
Multimedia, 221–235
    standards for, 222
    upgrade, 222
Multitasking, 3, 70–71
    with CD player, 231
My Computer, 3, 13, 90–91, 198–199
    browsing with, 93–94
    with network drives, 149, 153

Netscape, 242, 247–254
Network administrator, 148
Network Neighborhood, 148–150
New command, 97–98
Notebook computer, 216
Notepad accessory, 99, 117

Online help, 5–6
Online registration, 39–40, 166
Open command, 49–50
Open list box, 15
Option buttons, 15

Packet, 240
Page Setup command, 77
Paint accessory, 61–70
Password, protection of, 148
Paste command, 50, 58–60, 68
    transparent versus opaque pasting, 69
PC-compatible, 208
PCI bus, 214
Phone Dialer accessory, 160, 167–168
Pixel, 212
Point, 3
PPP connection, 240
Print command
    in Paint, 70
    in WordPad, 60
Printer, purchase of, 214
Printer server, 146
Prodigy®, 163

Program file, 92
Programs menu, 192
Properties, changing of, 95, 194
Pull-down menus, 14

Quick View, 106

RAM, 211
Random-access memory. *See* RAM
Recycle Bin, 3, 104, 112, 194, 201
Refresh rate, 213
Regional settings, 204
Rename command, 97
Reply command, in e-mail, 174, 179
Resolution
    changing of, 194, 212
    in sound files, 223
Restore button, 13, 19
Return receipt, in e-mail, 180
Right click, 5
RTF format
    in Microsoft Exchange, 174
    in WordPad, 49, 55
Run command, 193

Sampling rate, 223
Save command, 48–49
Save As command, 55, 76
Screen saver, 7
    implementation of, 11
Scroll bar, 13
Scrolling, 19–20
Selection area, 56
Select-then-do, 50
Send command, in e-mail, 174
Send To command, 110, 173
Server, 146
Settings menu, 193
Shift key, in Paintbrush, 65
Shortcuts, 29–30, 125–126, 130–131,
    202–203
Shutdown command, 12, 193
Size a window, 12–13, 18–19
SLIP connection, 240
Sound card, 215–216
Sound file
    MIDI file, 223, 228, 230
    WAV file, 223, 228, 229
Sound recorder, 226, 232–233
Sound settings, 204, 233–234
Start button, 3, 192
Start menu, modification of, 132
Status bar, 13
Super VGA, 212
System software, 2

Tabbed dialog box, 15
Taskbar, 3, 194, 196–197
    customization of, 31–32
    properties of, 195

TCP/IP protocol, 238, 240
Text box, 15
Tile command, 24–26, 28
Title bar, 12, 197
Toolbar
    in View menu, 17
    in WordPad, 51–52
Toolbox, in Paint, 61–62
ToolTip, 18, 51
Transfer rate, 215
Typeface, 50–51
Type size, 50–51, 56
Type style, 50–51

Undo command:
    with file operations, 108, 129
    multiple levels of, 202
    in Paint, 64
    in Windows 95, 29
    in WordPad, 58
Uniform Resource Locator, 240
    list of, 246
Upload, 156
URL. *See* Uniform Resource Locator

Vertical scroll bar, 13
VGA, 212
View menu, 17–18, 95–96, 198
Virus, threat of, 159
Volume Control, 226

WAV file. *See* Sound file
Web Crawler, 253
Whats This button, 15, 22, 196
Who Am I command, 150, 151
Window
    cascading, 24–26, 28
    components of, 12–13
    moving, 12–13, 18–19
    sizing, 12–13, 18–19
    tiling, 24–26, 28
Windows 3.1, migrating from, 191–206
Windows 95
    multimedia capability, 224–226
    registration of, 39–40, 166
    tour of, 192
Windows Explorer, 113–115, 199–200
WordPad Accessory, 48–61
Word Wrap, 54
Workstation, 146
World Wide Web, 241–255
    search of, 247, 252–254
    sites on, 246
Write protect, 104, 111
WYSIWYG, 47